CAVAILLÉ-COLL AND THE FRENCH ROMANTIC TRADITION

Frontispiece. Aristide Cavaillé-Coll (from E. and C. Cavaillé-Coll, *Aristide Cavaillé-Coll: Ses origines, sa vie, ses oeuvres*. Paris, 1929).

CAVAILLÉ-COLL AND THE FRENCH ROMANTIC TRADITION

FENNER DOUGLASS

YALE UNIVERSITY PRESS
NEW HAVEN AND LONDON

This is a new and expanded edition of
Cavaillé-Coll and the Musicians:
A Documented Account of His First Thirty Years in Organ Building,
Published in 1980 by the Sunbury Press.

Chapter 12 is reprinted with permission from
Albert Dunning, ed., *Visitatio Organorum: Feestbundel voor Maarten Albert Veute,*
© 1980 Vitgeverij Frits Knuf.

Set in Fairfield type
Printed in the United States of America

Library of Congress Cataloging-in-Publication Data
Douglass, Fenner.
Cavaillé-Coll and the French Romantic Tradition / Fenner Douglass.
p. cm.

English and French.
Enl. ed. of: Cavaillé-Coll and the Musicians. 1980.
Includes bibliographical references and index.

ISBN 0-300-07114-0 (alk. paper)

1. Cavaillé-Coll, Aristide, 1811-1899.
2. Cavaillé-Coll, (Firm).
3. Organ—Construction.
4. Organs—France.
5. Organists—France.
I. Douglass, Fenner. Cavaillé-Coll and the Musicians.
II. Title.

ML424.C2D7 1999   786.5'19'092—dc21 [b]   98-41897 CIP MN

To Jane
and the Children:
Stephen, Emily, and John

Contents

Illustrations follow page 82

"No subject will better reward study in the coming years than the career of Mr. Cavaillé-Coll. Honest and uncompromising, impassioned and consistent, it cannot but remind us of some of the lives of certain great artists of the past."

- La Semaine Réligieuse Historique et Littéraire de la Lorraine, V, 16, March 15, 1868, p. 8.

Preface

To a large extent, the documentation for this volume was photographed in 1971 from the library of Mme. Jean Lapresté of Paris, to whom I am deeply grateful. The dossier consists of sixteen bound volumes of letters, indexes, and contracts; dozens of unbound handwritten letters to Aristide Cavaillé-Coll from his father; and many more letters from Aristide to Lefébure-Wély, Philbert, and others. There are also several published monographs and drafts by Cavaillé-Coll himself. Because the pages of the volumes of letters and contracts are not numbered consistently throughout, references are made to volumes and numbering of items, as listed below. Microfilms are available in the library of the Oberlin College Conservatory of Music, and full-sized reprints may be found in the Perkins Library at Duke University. The Cavaillé-Coll office files were bound and identified as seen below, covering activities from the company's beginnings to December 1859:

Cited as	Actual Name
États des Orgues:	133 Archives 19/1, Etats des Orgues avant et aprés (1838-
Devis I:	Livre 13/3 9 Archives, Devis 1833-40
Devis II:	Livre 13/1 29 Archives, Devis 1841-45
Devis III:	Livre 13/2 31 d'Archives, No 3 Devis 6 Juillet 1844-31 Déc. 1849
Devis IV:	Livre 13/4, No. 4 Devis, 24 mars 1850-29 février 1856 Rappels du 1 Mars 1842 au 14 avril 1849
Devis V:	#5 Devis, 31 Mars 1856–11 nov. 1859 No. 2, Marchés, 28 février 1863-15 juin 1878 Repertoire des Marchés No. 14/1
Lettres I:	Livre No. 5/1, 23 d'Archives, #1 Copie de lettres, 6 janvier 1840-15 Nov. 1844
Lettres II:	Livre No. 5/2, 25 d'Archives, #2 Copie de Lettres, 15 Nov. 1844-21 Sept. 1848
Lettres III:	Livre No. 5/3, #3 Copie de Lettres, 24 Septembre 1848-28 Novembre 1851
Lettres IV:	#4 Lettres, 28 novembre 1851–10 Septembre 1855
Lettres V:	#5 Lettres, 10 Septembre 1855–13 Janvier 1859
Lettres VI:	#6 Lettres, 13 janvier 1859–26 décembre 1859

In addition, there are:

2 Lettres. Repertoire des Copies de Lettres, Nos. 21-47
Index of organ projects.

The extraordinary quality of printing for the first edition of *Cavaillé-Coll and the Musicians* (1980) may still be seen in this new publication. Richard Parsons, founder and proprietor of the Sunbury Press in Raleigh, North Carolina, used the equipment of his family business, the Bynum Printing Company. Thus the text and English translations of letters were set in Linotype and Ludlow hot metal, already an obsolete method, on an old 25-by-38-inch Babcock Optimus press. That very machine, later melted down for scrap, had been purchased secondhand in 1921 by Parsons's greatgrandfather. The Babcock Optimus press itself was invented early in the century by my grandfather, George Potter Fenner (d. 1915), president of the Babcock Printing Press Manufacturing Company in New London, Connecticut.

I acknowledge with gratitude the financial assistance of Oberlin College and the Mary Duke Biddle Foundation; the personal interest and direction offered by Marcel Dupré, Félix Raugel, and Cavaillé-Coll's genial grandson, André Cavaillé-Coll; the encouragement and generous help of the late Jacques Gommier and his wife, Marie-Claire Alain; and the substantial contribution of Prof. Charles Ferguson, whose gift of fluency in language has enlivened the English translations found in this volume.

Introduction

By the time he was thirty, Aristide Cavaillé-Coll had made the discoveries upon which he was to base his achievements as an artist and a craftsman. But he always delighted in devising new procedures, as well as adopting and improving the ideas of others. His position of strength as compared to his competitors was to change little during the last fifty years of his life. The restless searching of his genius kept his thoughts on a level above and beyond the mere concern for survival, even in times of political turmoil.

Never satisfied with the time he could devote to "things touching on theory of our art,"[1] he seized the opportunity of visiting organ builders in Germany and Holland, and he corresponded with the respected theorist Töpfer, of Weimar. Even more clearly than his theoretical writings, however, Cavaillé-Coll's business letters and contracts reveal his genius as an organ builder. Although in his workshop there were always stock or second-hand organs available for quick sale, Cavaillé-Coll carried out many of his experiments in organs built on contract. He ordered expensive and unauthorized changes, often at the last minute, expressing the hope that he would be reimbursed later. Thus the finished product sometimes differed substantially from the organ specified in the original contract. This was as true of his first great project, for the Royal Church of St.-Denis in 1834-41, as it was of the monumental "restoration" for the Church of St.-Sulpice in Paris, 1857-63.

Cavaillé-Coll's career, one of the longest in the history of organ building, is perhaps the most thoroughly documented as well. The reader is urged to search beyond this volume, for which only a small percentage of the available material was drawn. Only then may he realize fully what burdens must be assumed by any successful organ builder, and what a rare occurrence it is when all the requisite talents are found in one outstanding individual, who leaves a lasting imprint on his profession. The great expense of the art brought financial downfall to the less prudent Danjou, whose talents did not include business acumen and infinite patience. Despite his genius, even Cavaillé-Coll barely managed to survive the revolution of 1848. Since many of his most important contracts were funded by the government, we can imagine his despair when he wrote to Baron Seignier that his workshop had been closed for six months[2]; and a year later to the Mayor of Nîmes that "the very existence of our establishment is threatened."[3] Cavaillé-Coll was constantly in debt, awaiting for payment for organs already delivered, and he was always pressed to show a profit by those who advanced the funds to keep his shop in operation. He was not above entering controversy and even seemed to thrive on adversity, but he loved most to avoid both: "I hope, sir, that these considerations may bring about a solution that is both amiable and prompt. As an organ builder, I like things to be harmonious; and despite all the prestige that a victory might bring, I prefer peace."[4]

CHAPTER ONE

·

The Industrial Aftermath of the Revolution

The Revolution left French organs in ruins. Had the Reign of Terror (1792-94) continued to the end of the 18th century, it is likely that the art of organ building would have vanished from France altogether. The great builders were dead — LeFébure in 1784 and François-Henri Cliquot in 1791 — and the rest had dispersed to seek a livelihood in joinery. There was virtually no work for organ builders for more than a quarter-century. Countless organs were vandalized, or their pipes were melted down for bullets; confiscated churches were transformed into "Temples of Reason". Those instruments surviving the pillage were neglected and often unplayable. By the time of the Second Restoration (1815) only two experienced organ builders remained in Paris, the elder Dallery and Somer, the latter of whom would soon be succeeded by Louis Callinet. No one else in the capital was capable of reviving a tradition that had only recently (1790) produced Cliquot's masterpiece at the Cathedral of Poitiers, but since then had all but disappeared.

In the 1820's the government undertook the restoration of some cathedral organs, the aim probably being to seek favor from the clergy more than to preserve what was left of a national treasure. Enormous sums were allocated to the brothers Claude, of Mirecourt, whose deplorable activities contributed more to the destruction of French organs than to their preservation. At Tours, Le Mans, Nancy, and many other cathedrals, wind pressures were reduced and voicing mutilated, in order to hide the leaks in wind chests that the Claudes were being paid to repair. The wise counsel of the learned monk, Dom Bédos, went unheeded, and his monumental *L'Art du Facteur d'Orgues* (1770) was ignored.

But the Revolution had other consequences of immeasurable importance to the art of making musical instruments in France. The ancient guild system was destroyed and a new order established, providing the atmosphere for rapid development in the forthcoming industrial age. The Industrial Revolution had come first to England in the 18th century, a circumstance that strengthened her prosperity after the victory at Waterloo. Now, France would be the first on the Continent to feel the impact of machine tools and mass production. The craftsman's traditional practices and forms were given up wherever a machine was thought to improve the final product. The products of machine tools — uniform, superhuman — were set up as models against which artisans and handworkers were forced to compete.

The Restoration monarchy in France (1814-30) sought to develop industrial competition with the ancient foe across the Channel. From 1820 on, subsidies were provided to support industrial exhibitions, encouraging a fever of competitive activity and innovation to spread into the world of music. Musical instruments of all descriptions were prominently displayed, such as various models of the piano: the upright, square, grand and upright grand pianos; the oblique and the cottage piano, and the piccolo piano. Improvements in the action were patented in dozens by Érard, Broadwood, Streicher, Lord, Currier, Dodd, and many others. In 1834, Camille Pleyel and his partner, Kalkbrenner, employing two hundred and fifty workmen, manufactured over a thousand pianos. Is it surprising that at the new *Conservatoire National Supérieur de Musique* hundreds of harpsichords, plundered from the nobles during the Revolution, were piled up and burned as worthless?

The harpsichord and clavichord were forsaken, yielding to a successor, the pianoforte. For a time, to be sure, they could be recognized as close relatives, but each new improvement for the piano emphasized the dissimilarities. Such also was the fate of the organ in the same period. However, keyed instruments with pipes, no matter how unlike their ancestors, never lost their generic name. The longing for "expression" on the organ was coupled to the search for greatly increased sonority to form the basis for the development of the Romantic organ, which differs as much from its classical ancestors as the 19th century piano differs from the harpsichord or clavichord.

Toward the end of the 18th century there came into being a new keyed instrument that was to have a profound effect on the development of the organ: the harmonium, or free reed instrument. The principle of free reeds may have been adapted from the Chinese *cheng*, an instrument making use of many small free reeds of brass. In 1788, the eccentric Abbé Vogler learned of the free reed in St. Petersburg. By 1790, in Holland, he had developed it for the organ. Meanwhile, Sébastien Érard (1752-1831), the inventive piano maker in Paris, was searching for a way to give the organ "expressive" attributes, while keeping its ability to sustain sounds. His *pianos organisés avec deux claviers* combined the organ and piano under the control of one player, the keyboards being playable separately, or coupled together. Despite the popularity of the *piano organisé* in Paris, Érard was not satisfied until he discovered a means by which the player at the organ keyboard might transmit the "impressions of his soul" through the fingertips and keys. Just before the Revolution he achieved his aim in an instrument commissioned for Marie-Antoinette. Abbé Vogler controlled the wind for his free reeds with a pedal; Érard had devised a method of controlling their dynamic power by pressure on the keys themselves, connecting them to the wind system. This was the first such attempt, but the instrument was never finished. Fate claimed Marie-Antoinette, and Érard fled to England.

A few years later, Gabriel Joseph Grenié (d. 1837), who knew of Érard's work, used a pedal to control the wind pressure on free reeds. Many such harmoniums with pedal "expression" were made in Germany during the first decade of the 19th century under the trade names *Eolian* and *Physharmonica.* Meanwhile Érard, in England during the Terror (1792), occupied his time with improvements on the harp, resulting in his famed *harpe à double mouvement,* and later in France, he built the epoch-making double escapement action for the piano (1821).

The harmonium, or *orgue expressif,* and free reed stops in otherwise conventional pipe organs enjoyed an immense popularity in the 19th century. We shall see that Cavaillé-Coll's *Poïkilorgue* sparked Rossini's interest in the young craftsman, a circumstance that determined the timing of Aristide's pilgrimage to Paris. The Cavaillé-Colls knew that free reed instruments seemed to answer the demand for "expression" in the organ, and they were among the first to patent a type of harmonium. They were also among the first in France to install the swell. A brief account of the contrasting musical characteristics of free as against conventional organ reeds is indispensable at this point, even though Cavaillé-Coll's solution to problems of "expression" ultimately involved rejection of the free reed principle.

Since the 16th century the organ has made use not only of flue pipes — principals and flutes — but also of reed pipes, which can be compared in terms of sound production to oboes, clarinets, or bassoons. These conventional or "striking" reeds consist of metal tongues that beat against openings in the shallot, or reed. The shallot is a downward extension of the pipe resonator, and air is admitted at a theoretically constant pressure by a valve inside the chest. This is an essential condition for the success of striking reeds, as the main strength of their sound comes from the air in the pipe, rather than from the vibration of the tongue. That is, the pitch generated by the tongue and reed is amplified and reinforced harmonically by the pipe, which is in resonance with the reed's vibration. It is the reinforcement of the reed's harmonics that gives the sound its timbre and brilliance. A conical resonator, such as is used for *Trompettes,* will respond equally to all harmoncis, while a cylindrical resonator, for Clarinets, *Cromornes,* or Dulcians, will reinforce only the odd-numbered harmonics.

Free reeds differ from conventional organ reeds in that their tongues vibrate in both directions, rather than beating against an opening in the shallot. The tongue of a free reed, on the other hand, is screwed to a metal plate so that it may swing back and forth on both sides of an opening in the plate, and it must be fitted so that it is not hindered in its vibrations. A spring, or tuning clip, exerts some control on the reed's activity by lengthening or shortening its vibrating portion. While the pitch of the ordinary striking reed changes markedly with the slightest fluctuation of wind pressure, the frequency of vibration in free reeds does not change at all as the wind pressure is increased or decreased. Thus, the dynamic range of free reeds, due to the pendular motion of the tongue, affords a very wide "expressive" range, dependent only upon the limits of wind pressure that may be applied. In much the same manner, we may observe no change of pitch in the vibrating arms of a tuning fork, no matter how sharply it may be struck. Because of these characteristics of constant pitch and considerable dynamic power, it was discovered that free reeds could generate low pitches of great force. When attached to normal pipe resonators, the free reeds were enclosed in oversized boots, so as to provide them with a substantial volume of wind.

As the French harmonium operates on wind pressure, rather than on partial vacuum, the valve setting the reed in motion was above the reed, and not inside the chest. That is the secret of its wide dynamic range. The so-called "American organ", or "parlor organ" is a harmonium with suction bellows, like a harmonica, and its sound is therefore softer and slower to respond. The operation of the harmonium as Cavaillé-Coll knew it is described thus by Sir James Jeans: "The reed . . . consists of a spring of metal which is screwed down tightly at one end, and is shaped to fit closely into an aperture in a rigid piece of metal, which lies between a lower wind-chest and an upper wind-chest. When the appropriate stop of the harmonium is drawn, air under pressure fills the wind-chest and spreads round the reed into the upper wind-chest. But before the pressures in the two chests have become fully equalized, the elasticity of the reed carries it back to its original position, so that the flow of air is checked and the pressure again increases. By a continued repetition of this process, the reed is set into violent vibration, with a period equal to that of its free vibration."[1]

Curt Sachs has said: "Romanticism vibrated between two poles of expression. At one end of its sphere were mysticism and sentimentality, and at the other violence and passion. This contrast required the overwhelming power and strong accents of wind instruments."[2]

The harmonium seemed for a time to answer the requirement for such dynamic expression, and organ builders delighted in incorporating free reed registers.[3] Thousands of harmoniums were manufactured under a variety of trade names. In 1856, Adrien LaFage listed the following free reed instruments that had been on the market: *typotone, accordéon, éolodicon, physharmonica, antiphonel, poïkilorgue, aéronino, harmoniphon, séraphina, concertina,* and *organino.* In addition, there were chord-organs for the accompaniment of chant in small churches, playable with one finger: the *symphonista-Guichené;* the *orgue Cabias,* displayed in the Exhibition of 1834, and the *milacor.*

The influential Fétis, publisher of *La Revue Musicale,* was convinced that the *orgue expressif* signalled a revolution in the history of the organ. In a series of articles in 1829 he described what must have been a remarkable *grand orgue expressif,* designed by the indomitable Sébastien Érard for Charles X. Érard, internationally famous because of his escapement action for the piano and his harp with pedals, had decided to re-enter the field of organ building in 1826. Realizing that his ideas could not be put into concrete form without the aid of an experienced organ builder, he persuaded John Abbey (1785- ?) to move from London to Paris under his protection, and to build for him a free reed organ for the *Exposition des produits de l'industrie nationale* (1827). Another followed for the *Couvent de la Légion d'Honneur* at St.-Denis. King Charles X was so impressed with Érard's exhibition instrument that he ordered a *grand orgue expressif* for the Royal Chapel at the Tuileries. The royal order was executed for Érard by John Abbey in 1829. Unfortunately, that instrument, which inspired Fétis' articles, was destroyed with the Tuileries during the revolution of 1830. It is possible that the young Aristide Cavaillé-Coll, working in Lérida, read and absorbed Fetis' description, taking special note of Érard's pedal controls for stops, his use of Cumming's inverted-fold bellows, and the Venetian swell. These matters had already attracted Cavaillé-Coll's attention in his eighteenth year.

Fétis described Érard's *grand orgue expressif* as "the most successful one that has been built thus far, and perhaps the *nec plus ultra* of all possible improvements".[4] He identified the roots of this new revolution in musical expression in the dramatic compositions of the late 16th century. There was at that time a conflict between the dominant sacred music of Palestrina, serious and severe, and the intruding dramatic styles as later exemplified in the works of Bach and Handel. Now that dramatic expressive styles of composition had won the day in sacred music there was an urgent necessity for a revolution in musical instruments of the church, particularly the organ. The organ of classical times, in his opinion, lacked the capability for accent, no matter how majestic its sonority. The intrinsic absence of accent, or modification in intensity of sound, had made the conventional organ ineffectual for expressive music. Thus, the *orgue expressif* of Érard was to Fétis "the signal" that Bach could be reborn, rather than abandoned.

Whether Érard shared Fétis' extravagant claims for his *grandes orgues expressives* is not known. But at seventy-seven he was determined to provide the *Chapelle du Roi* with the full sound of a *grand orgue,* generated from an instrument of relatively small dimension. The key to his "success" lay in the expressive manual with finger control for the wind pressure, which for all its merits never fulfilled Fétis' promises for it. The instrument was disposed as follows:

Manual compass: 6½ octaves

Pedal compass: 2 octaves

Wind supply: two rectangular bellows in the English style, arranged vertically and moved by one lever, requiring one-third or one-quarter the space needed for a conventional cuneiform system.

Three manuals, of which the first and second were enclosed behind Venetian shutters, and the third was "expressive".

Couplers: II + I; III + II; III + 1; Ped + 1

Eleven pedal pistons operating the stops, on or off.

Stoplist:

1. Flûte ouverte 8'	7. Quinte
2. Flûte 4'	8. Fourniture IV
3. Bourdon 16'	9. Trompette
4. Bourdon 8'	10. Chromorne (*sic*)
5. Prestant	11. Hautbois
6. Doublette	12. Basson

Hamel described the operation of Érard's expressive keyboard as follows:

"The organ in the chapel of The Tuileries was built according to the same design, having moreover but one manual for a stop made expressive by finger pressure alone. Plate 43, figs. 974 and 975, shows the elevation and plan of the articulated pallets used by Érard: the arrangement of the pallets is the only difference between his instrument and Grenié's. All sections of the pallet are attached to a single strip of leather, and they bear against part *o*. The latter is bored with holes *g*, *h*, *i*, and *j*, of different sizes, through which wind enters the channel. The pallet sections are held closed by springs *k*, secured by a screw at *p*. Part *o*, carrying the pallets and springs, is attached beneath the channel by a screw at one end, and at the other by a dovetail, *s*, engaging a slot in the cut chest. A sticker, controlled by the key, bears against pallet *f* and opens sections *e d c b* in succession, according to the degree to which the key is depressed. However ingenius this invention may have been, and whatever praise it may have received, this scheme has disadvantages that preclude its use in organs: therefore, it has remained unsuccessful."[5]

"Sébastien Érard was too old and too inexperienced in organ building to deliver it singlehanded from its classical fetters. Nevertheless, he had made a valuable contribution towards bringing the French organ up to date. Through his influence, John Abbey had introduced Paris to Cummings new, improved wind system, which consisted of feeder bellows and wind reservoirs making use of inverted folds for increased stabilization of the wind at all positions.[6] Érard was the first in Paris to use the Venetian swell, which was already familiar to the Cavaillé-Colls in the southern provinces. Érard's legacy included some of the first experiments with free reeds, the first successful control of their volume by the manual keys themselves, the first *piano organisé*, the use of full piano compass for organ manuals, and the invention of pedal controls for the stop action.

By 1830, pianos and harmoniums were being turned out by the thousands, whereas most organ builders had not yet felt the nervous turbulence of the industrial age. To arouse and regenerate the art of organ building would demand the creative energy of a young man, brilliant and firmly disciplined in the ancient tradition. That person was to be Aristide Cavaillé-Coll, who was swept into the mainstream of cultural life in the capital, as though foreordained.

CHAPTER TWO

Aristide Cavaillé-Coll Goes To Paris.

It was from a set of seemingly fortuitous conditions that the longest and most illustrious career in 19th century organ building emerged. By accident, Aristide Cavaillé-Coll, born in a remote corner of France, was thrust unexpectedly into the rapid and continuing current of change in Paris. But it was neither he alone nor Érard, nor Rossini who set the Romantic era in motion. Organ building was behind the times, and the level of performance in church music disgraceful. Consider the report of Felix Mendelssohn, a conservative when it came to organs, who visited the Church of St.-Sulpice in Paris less than a year before Cavaillé-Coll embarked from Toulouse:

"I have just come from St.-Sulpice, where the organist showed off his organ to me; it sounded like a full chorus of old women's voices; but they maintain that it is the finest organ in Europe if it were only put into proper order, which would cost 30,000 fr. The effect of the *canto fermo*, accompanied by the serpent, those who have not heard it could scarcely conceive, and clumsy bells are ringing all the time."[1]

When Cavaillé-Coll settled in Paris, the railroad was still hardly known on the Continent. Early in 1832, Mendelssohn travelled by stagecoach, even though there were over 1200 miles of canals in France. So rapid was the change in modes and speed of communication that by the time Cavaillé-Coll needed to do so, he could count on the railroad for keeping in touch with his brother in the south. Aristide moved about the country with unprecedented speed, overseeing organ projects progressing in several provinces at the same time. The shops of musical instrument makers were constantly expanding, to keep up with the new tempo of commerce. For instance, Alexandre, maker of harmoniums, employed over four hundred workers by the middle of the century. While Cavaillé-Coll never saw fit to expand his work force to such numbers, his entry into the musical world came at a moment when conservative thinking was all but unacceptable. Had he waited ten years, the initiative would have been seized by another, Félix Danjou, two years his junior. Had he been earlier, he could not have benefited from the priceless innovations of Sébastien Érard and John Abbey.

The first Cavaillé to become an organ builder was Joseph, a Dominican monk of the 18th century who was associated with Isnard in the construction of several organs in the south of France. Joseph trained his orphaned nephew, Jean-Pierre, and the two worked together until 1765, when the younger man sojourned alone in Barcelona. There Jean-Pierre built two organs, and on February 12, 1767, married a Spanish girl, Marie-Françoise Coll. Their son, Dominique-Hyacinthe Cavaillé-Coll (1771-1862) was born in Toulouse, but he spent his early years in Barcelona, where he first learned to read in his mother's native language, Catalan. Jean-Pierre built the organ in St.-Michael, Castelnaudary, known to Dom Bédos. He also restored the instrument in the Cathedral of Carcassonne, and built those at St.-Guilhem-du-Desert and in the Cathedral of Montréal (Aude). For the latter, in 1785, his collaborator was his son Dominique, then fourteen years old. During the Revolution the Cavaillé-Colls escaped to Barcelona. In 1806, Dominique was back again in Toulouse at the church of the Cordeliers restoring the organ, originally built by his father and Lépine. After his marriage in 1807, Dominique established the family in Montpellier, where two sons were born: Vincent, on October 9, 1808, and Aristide, on February 4, 1811. But the events of 1815 drove them once more across the border to Spain, where Dominique worked on several organs, including the restoration of the great instrument at the Cathedral of Lérida. Aristide, then, had his first schooling in Spanish. But in 1822 a plague sent them all back to France.

Aristide and his brother apprenticed to their father at St.-Michel-de-Gaillac from 1824 to 1827. In 1829, Aristide was sent alone to Lerida, charged with completing the restoration of the Cathedral organ which had been suspended in 1822. There he became absorbed with problems that were to engage his attention for many years to come. At eighteen he was already seeking to stabilize the wind by maintaining the parallelism of folds in the bellows in order to equalize their action while opening and closing. He also devised and installed a pedal control for coupling and uncoupling the manuals. This relieved the player of the necessity of removing both hands from the keys to slide the keyboard itself.[2] Back in Toulouse in 1831, he applied himself to the study of mathematics and the invention of a type of harmonium, the *Poïkilorgue,* which was produced successfully for some years.

Aristide Cavaillé-Coll at eighteen was seen by his father to possess the disposition and aptitude that would qualify him for success as an organ builder. He was a child of the new century, gifted in mathematics and physics, endowed with the power to conceive and present new combinations of facts or to re-interpret known combinations, and highly motivated in devising new methods and in convincing others of their intrinsic worth. Moreover, Aristide was an assiduous worker, a persistent salesman, a keen politician, and a patient and lovable man. Nor had he to suffer the frustrations that come from having been born too soon, as did his counterpart in the world of the piano, Sébastien Érard.

By mere chance, it was Gioacchino Rossini (1792-1868), the idol of Parisian opera circles, who accelerated the most striking stylistic change in the history of

French organ building. The story is told by Cecile Cavaillé-Coll, taken from her father's correspondence. Rossini arrived in Toulouse in September, 1832, to direct Meyerbeer's new opera, *Robert le Diable*, which had created a sensation a year earlier. Coincidentally, this was the first opera calling for an organ with the orchestral accompaniment. As the theater in Toulouse lacked a pipe organ in the pit, a Cavaillé-Coll *Poïkilorgue* had been supplied by its enterprising builder. The distinguished visitor was so taken with the sound of Aristide's harmonium that he sought to acquaint himself with its makers. Is it possible that Rossini had never before heard a harmonium? The composer urged Aristide, who was just twenty-one years old, to go to Paris, suggesting that he was wasting his talents in the provinces.

A year later, on September 17, 1833, Aristide set off for Paris, armed with letters of introduction to Baron de Prony, Lacroix, Cagniard de la Tour, Cherubini, Berton, and the organ builders Érard, Callinet, Davrainville, and Dallery. Starting on September 23 he made his visits, but the last proved to be decisive. Henri Berton was a professor at the *Conservatoire de Musique* and conductor of the orchestra at the *Théâtre Italien*, where Rossini had been director from 1824 to 1826. It happened that Berton had been named president of a special commission from the Academy of Fine Arts, to choose the builder of a large organ for the Royal Church of St.-Denis. According to Cecile Cavaillé-Coll's account, which cannot be denied, Berton suggested in that first interview with Aristide Cavaillé-Coll that there was still time for him to enter the competition for this monumental project. He immediately dispatched the young man to St.-Denis to take measurements. In the three days remaining, Cavaillé-Coll composed the winning proposal, using for an office his room in an old hotel on Quai Voltaire. The award, announced on October 2, must have been a terrible shock to the losing competitors: Pierre Érard, John Abbey, Louis Callinet, and Dallery, who is said to have turned Aristide away from his door only a few days earlier.

The loss of the contract for St.-Denis to a young *parvenu* was painful to them all, who knew the winner would gain immense prestige from this sort of recognition. The ancient basilica of St.-Denis, named after the first Bishop of Paris and burial place of French monarchs, was to be entirely restored at government expense. The organ would be the largest and most prestigious in France, leading to further important contracts. Such was indeed the case, for only two days after Cavaillé-Coll was announced the winner at St.-Denis, the priest of the fashionable Parisian church of Notre-Dame-de-Lorette invited him to submit a proposal for an organ of considerable size.

With neither a workshop nor the credit to rent one, the twenty-two-year-old Cavaillé-Coll had established himself as the most favored organ builder in the realm. His father rushed to Paris. A workshop was rented at 14 rue Neuve-St.-Georges (renamed and renumbered in 1835, 42 rue Notre-Dame-de-Lorette). Aristide's older brother, Vincent, arrived with an old friend, Jean Puig, of Barcelona, to set the new shop in motion. Dominique established himself in the church at St.-Denis, where he commenced making pipes for both organs.

The reactions of the press were less than enthusiastic, as noted in the *Revue Musicale,* December 14, 1833:

"The Building of an Organ in the Church of Saint-Denis.

"It is a tradition with the *Revue musicale* to speak out whenever the cause of music is at issue, since the *Revue* is the only publication devoted to that art. An occasion has arisen which is serious enough to warrant informing our readers briefly concerning it.

"The French government has appropriated a sizable sum of money for the purpose of building an organ in the church of Saint-Denis. There has never, perhaps, been a better opportunity for erecting the handsomest and most fully developed of instruments: but in order that this goal might be attained, the task should have been entrusted to one or more builders whose work is available for inspection. Apparently, the Minister felt he should leave the choice of a builder and the evaluation of his project to a committee made up of members of the Music Section of the Institute.

"Of course, no one respects the talent of Messrs. Cherubini, Berton, and the other committee members more than we do, but this is a matter entirely foreign to them, requiring the knowledge of an engineer, an organist, and an organ builder combined. To consider the committee members capable of making decisions in such a matter would indeed be an insult to them, since it assumes they have squandered on extraneous studies the precious time they could have spent composing masterpieces. Furthermore, I doubt that a single member of the committee has made organ music his specialty.

"What has been the consequence of the Minister's trust? The gentlemen of the committee have singled out a builder from the provinces whose work they are unacquainted with, and who apparently was armed with endorsements and perhaps even influential patronage. In any event, it is said that without having inspected even one of his instruments, the committee awarded him 80,000 fr. worth of work at Saint-Denis.

"Next, swayed by the committee's decision, the parish priest of Notre-Dame-de-Lorette is having the same individual build a 30,000-fr. organ. There were two builders in Paris, Messrs. Callinet and Dallery, who have built several large instruments: their work should have been inspected and judged, in order to make the award to one of them.

"Fashion holds such sway in Paris that it would be no surprise if this builder — whose worth, I repeat, is entirely unknown — were soon charged with more tasks than he could complete in his entire lifetime.

"We shall go no further with these disheartening remarks. If, as we greatly fear, this builder does not perform what is expected of him, we reserve the right to remind the gentlemen of the committee that they should have declined to assume responsibility in a matter wholly foreign to their competence."[3]

Five years intervened before the inauguration of the first of the two organs to be completed, Notre-Dame-de-Lorette. The *Revue Musicale* took note of the event on October 28, 1838. Now, harsh words were addressed to the players, while Cavaillé-Coll received nothing but extravagant praise:

"The organ in Notre-Dame-de-Lorette was inaugurated last Monday, before a large and distinguished audience. On seeing the stylish assembly in that church whose décor is as lavish as it is worldly, we might have mistaken the occasion for a concert in *rue Vivienne:* the pieces performed on the organ were not such as to dispel the illusion. Waltzes and coy, clever melodies, reminiscent of the *Opéra* and *Salle Musard,* were played by the *pianists* who tried the new instrument. It is a sad fact, but we must face it: organ playing is in utter decadence today.

As for Messrs. Cavaillé, we have long recognized them to be skillful and scrupulous organ builders. The instrument they have just completed could not fail to be satisfactory. Especially if we consider the difficulties they had to resolve in this installation, we must acknowledge their skill and the quality of their work.

Messrs. Cavaillé recently built an organ at Lorient, and we have in hand a most favorable account of it. We have learned with pleasure that other major projects have been awarded to them. May numerous contracts reward them for the untiring dedication with which they advance their craft."[4]

In five days Cavaillé-Coll had established a career in Paris. In five years he had overcome the power of the opposition. And still there were more than fifty years of virtually uninterrupted productive time ahead.

CHAPTER THREE

The Organ for St. Denis and the Barker Machine

The text of Cavaillé-Coll's winning proposal for St.-Denis appears in the first book of his contracts, dated October 7, 1833 (see Appendix C). It is an odd combination of classical requirements with eccentric "modern improvements", all of which could fit only into an instrument of immense size. A second document followed close by, on January 10, 1834, after old Dominique arrived in Paris. The number of stops dropped from eighty-four to seventy-one, while the price rose from 80,000 fr. to 85,000 fr. Was it Dominique who forced economies in the plan? A comparison of the two stoplists follows:

St. Denis, October 2, 1833
Pédale (2 octaves)
1. Flûte ouverte 32
2. Flûte 16′
3. Flûte 16′ octaviante
    (8′ pitch)
4. Flûte 8′
5. Flûte 8′, octaviante
    (4′ pitch)
6. Flûte 4′
7. Flûte 4′, octaviante
    (2′ pitch)
8. Gros nazard octaviant
    (at the 5th of the Prestant)
9. Bombarde
10. Trompette
11. Cor de chasse
12. Clairon
13. Clairon, octave higher
14. Clairon, two octaves higher
15. Grosse caisse, Cymbales, and
    Chapeau chinois
16. Caisse roulante

St. Denis, January 10, 1834
Pédale (2 octaves, F to F) 25 notes
1. Flûte 32′
2. Flûte 16′ (to 24′)
3. Flûte 8′ (to 12′)
4. Flûte 4′ (to 6′)
5. Nazard, at the fifth of the
    8′ stops
6. Bombarde 24′, wood
7. Basson 12′, wood
8. Bombarde 12′, tin
9. Première Trompette 8′
10. Seconde Trompette 8′
11. Clairon
12. Clairon octave

1833

Positif (Manual I) 54 notes
 1. Cornet V
 2. Montre 8'
 3. Prestant 4'
 4. Bourdon 16'
 5. Flûte 8'
 6. Flûte 4'
 7. Nazard
 8. Quarte
 9. Tierce
10. Larigot
11. Doublette
12. Fourniture V
13. Cymbale IV
14. Trompette
15. Basson

Grand Orgue (Manual II) 54 notes
 1. Grand Cornet IX
 2. Montre 32', from 24' F
 3. Montre 16'
 4. Montre 8'
 5. Violoncelle 8'
 6. Bourdon 16'
 7. Bourdon 8'
 8. Flûte ouverte 8'
 9. Gros nazard 8' (sic)
10. Prestant 4'
11. Flûte 4'
12. Nazard
13. Quarte
14. Tierce
15. Doublette
16. Grosse fourniture IV
17. Grosse cymbale IV
18. Fourniture IV
19. Cymbale VI
20. Trompette à pavillon

Bombarde (Manual III) 54 notes
 1. Grand Cornet IX
 2. Flûte 16'
 3. Flûte 8'
 4. Flûte 4'
 5. Prestant

1834

Positif (Manual I) 54 notes
 1. Bourdon 16'
 2. Montre 8'
 3. Prestant 4'
 4. Bourdon 8'
 5. Flûte 4'
 6. Nazard
 7. Doublette 2'
 8. Tierce
 9. Cymbale IV
10. Fourniture IV
11. Flûte octaviante 8'
12. Flûte octaviante 4'
13. Flûte 2'
14. Trompette 8'
15. Cor d'harmonie / Hautbois
16. Cromorne 8'
17. Clairon 4'

Grand Orgue (Manual II) 54 notes
 1. Grand Cornet III
 2. Montre 32'
 3. Montre 16'
 4. Montre 8'
 5. Prestant 4'
 6. Bourdon 16'
 7. Bourdon 8'
 8. Dessus de flûte (traversière)
 9. Flûte (Viole)
10. Nazard
11. Flûte octaviante
12. Doublette
13. Grosse Fourniture III
14. Grosse Cymbale III
15. Fourniture III
16. Cymbale III
17. Trompette (à pavillon) to 16' C
18. Basson / Cor anglais
19. Clairon
20. Voix humaine

Bombarde (Manual III) 54 notes
 1. Grand Cornet IX
 2. Bourdon 16'
 3. Bourdon 8'
 4. Flûte 8'
 5. Prestant 4'

1833
  6. Nazard
  7. Quarte
  8. Tierce
  9. Bombarde
  10. Trompette
  11. Clairon

Stops mounted horizontally
       outside the organ case
  12. Trompette
  13. Clairon, with one break
  14. Clairon, octave higher, with two breaks
  15. Clairon, two octaves higher, with three breaks

1834
  6. Flûte 4′
  7. Quarte 2′
  8. Bombarde
  9. Première Trompette de Bombarde
  10. Seconde Trompette de Bombarde
  11. Premier Clairon
  12. Second Clairon

Récit (Manual IV) 37 notes, F to F
  1. Flûte conique 8′
  2. Bourdon 8′
  3. Cornet VI
  4. Trompette
  5. Hautbois
Jeux expressifs, mounted on the
       Récit chest
  6. Basson
  7. Cor anglais / Hautbois
  8. Voix humaine
  9. Trompette expressive mounted outside
  10. Set of Bells, played from Manual IV

Récit and Echo (Manual IV) 54 notes
  1. Flûte (harmonique) 8′
  2. Prestant 4′ (replaced by Flûte
       octaviante)
  3. Bourdon 8′
  4. Flûte octaviante 4′
  5. Doublette 2′
  6. Trompette (harmonique)
  7. Clairon (harmonique)
  8. Voix humaine (harmonique)

Echo (Manual V) 37 notes, F to F
  1. Bourdon 16′
  2. Flûte 8 (ouverte)
  3. Flûte 4′
  4. Cornet V
  5. Violon
  6. Clarinette
  7. Voix humaine 16′ pitch
  8. Flûte traversière

Three pedal controls, "permitting
       coupling two or three manuals
       together"
Three pedals controlling:
    a. Grosse caisse, cymbale, and chapeau chinois
    b. Caisse roulante
    c. Echo shutters
Pedal for controlling wind on *jeux expressifs*

Jeux expressifs (Manual V) 54 notes
  1. Cor anglais
  2. Voix humaine

Couplers: I + II
             II + III
             III + IV
             IV + V
             Pedal for Récit shutters
             Pedal for controlling
             wind on *jeux expressifs*

Noteworthy items in the project of 1833

1   The pedal, *Grand Orgue,* and *Bombarde* chests were to be given double pallet boxes, so that reeds could be on higher wind pressures than flues ("required by the tone-quality of the various wind instruments to be imitated").

2.   The *Positif* would be a *Positif-de-dos,* situated traditionally behind the player.

3.   Cuneiform bellows with compensating weights were defined as superior to the new style feeders and bellows.

4.   Harmonic, or double length, flutes were to be used in the pedal at 8′, 4′, and 2′ pitches. This was the first of many statements by Cavaillé-Coll on the advantages of harmonic pipes, and the only one defending their use in the bass range. Subsequently, they appeared only in the trebles. He said:

"The three overblowing stops placed in the *Pédale* may raise a question as to why I have used such large pipes to produce sounds which might be obtained from pipes half their size. My answer is that they are not the same sounds, and they can be distinguished by their characteristic timbres. The latter are produced by a vibrating column of air with a node at its mid-point, so that although the pitch is the same, the tone is more aggressive and the volume greater. If we take the volume of air as an index of the volume of sound, the ratio with a conventional pipe of the same pitch is $1:2^3$, or $1:8$. Therefore, the sound of overblown pipes is eight times greater than that of conventional pipes at the same pitches; so if I devote space to these larger pipes, I obtain greater effects from them." (*Devis* I, 2, October 7, 1833)

5.   Resonators for reed pipes were to be made in shapes resembling their orchestral counterparts, rather than the customarily plain cone-shaped resonators.

6.   Four horizontal trumpet stops in the Spanish style were to be installed in the *Bombarde;* also, the *Trompette expressive* would be mounted horizontally.

7.   The *Récit* was to be unenclosed in the classical manner, but with double pallet boxes on the chest to accommodate the *jeux expressifs* played from the same keyboard.

8.   The *Echo,* enclosed behind shutters operated by foot, would lack powerful reeds.

9.   The classical layout of flute mutation ranks was not yet given up, as there were no harmonic flutes in the manuals for this plan. Clearly, the two *Grands Cornets* IX were looked upon as strengthening features for the trebles of the trumpets. The *Echo,* despite its *Cornet V,* was given two unconventional reed voices: the *Clarinette,* and the *Voix humaine* 16′.

10.   Manual coupling was to be operated by pedal levers, just as Cavaillé-Coll had provided them at Lérida before he was twenty years old. Thus, all manual keyboards would be stationary, "permitting coupling two or three manuals together, without interruption in performance".

11.   All metal pipes were to be hammered, for "improved tone quality".

12.   The pedalboard, though French in compass with *ravalement,* would be made in the German style, with long keys, to allow "playing legato scales with the same foot".

13.   The five manual keyboards would be made "like those of the best pianos".

Noteworthy items in the project of 1834

1. There was a marked reduction in the number of mutation ranks, favoring instead stronger batteries of reeds and the substitution of harmonic flutes in the manuals.

2. The traditional location of *Positif* would be abandoned; its new location was to be in the "lower part of the organ case".

3. The cumbersome harmonic flue pipes from the *Pédale* were eliminated.

4. The wind system was revised. Previous arguments for cuneiform bellows were abandoned in favor of eight rectangular reservoirs with feeders.

5. Cavaillé-Coll defended the two-octave pedal compass as superior to a three-octave compass as listed in the official requirements.

6. The *Echo* was suppressed, and the *Récit* enclosed. Powerful harmonic reeds were added to the *Récit*. Note that it was not until Cavaillé-Coll's 1839 proposal (quoted below) that he decided to use double walls for the swell box, with sawdust between, and double shutters on the front.

7. The compass of the *Récit* was expanded from 37 to 54 keys.

8. All but two of the *jeux expressifs* were abandoned. Did this signal Cavaillé-Coll's growing disillusionment with free reeds? Or did Dominique prevail against too many expensive and dangerous experiments?

9. Horizontal reeds were given up.

10. The *Montre* 32 was carried to low C.

11. The total number of pipes was reduced from 5621 to 5301.

12. Bells and other sound effects were eliminated.

13. Additional couplers would make all five manuals playable together. This was a bold and dangerous provision.

Delivery had been promised in three years. It was to Cavaillé-Coll's eventual great advantage that it would be seven before the organ was finished, due to delays in completion of the architectural restoration of the church. Even though the letters show financial difficulties stemming from the delay[1], priceless time was gained for experimentation and study. The elder Cavaillé-Coll understood that an organ of such gigantic size, incorporating several wind-hungry innovations, could not be played comfortably with all five manuals coupled together, nor even with three, or two. Aristide's brilliant, visionary ideas had captured the contract, but how could he be sure that the instrument would be a success? His reputation was strengthened by the completion of several other projects before 1839 — Notre-Dame-de-Lorette in Paris, Lorient, Pontivy, and Dinan — but it would rest ultimately on the results at St.-Denis.

The year 1839 proved to be second only to 1833 for its unexpected good fortune; it was certainly the most important in the history of Romantic organ building. An Englishman, Charles Spackman Barker (1806-79), took a patent in France on a pneumatic machine designed to lighten the manual key action in the organ. Discouraged by refusals on the part of English organ builders, he had gone to Paris to seek support. Precisely at that moment, Cavaillé-Coll needed him most. His own attempts to "modify the pallets so as to decrease the wind pressure on them" had proven unsuccessful. The Barker machine, on the contrary, would do the work of opening the pallets, a development that would eventually make enormous new demands on the wind supply in the organ. But we will best learn of this from Aristide himself, who submitted the following proposal on December 2, 1839.[2] The acceptance of the changes outlined in this document provided the key to vindicating his bold claims for harmonic pipes and varying wind pressures.

"December 2, 1839
Royal Church of Saint-Denis
"An Account of Certain Major Improvements and their Application to the Organ in the Royal Church of Saint-Denis.

Contents

1. Bellows
2. Harmonic, or Overblown Stops
3. Stiffness, or Heaviness of Key-action
4. *Récit* and *Echo: Jeux expressifs*
5. Itemized Estimates of the Cost of the Improvements Discussed in this Paper, as Applied to the Organ in the Royal Church of Saint-Denis.

"Part I.

Bellows

"The bellows of a pipe organ is indisputably the most important part of this gigantic instrument, for the wind supplied by the bellows is the source of the sound: therefore, the bellows brings to life all the pipes that constitute the various instruments that the organ draws upon. The timbre, tone quality, and character of these instruments depend chiefly on the bellows; the correct intonation and pitch of the organ are unattainable unless the bellows possesses all the necessary qualities that we have just mentioned.

"One of the first requirements for the bellows is that they supply steady and continuous wind, for the pitch of the pipes varies with the pressure of the wind: when the pressure increases, the pitch rises; and *vice versa*. Thus, an organ cannot play in tune unless the wind is perfectly even.

"Old-fashioned bellows, such as still exist in most organs in France, do not achieve this goal: the ribs forming the sides of the bellows add their weight to that of the bellows, as the latter opens; thus, the wind-pressure varies.

"Reservoirs presented the same disadvantage for a long time; namely, that the added weight of the ribs increased the wind-pressure. In addition, reservoirs required steadying by a slide mechanism, whose friction aggravated the irregularity of the wind.

"A series of improvements that we have made in reservoir construction enable us to achieve the requisite evenness of pressure: an iron pantograph mechanism of our design, fitted to each reservoir, makes its movement even and as free as possible from friction; and a set of levers, also of our design, fitted inside the reservoirs, causes the ribs to open simultaneously: the variation in pressure once caused by their weight is cancelled by this new device.

"These improvements, without which the organ cannot sound at a stable pitch, are not the only ones demanded by this instrument. The volume and quality of tone, in most of its stops, can be greatly improved. Indeed, if we consider that the powerful, beautiful tone of an orchestra made up of thirty odd instruments outshines the weak, thin tones of an instrument containing several thousand pipes, we are astonished to see that the organ, even with its greater resources, produces no greater power in proportion to its size. The chief cause of this weakness lies in the bellows, where none of the designs known to date gives the instrument either the volume or quality it ought to possess.

"Until now, the wind-pressure used in organs has been no greater than 5 to 10 cm. of water: these figures are the limits between which all the instruments that we have measured with a wind-gauge have been voiced. Indeed, flue stops seem likely to speak well at these pressures, but it is obvious that reed stops require greater pressure, particularly in the upper registers.

"Nevertheless, organ building habitually ignores this essential point: each builder chooses the pressure he deems appropriate to his instrument, so that the same wind-pressure is used for every stop, without distinction. The result is that the flue stops are in danger of being overblown; while the reeds, in contrast, are undersupplied.

"Here is the chief reason why the *Trompette,* the *Clairon,* and other such stops do not possess the character of the instruments whose names they bear. One reason of course lies in the fact that a metal shallot takes the place of the lips, but another is the wind pressure required to sound these instruments.

"It may readily be seen, by blowing on a wind-gauge, that the lungs furnish 50 cm. of wind and more: I have proved that vigorous blowing can produce a pressure of 100 cm.

"Now if we blow on a wind instrument such as the French horn or trumpet, we readily observe that 50 cm. and more are required to make them sound. High pitches demand the greatest pressures, low pitches the least, and the intermediate pitches require pressures between the two extremes.

"These observations suffice to account for the weakness of organ stops in comparison with orchestral instruments: we have just seen that the highest wind pressure used in organs so far is 10 cm., whereas wind instruments require pressures four or five times greater.

"Surely, an organ's effectiveness would be greatly increased if the flue stops were winded at the proper pressure, and the reeds at higher pressures, as they require. Better still, each octave in the compass should receive wind at the pressure suited to the volume of sound which that range should produce.

"In order to achieve this end, a wind supply had to be devised whereby each octave of each stop received the appropriate wind pressure.

"At first glance, this seems easy to accomplish merely by installing a reservoir for each pressure desired. However, if we consider the disadvantages of such an arrangement, the problem proves to be more complex.

"First of all, the large number of bellows required would take up vast amounts of room, making this scheme impossible in most instances.

"Then, since wind is not used evenly but according to the number of stops drawn and the range in which the organist plays: low, high or medium; it could easily come about that one reservoir was exhausted while others were full. Thus the organist might find certain keys silent while others continued to sound.

"Fully aware of these disadvantages, we have designed a new wind supply that meets all the requirements listed above.

"This system is made up of tiered reservoirs, as many as are required for the number of different pressures to be obtained. Although these reservoirs are fed by the same pistons or plungers, the wind pressure derived from each cannot be altered by inept blowing.

"These reservoirs are arranged in such a way that although each supplies wind at a different pressure, a small device allows them to be replenished simultaneously, with no variation in pressure, and with no exhaustion of one reservoir so long as any contains wind.

"This wind supply can have a profound influence on the volume and quality of the organ's tone. By using only two different pressures in the organ we built for the Exhibition, we achieved more satisfactory results as regards volume and uniformity of tone, reinforcement of the trebles of reeds, and — thanks to the ease of dividing the wind among flues and reeds, treble and bass — freedom from the quavering sometimes produced in the melody by certain accompaniments.

"Since the principles underlying this new system permit using as many different wind pressures as may be desired, we may assume that an organ built according to this scheme would produce sounds of an impressive and altogether original character.

"Part 2.   Harmonic, or Overblown Stops

"Organ stops, as made hitherto, consist of pipes which speak the fundamental pitch. In the low register, these stops possess adequate tone; but the higher the pitch, the thinner and shriller their tone becomes. This shortcoming is observed even in the best built organs, for it results from the design of the pipes themselves, as these pipes have always been made.

"Everyone knows that each stop is made up of a set of pipes, one for each note of the keyboard. Each pipe sounds the pitch of the corresponding key. We also know that the dimensions of each pipe are approximately in inverse proportion to the frequency of that pipe. Consequently, the volumes of the pipes vary as the cube of their linear dimensions.

"Taking low C and 1, we have the following figures:

Pitch	CC	C	c	c^1	c^2
Frequency	1	2	4	8	16
Linear dimensions	1	1/2	1/4	1/8	1/16
Volume	1	1/8	1/64	1/512	1/4096

"Now, aside from character and tone, if we admit that the volume of sound produced by a pipe varies as the volume of air contained in the pipe, it will be seen in the above table that the volume of a stop decreases from bass to treble: it is no longer surprising that high pitches in the organ are thin and weak compared to the bass.

"It must be acknowledged that in several organs this defect is somewhat corrected by voicing the bass pipes soft and the trebles loud; but this practice reduces the effectiveness of the bass while making the treble harsh and dry, and no stop has that uniformity of tone which distinguishes a good musical instrument.

"Although they have long been known and studied by physicists, the harmonics of pipes have never yet been used in organ building. We know that harmonics give a fullness and power not found in pipes which speak only the fundamental. The air-column in pipes sounding the harmonics is divided into as many portions as there are harmonics: thus modified, the column modifies the tone, giving it better quality, and increasing its volume without shrillness.

"The wind instruments in the orchestra afford a clear idea of the advantages of harmonic tone over the fundamental.

"In the French horn, for example, the sound is produced by the same resonating body, the different pitches being accomplished by harmonics. We note that the tone of this instrument becomes purer and more beautiful as the pitches rise: the air column is divided into a greater number of segments.

"The trumpet, the cornet, and other instruments in the brass family, of smaller dimensions than the horn, do not have the same smoothness or fullness. Here the air column is smaller, and the volume of sound is accordingly less.

"The sound of the transverse flute, compared to that of an ordinary flute or recorder, again shows us the superiority of tone produced by an instrument containing several times as much air as a smaller instrument of the same kind. Indeed, the same pitches played on each flute, all other things being equal, reveal a volume and purity in the transverse flute that the smaller flute cannot equal.

"The above observations, which anyone can make for himself, bring us to the conclusion that sound increases in fullness and volume as the air column is increased.

"As we have already commented, the low notes in the various stops produce a suitable volume of sound, by means of the fundamental pitch of each pipe. However, in the tenor and treble ranges, the notes lose fullness and volume as the pitches rise. To remedy this defect, we have made several stops as follows: the lowest octave speaks the fundamental; the next octave, the first harmonic; and the third octave, the second harmonic; the fourth, the third harmonic, and so forth.

"Thus, as the pitches rise, the air columns become larger in proportion, and the tone quality is made uniform throughout the compass of the stop.

"Note that the wind pressure required is greater in proportion to the number of harmonics being sounded in the air column.

"In reed stops especially, this increase in pressure is necessary to insure all the fullness and power of which these stops are capable.

"The new system of multiple-pressure bellows mentioned above, apart from the influence it may have on conventional stops, would at the same time be most helpful in securing the most beautiful tone possible in harmonic stops.

"Various experiments which we have already performed with these new stops, and the use of several such stops in the organ we built for the 1839 Exhibition — which organ caused the judges to award us a medal — might well demonstrate the superiority of these stops over those employed until the present time. Not only would the power of the organ be doubled by their use, but the tone would possess an immediacy and purity which cannot be obtained by conventional methods.

"Part 3.   Stiffness, or Heaviness of Key Action

"Organists and builders generally agree that the larger the organ the stiffer the key action. A brief explanation will show that this must be so for reasons of construction, and that of two organs equal in size, the more powerful instrument must have the stiffer manual action.

"The manual keys, when depressed by the organist's fingers, operate a relay mechanism and open the pallets, which allow wind supplied by the bellows to reach the pipes. The pallets are enclosed in a box, called the pallet box, which is connected to the bellows, and they cover the passages through which the wind must reach the pipes. Now if we inquire as to the causes of heavy action, we find (1) the springs holding the pallets closed, and the friction in the mechanism linking keys to pallets, and (2) the pressure exerted on the pallets by the wind from the bellows.

"The first of these causes may be reduced by careful design and construction, but the second cannot. We know that gases exert on the surface of container a pressure equal to that brought to bear on them. Now since each pallet must supply all the pipes corresponding to a given key, it follows that the larger the organ, the greater the wind pressure on each pallet.

"To overcome this obstacle, two methods have been used until the present time. The first consists of increasing the mechanical advantage of the lever-arm formed by the key: in this case, the key dip becomes so great as to hamper the performer. The second method limits the size of the pallets; but then they cannot admit all the wind necessary to supply the pipes adequately, and the pipes do not speak with suitable power. From the above it may be deduced that a large organ with light action must lack volume; otherwise, the excessive key dip is just as serious a handicap, for it does not allow the performer to exploit fully the resources of a large instrument.

"Fully aware of the disadvantages mentioned above, and after studying the methods used to date by the best builders but without success, we determined to find a new method for solving this problem.

"A few experienced builders have attempted to modify the pallets so as to decrease the wind pressure on them. We were also engaged in this attempt when Mr. Barker brought us an appliance of his invention, patented in France, which appliance gives the keyboard all the lightness one might desire, reduces the key dip, and makes no change in the design of the pallets.

"Based on the elasticity of air, this appliance uses the very wind supplied by the bellows.

"Instead of directly overcoming the resistance of the pallet, each key serves as a kind of trigger or detent controlling the action of this device, which in turn opens and closes the pallet.

"For each manual key there is provided a small bellows, connected to the pull-down of a pallet in the chest. These little bellows are so designed that when a key is depressed, the corresponding bellows fills with wind from the main supply. Since air is elastic, the little bellows immediately fills with wind, and it opens the pallet connected to it. When the key is released, the little bellows collapses, and the pallet immediately closes.

"This new device not only allows us to decrease the stiffness of the key action; it also allows us to increase the size of the pallets and thus to supply the pipes with all the wind they need to speak with characteristic power. Finally, it will be observed that this device is a valuable resource where the action of coupled manuals is concerned.

"It is common knowledge that pipe organs are fitted with several keyboards, each of which controls a certain number of stops; and that the full power of the organ can be obtained only by coupling the keyboards in such a way that one of them operates all the others. In this case, the organist is faced with the greatest difficulty, for each keyboard coupled increases the heaviness of the action.

"By using this new scheme, we obtain all the advantages of coupling and none of the disadvantages: since all coupling is done with the aid of the pneumatic device just described, the lightness of the key action is in no way affected by the various combinations.

"Another system of couplers involving this device allows the organist to increase the resources at his disposal and thus double the usual power of the organ.

Récit and Echo: Jeux Expressifs

"We may distinguish two main categories of sound which the organ can produce: (1) those peculiar to the organ, which are made chiefly by foundation stops: their majestic tone is imitated by no other instrument; (2) those which more or less successfully imitate the various instruments in the orchestra.

"True, the latter stops give only an imprecise imitation of the instruments whose names they bear, and they are capable of great improvement in tone quality, as we have pointed out in connection with the bellows and harmonic stops. A further essential quality to be mentioned here is the ability to increase in volume as desired, so as to perfect the imitation of orchestral instruments.

"Not only in our time have efforts been made to give the organ this capability: indeed, old organs frequently bear witness to attempts made long ago towards this goal.

"Thus, a few stops placed in a location unfavorable to the exit of sound were called Echo. Later, these stops were placed in a box, whose lid or side could be opened at will by means of a pedal: thus, shadings were obtained in the volume of sound. Still later, shutters took the place of one side of the box, affording a more precise response to the slightest movement of the pedal, and imparting to the stops whose sound the shutters affected a certain shading which imitated the expression of orchestra instruments.

"However, these stops are usually too limited in number and compass, with reference to the rest of the organ; the powerful low range of the latter overshadows the nuances of the stops contained in the box.

"Now by increasing the number and compass of the stops placed under expression, this division of the organ may be given greater power; but we must point out that in this case the design and even the construction of the box are inadequate to reduce the volume: the sound waves are transmitted by the sides of the box, and the range from loud to soft is reduced to almost nothing.

"We shall now describe a new construction method whose purpose is to give this division much more power and greater range of expression than is possible by conventional means.

"In this scheme, the *Récit* manual is extended so that its compass equals that of the *Grand orgue*. This manual controls stops of the greatest power, and they all have full manual compass. This extension in range is a great advantage for solo stops, and when they are coupled to the *Grand orgue,* they lend greater brilliance to the latter division. The chief improvement, however, lies in the actual construction of the box containing these stops.

"The walls of the box comprise two panels with a space between, the space being filled with sawdust or any other sound-insulating material. The box also possesses two sets of shutters arranged in such a way that one opens before the other, thus allowing every possible gradation of volume. Since the walls of the box are impervious to sound waves, the volume may be reduced or augmented as much as may be desired.

"Thereby, the stops in this division take on all the expressive qualities of orchestra instruments: by virtue of their compass and power, their qualities seem to influence all the stops in the organ, when the latter are played together with the stops under expression.

"Part 5.   Itemized Estimate of the Cost of the Improvements discussed in this
         Paper, as Applied to the Organ in the Royal Church of Saint-Denis.

"I.   Multi-Pressure Bellows

"In order to modify the present bellows in accordance with Part 1 of this paper, various additions would be required as well as alterations in the original construction.

"The additional work would consist of the following:

"1) Adding mechanisms to ensure that the ribs open simultaneously, and not in succession as in conventional bellows, thus contributing to the pitch stability of the organ.

"2) Fitting a new set of wind trunks so as to connect the reservoirs to one another, without changing the pressure created by each.

"3) Increasing the number of wind trunks, as required to supply wind at different pressures to the various chests.

"4) Modifying the wind chests themselves so that they may receive a different wind pressure for each octave in their compass.

"5) Finally, building a new *high-pressure* bellows to supply wind to the treble range of the reed stops as well as to the pneumatic device described in Part 3 of this paper.

"The additions listed above would cost 6,000 francs.

"II Harmonic, or Overblown Stops.

"The harmonic stops described in Part 2 of this paper would require additional labor and expense compared to conventional stops, first because of their greater dimensions, and second because they are more difficult to voice and tune.

"The new stops would be installed as follows:

"In the *Positif*, a *Flûte harmonique*, a *Flûte octaviante* and a *Seconde Flûte octaviante*, a *Trompette harmonique*, and a *Clairon octaviant*.

"In the *Grand orgue*, a *Trompette harmonique à pavillon*: in general, all the reed stops and the chief foundation stops would speak harmonics rather than the fundamental, in the treble range.

"In the *Bombarde*, the same alteration would be made in the treble range of the reed stops.

"In the *Récit*, a high-pressure *Trompette d'harmonie* and *Clairon*, a *Flûte traversière*, a *Flûte octaviante*, and a *Petite Flûte*.

"In the *Pédale*, a *Trompette harmonique*, a *Clairon harmonique*, and a *Second Clairon octaviant*.

"The alteration listed above would cost 8,000 francs.

"III Manuals

"The major improvements described in Part 3 of this paper have as their purpose to eliminate the stiffness usually found in organ actions: they would entail certain alterations in the arrangement of the manuals as already described. This labor, together with building the pneumatic appliance described in this paper, would cost 5,000 francs.

Récit and *Echo: Jeux expressifs*

"The improvements listed in Part 4 of this paper entail further work on the mechanism of this division, and so would cost 1,000 francs.

Total   20,000 francs"

Authorization for the additional work and alterations was granted by the Minister of Public Works in June, 1840. Sensing the urgency, Cavaillé-Coll had already written to his friend Ménard, in Coutances, asking him to come to Paris to make "reed stops and others for St. Denis."[3] By the end of August, he could report to the Minister that "the work . . . is completely finished, and the additional improvements . . . are also about to be terminated."[4] The *Montres* 8′ and 16′ were playable by September;[5] and the organ, though incomplete, was being used for services in October.

The innovations of the 1839 project, outlined above, were put into effect after much of the organ had been built. They were (1) radical alteration of the wind supply to accommodate various wind pressures: a different wind pressure would be supplied for each octave of the compass. The highest pressure would be generated from a new high-pressure bellows, to supply the trebles of the reed stops. (2) Addition of numerous harmonic trebles for flutes and reeds. (3) Reduction from five to four manuals. (4) Redesign of the pedal controls for couplers, etc. It is significant to recall Cavaillé-Coll's statement: "in general, all the reed stops and the chief foundation stops would speak harmonics rather than the fundamental in the treble range".

The instrument as delivered was still smaller than the 1834 project: 4506 pipes and 69 stops, as against 5301 and 71 stops. But the new authorization of 18,000 fr. did not prove sufficient to cover Cavaillé-Coll's extra costs, as seen in his request for an additional 22,000 fr. dated October 19, 1841,[6] one month after the ceremonies of inauguration. The final stoplist follows:

Pédale, F to F, 2 octaves

Flutes	Pipes	*Ravalement* to:
1. Flûte ouverte 32′	25	
2. Flûte ouverte 16′	25	24′
3. Flûte ouverte 8′	25	12′
4. Flûte ouverte 4′	25	6′
5. Gros nasard ou quinte de 8	25	
Reeds		
6. Basse-contre 16′	25	24′
7. Basson 8′	25	12′
8. Bombarde 16′	25	24′
9. Première trompette 8′	25	12′
10. Deuxième trompette 8′	25	12′
11. Premier clarion 4′	25	6′
12. Deuxième clairon 4′	25	6′

Positif, 4½ octaves from C to F

Flutes	*Pipes*
1. Bourdon 16′	54
2. Salicional 8′	54
3. Bourdon 8′	54
4. Prestant 4′	54
5. Flûte 4′	54
6. Nasard ou quinte 3′	54
7. Doublette 2′	54
8. Tierce	54
9. Cymbale IV	216
10. Fourniture IV	216
Reeds and Harmonic stops	
1. Flûte harmonique 8′	54
2. Flûte octaviante 4′	54
3. Flageolet harmonique 2′	54
4. Trompette harmonique 8′	54

  5. Cor d'harmonie et hautbois 8'   54
  6. Cromorne 8'   54
  7. Clairon octaviant 4'   54
  8. Tremblant

Grand Orgue, 4½ octaves, from C to F

	Flutes	*Pipes*
1.	Montre 32'	54
2.	Montre 16'	54
3.	Montre 8'	54
4.	Viole 8'	54
5.	Bourdon 16'	54
6.	Bourdon 8'	54
7.	Flûte traversière harmonique 8'	54
8.	Flûte octaviante harmonique 4'	54
9.	Prestant 4'	54
10.	Nasard ou quinte 3'	54
11.	Doublette 2'	54
12.	Grosse fourniture IV	216
13.	Grosse cymbale IV	216
14.	Fourniture IV	216
15.	Cymbale IV	216
	Reeds	
16.	Première trompette harmonique 8'	54
17.	Deuxième trompette harmonique 8'	54
18.	Basson et cor anglais 8'	54
19.	Clairon octaviant 4'	54
20.	Cornet à pavaillon 8'	54

Bombarde, 4½ octaves, from C to F

	Flutes	*Pipes*
1.	Grand cornet VII	210
2.	Bourdon 16'	54
3.	Bourdon 8'	54
4.	Flûte 8'	54
5.	Prestant 4'	54
6.	Nasard ou quinte 3'	54
7.	Doublette 2'	54
	Reeds	
8.	Bombarde 16'	54
9.	Première trompette de bombarde 8'	54
10.	Deuxième trompette harmonique 8'	54
11.	Premier clairon harmonique 4'	54
12.	Deuxième clairon octaviant 4'	54

Récit-Echo Expressive, 4½ octaves, from C to F

	Flutes	Pipes
1.	Bourdon 8′	54
2.	Flûte harmonique 8′	54
3.	Flûte octaviante harmonique 4′	54
4.	Octavin harmonique 2′	54
5.	Quinte	54
	Reeds	
6.	Trompette harmonique 8′	54
7.	Clairon harmonique 4′	54
8.	Voix humaine harmonique 8′	54

Pédales de combinaison

1. Expression pedal, *Récit.*
2. *Récit* to manual II.
3. *Bombarde* to manual II.
4. *Grand Orgue* to manual II.
5. *Positif* to manual II.
6. *Pédale des dessus,* coupling trebles of reeds and harmonic flutes to the foundations of the *Positif.*
7. *Pédale des basses,* combining basses of reeds and harmonic flutes to the foundations of the *Positif.*
8. *Pédale de tirasse,* coupling basses of all manuals to pedal.
9. *Pédale d'octaves,* coupling all keyboards to the octave below.

The influence of wind requirements on the size, number, and operation of the pallets in the wind chests was explained in Cavaillé-Coll's proposal of 1839 quoted above.[7] It was an accepted fact that the size and dynamic power of an organ must be limited by the ability of human fingers to open the pallets connected to the manual keys. A player was most comfortable opening one pallet per manual key, but he could control two, three, or even four when double pallets and couplers were engaged. Cavaillé-Coll must have known in 1834 that it would be virtually impossible for most organists to play the organ at St.-Denis with five manuals coupled together. In the five years between 1834 and 1839, he had been searching for a solution, we are told, without success. Then Barker appeared.

The Barker machine brought success to Cavaillé-Coll at St.-Denis and assured him the means by which he could continue to modify and increase the organ's sonority. By the application of one Barker pneumatic machine per key on the *Grand Orgue,* the *Grand Orgue* manual could engage the action of all the other manuals through couplers, without the player's noticing the slightest increase in resistance. Potentially the *Grand Orgue* could be coupled to itself at the octaves below or above, thus operating ten, twenty or even more than twenty pallets by the action of one key. Until the machines were applied to the actions of the other keyboards as well, the *Positif* and *Récit* (or others) would continue to operate with the old mechanical action. At St.-Denis in 1841, just as at Ste.-Clotilde in 1859, fifty-four machines responded to the fifty-four keys of the *Grand Orgue*. Only in very large organs did Cavaillé-Coll propose that the Barker device be used for the other keyboards and pedals.[8]

In *Grand Orgue* divisions equipped with the Barker lever, the keys were tripping pneumatic pouches. On the other manuals they were still opening and closing pallets at differing speeds and with differing musical results. No one seemed to care. It was surely not uppermost in musicians' minds to preserve the traditional intimacy between player and sound source upon which our own classical revival bases its *credo*. Rather, the pneumatic device was viewed by Cavaillé-Coll's friends and enemies alike as a scientific marvel that would release the organ at last from primitive restraints. And Cavaillé-Coll himself discounted, probably unwittingly, the value of variable articulateness when he argued that the Barker machine "has as its purpose the lessening of stiffness in the keyboard action as well as increased precision in the prompt speech of the instrument."[9]

Barker's drawing is shown in Plate XVI, as reproduced in the Encyclopédie-Roret.[10]

"The wind in pallet-box *a* rushes into channel *k* as soon as pallet *e* opens, and it inflates pneumatic *q*. This pneumatic has a surface area twice or three times greater than that of the pallets (in the chests). Therefore, by means of a suitable mechanism, the pneumatic can open all the pallets simultaneously as soon as the key opens pallet *e*, which is the only resistance the key must overcome. As soon as the finger releases the key, inlet pallet *e* closes and exhaust pallet *o* opens, so that the pneumatic may collapse immediately. The rise and fall of the top-board of the pneumatic are so prompt that they can scarcely be measured."

Roret, 1905, p. 106.

An eloquent defense of the Barker lever, as improved by Cavaillé-Coll, appeared in a booklet written by Aristide's close friend, Philbert:[11]

"Between the key and the pipes, he added a very small cuneiform bellows, one or two square decimeters only in area, equipped with two small valves, each having a different function. One valve admits wind to the bellows, and the other lets the wind escape. When depressed by the finger, the key opens the former valve and closes the latter. Wind rushes into the bellows, instantly inflating it, and keeps it inflated as long as the second valve remains closed. As soon as the key returns to rest, the opposite occurs: the inlet valve closes, and the exhaust valve simultaneously opens. The wind escapes from the bellows, and the top board falls as promptly as it rose. In a bellows with the dimensions we have mentioned, and at a suitable wind pressure, the top board rises and falls so quickly that the motion is calculated to last only a few thousandths of a second. The most accomplished performer could not guarantee such rapidity when pitted against straight mechanical action, while a further advantage in fast-moving passages is precise regularity of touch: the key cannot be depressed even slightly without opening the bellows *fully*, thus playing the note to *capacity*.

"All the resistance which in a conventional organ must be overcome by means of the key alone is linked through suitable action to the top board of the small bellows. When its dimensions have been properly determined according to the wind pressure, it actuates the entire mechanism promptly and precisely, as we have just stated. However, there is a further advantage in this device, one that is particularly valuable and entirely exclusive to this remarkable machine. Whatever variation there may be in resistance as a result of coupling or uncoupling manuals, be it one or two pallets or *twenty* to *twenty-five* opening simultaneously in some large new organs, the player's finger need never vary its exertion. All the finger need ever do is overcome the slight, always uniform resistance of a single tiny valve: even at the least touch of the key, the valve admits air to the small bellows. In this way the key action of the most enormous organs is made as light, even, and responsive as that of the finest concert grand piano.

"Such is the boon, if we may be allowed the term, of the pneumatic lever for the organist. Henceforth, the performer need only *play*, instead of having to accomplish a feat of strength, sometimes as exhausting and even painful physically as it is disruptive of spontaneity and inspiration. It would take the fingers of Milo of Crotona and nerves of the strongest steel to keep freshness and clarity of interpretation while struggling with the manuals of certain organs with old-fashioned action, without being concerned and even obsessed with the constant disfigurement of one's interpretation by an unresponsive medium.

"While the pneumatic lever affords the organist such effective aid, the builder derives no less benefit from it. With conventional action, in order to avoid a resistance that is quite impossible to overcome, he must limit as strictly as possible both the wind pressure and the number of pallets, using the lightest possible springs to keep the pallets closed. As a first consequence, the pipes receive only weak and barely adequate wind. In addition, however, so as to relay the finger's motion to the pallet with all desirable speed and precision, great accuracy must be achieved in regulating the trackers, although they may be extremely long. By virtue of the short travel of the key and the pallet itself, and by virtue of the requirement that a pipe speak the instant the key begins to move, no motion must be lost, and no compromise must be made with accurate regulation by leaving a bit of play in the action. At the same time as the action is regulated "close" (as builders say), the slightest friction must be avoided at every point, so as not to burden an already weak pallet-spring and keep perfect freedom of movement in every part of the action. But if the motion is hindered in the slightest or friction is the least bit increased, whether by a change in humidity, a speck of dirt, a threaded wire, or any other cause, the pallet does not close fully. Remaining partly open, it causes — sometimes with maddening persistence — that frequent and unpleasant disorder known as a *cipher*: the finger releases the key, but the note keeps sounding indefinitely.

"With the pneumatic lever, we control considerable energy, one quite independent of the organist and the keyboard. We may therefore install pallet-springs of considerable tension; and if necessary, we may increase the number of pallets and the wind pressure. Thus, the pipe is properly winded, and the action returns to rest promptly and reliably. Secondly, since the tracker is no longer limited to a travel of but a few millimeters, and since a slight delay is not noticeable in the long tracker behind the action, between the lever and the pipes, enough play may be left in this tracker to offset any unforeseen change in regulation.

"The short trackers in front of the action, between the keys and the pneumatic machine, are utterly simple. Since the manual and the machine may be located in proximity to each other, the trackers are very short, and thereby less affected by accidental disturbance. They are, moreover, quite light and responsive, since much weight and friction can be avoided by placing each pneumatic lever opposite its key and doing away with the horizontal relays called *rollers*. Therefore, these trackers can be precisely regulated with no risk, the more so because there are few parts and thus few adjusting nuts: in contrast to the long trackers, these are easily visible and accessible in a single group. Finally, since they control valves fitted with very light springs, these trackers do not wear and they retain their accuracy all the longer.

"Like all useful inventions, the two innovations we have just described had ardent opponents.

"Despite the example set by England in making widespread use of parallel reservoirs, the Continent long persisted in tormenting the poor old cuneiform bellows, trying to obtain from it what it cannot provide, namely, a perfectly even wind.

"But especially the pneumatic lever encountered the most ardent opponents. The English builders, who were later to take advantage of it, first utterly scorned the work of a bold novice who dared interfere with the arcana of their routines. Examining the invention would have required time and effort: it was easier to criticize faults they honestly believed it possessed, if only out of courtesy towards its distinguished detractors. This simplest of devices was condemned as very complicated; although sturdy, it was called fragile; and its responsiveness was pronounced sluggish. It was even claimed that the lightness of its key action would encourage organists to play too fast. However, all these objections vanished as if by magic as soon as the machine had been observed, as installed in the organ where it was first used, together with a splendid improved wind system with parallel reservoirs."

CHAPTER FOUR

Danjou's Challenge and the Disaster at St.-Eustache

We are told that Cavaillé-Coll did not try to monopolize Barker's invention, but instead was content with making improvements upon it. This is an oversimplification of the facts, if not a falsehood. Within a year of the inauguration at St.-Denis, Barker abandoned the alliance with Cavaillé-Coll to become technical director of the rival firm, Daublaine-Callinet, also ceding to them the right to use the pneumatic lever. It cost Cavaillé-Coll 2,000 fr. to use the Barker device for the second time at St.-Roch (Paris).[1] Then he learned, to his great discomfort, that Daublaine-Callinet was paying only 500 fr. for the very device Cavaillé-Coll had put on the market. With annoyance, he wrote: "To Mr. Barker at Bordeaux: . . . I won't hide the fact that I consider it unjust for you to grant others the rights to your machine for one quarter the amount you charge me . . . if you decreased your price to 1,000 fr., I believe it would be to your advantage as well as my own."[2]

This approach met with no success. Not until 1845 was a formal agreement proposed by Cavaillé-Coll, by which Barker would sell the right to use the system to Cavaillé-Coll's financial agent. The price was 4,500 fr. The two companies, Cavaillé-Coll and Daublaine-Callinet, would reserve for themselves the exclusive right to use the machine.[3]

At Daublaine-Callinet, it had been Félix Danjou who recognized the merits of the Barker lever. Danjou, two years Cavaillé-Coll's junior and the most zealous reformer among organ builders of his time, had actually been the organizer of the Daublaine-Callinet firm, as well as its artistic director. His importance in the development of organ building has been all but neglected to this day, even though Hamel stated in 1849 that it was to Danjou "that organ building owes the spectacular progress it has made in our time."[4]

Jean-Louis-Félix Danjou (1812-66), a Parisian, began his career as organist at age seventeen for the church of Notre-Dame-des-Blancs-Manteaux, having earlier been taught by the clergy of that parish, then by Benoît at the *Conservatoire*. At twenty, he contributed an article to the *Revue Musicale*, "Sur l'origine de l'orgue",[5] and a review of Rinck's *Orgelschule*, "Méthode elémentaire pour l'orgue," in which Danjou proclaimed the superiority of German organists over the French.[6] In 1834 he was named organist at the church of St.-Eustache. During the same winter, when Cavaillé-Coll was setting up his Paris workshop, Danjou was setting goals for his life's work. In addition to his duties at St.-Eustache, he later took on the post at Notre-Dame-de-Paris (1840); and, in order to gain access to ancient manuscript sources for his studies in chant, took a position at the *Bibliothèque Royale*. At St.-Eustache, he found a congenial colleague in Louis Dietsch, the choir director, who was working towards reform in church music. Inspired by a receptive clergy and the group of zealots that quickly formed about him, Danjou soon found himself the leader of a movement for reform, the purposes of which were to restore sacred chant to its ancient dignity, to act against prevailing bad taste and secularization in church music, to organize societies in the provinces to promote those aims, to publish articles and unknown musical masterpieces from the Renaissance and Baroque eras, to raise the standards of organ building and organ repair, and to train a new school of organists who would be capable of reviving the great traditions of the past.[7]

Danjou travelled in Holland, Germany, and Belgium, seeking to improve his knowledge as historian, musical archeologist, and organist, and to perfect the disciplines that would enable him to inspire others through his own performance. He published *Chants sacrés de l'Office divin*, *Repertoire de Musique Sacrée*, and a pamphlet entitled *L'Etat et l'avenir du chant, ecclésiastique* (1844). He also edited a periodical, *Revue de la musique religieuse populaire et classique*, which endured from 1845 until the Revolution of 1848. In 1847, the Minister of Instruction sent him to Italy to seek source materials for his work. On his return, he discovered the famous Montpellier manuscript.

The Daublaine-Callinet firm, formed by Danjou in 1838, was essentially a reorganization of earlier ventures in organ building, which were to be funded by Daublaine. Danjou combed England and Germany for talented workmen, setting up two workshops, one in Paris under the management of Louis Callinet, and the other in Lyon with Theodore Sauer in charge. As artistic director, Danjou travelled about France persuading clergymen to replace their serpents and ophicleides with *orgues de choeur*, small instruments in the chancel for the accompaniment of chant. In its short life (1834-45), the Daublaine-Callinet firm is said to have built or restored over four hundred organs.

Hamel relates that Danjou was plagued by misfortune and misunderstanding through much of his life. The failure of his organ building enterprise was one of the catastrophes. Intent on reforming the world singlehanded, he inevitably jeopardized his cause by mercilessly attacking abuse, errors, and ignorance, until ultimately his support faded away. By contrast, Cavaillé-Coll seemed usually to be in the right place at the right time, seeking and finding the most powerful support, and devoting his energies to scientific pursuits that were of interest to his contemporaries.

Soon after Barker joined Daublaine-Callinet as technical director, the firm was engaged to rebuild the organ at St.-Eustache, one of the most beautiful churches in Paris and the center of Danjou's and Dietsch's musical reform. This "restored" instrument was clearly intended to be Danjou's response and challenge to Cavaillé-Coll's organ at St.-Denis. Barker's participation was to guarantee the technical details, while Danjou's musical experience would insure tonal excellence. As completed in 1844, the organ contained sixty-nine stops—the very number found in Cavaillé-Coll's instrument at St.-Denis.

In January, 1802, the church of St.-Eustache had been awarded an old Cliquot organ from the Abbey of St.-Germain-des-Près, closed during the Revolution.[8] The Clicquot instrument was the one "restored" by Daublaine-Callinet under Danjou's artistic direction. There were four manual keyboards, and two complete and tonally independent pedalboards, one French and the other German.

Church of St.-Eustache, 1844
Positif (54 notes)

1. Flûte 8′ en montre
2. Bourdon 8′
3. Cornet
4. Salicional 8′
5. Prestant 4′
6. Clarabella
7. Nazard
8. Doublette
9. Plein-jeu
10. Trompette 8′
11. Clairon 4′
12. Basson 8′
13. Cromorne 8′

Grand Orgue (54 notes) wind pressure: 103 mm.

1. Montre 16′
2. Montre 8′
3. Gambe 16′
4. Bourdon 8′
5. Gambe 8′
6. Flûte 8′
7. Prestant
8. Nazard
9. Doublette
10. Gambe 4′
11. Fourniture
12. Cymbale
13. Cornet
14. Première trompette 8′
15. Deuxième trompette 8′
16. Euphone 8′
17. Clairon 4′

Bombarde (54 notes)

1. Bourdon 16′
2. Cornet VII
3. Flûte 8′
4. Deuxième flûte
5. Bombarde
6. Trompette
7. Clairon

Récit (42 notes from C) enclosed; wind pressure: 152 mm.

1. Quintaton 16′	9. Euphone 8′
2. Bourdon 8′	10. Euphone 4′
3. Flûte harmonique	11. Trompette
4. Flûte 8′	12. Clairon
5. Prestant	13. Hautbois
6. Nazard	14. Cor anglais
7. Doublette	15. Voix humaine
8. Euphone 16′	

Pédale I, à la française (28 notes, from AA to C)

1. Flûte 16′	6. Quinte 12′
2. Bourdon 16′	7. Bombarde
3. Première flûte 8′	8. Trompette
4. Deuxième flûte 8′	9. Deuxième bombarde
5. Flûte 4′	10. Clairon

Pédale II, à l'allemande (28 notes, from AA to C)

1. Contre-basse 16′	5. Euphone 16′
2. Flûte 8′	6. Trompette
3. Violoncelle 8′	7. Euphone 8′
4. Flûte 4′	

According to Georges Schmitt and Charles Simon[9] it was Barker who made the decision to install two pedal keyboards, following certain innovative German models. Danjou is said to have disagreed on the grounds that the arrangement introduced unnecessary complications. More likely, Danjou objected for a different reason, namely, that identical compasses for two adjacent pedal keyboards could suit only one of them when it came to playing the literature. The French compass, AA to c′ (28 notes), was quite inappropriate for the toccatas and fugues of Johann Sebastian Bach, for which the German pedals had been introduced at St.-Eustache. It seems, however, that Adolphe Hesse did manage to perform Bach's Toccata in F with brilliance, despite the handicap of a German pedalboard whose top key was middle C.

Just as Cavaillé-Coll had done before the inauguration of the organ at St.-Denis, Danjou mailed hundreds of invitations and caused placards to be posted on the kiosks. He also arranged with a close associate, Stephen Morelot, to report on the first concert for the influential *Revue et Gazette Musicale de Paris.*[10] Seven thousand people filled the church to hear choral music, chants, speeches, and solo performances by no fewer than five Parisian organists: Fessy, Lefébure-Wély, Séjan, Boëly, and Benoît. But the main performer was the newcomer from Germany, Adolphe Hesse, acclaimed as a great interpreter of the works of J. S. Bach. It was clearly Danjou's aim to use the occasion to promote the traditional style of German organ playing, which was quite unknown in Paris. Morelot's review, of course, served this end. But outside the small group surrounding the musicians at St.-Eustache, it seems that Hesse's meticulous virtuosity was not much appreciated: "the audience of 7,000 did not find them to its liking, and this great artist was not as successful as his talent led one to expect. The audience preferred the style of the like of Fessy, Lefébure, Séjan, and Boëly: their half-religious, half-worldly manner was better suited to French frivolity."

Danjou had shown poor judgment by choosing to introduce Paris to Hesse and the works of Bach on that occasion. He should have known the crowd would be more pleased with their own Fessy and especially the colorful Lefébure-Wély, who always bowed to popular taste in his improvisations on well-known tunes. Hesse was apparently not skilled in extemporaneous performance. Recalling Hesse's Paris début, LaFage said: "Several years ago when Mr. Hesse came to Paris, we were very surprised to hear that he played only composed music."[11]

In his critique for the *Revue Musicale,* Morelot took the opportunity to sketch the aims of Danjou's reform movement by emphasizing stylistic differences between two sorts of performers at the concert at St.-Eustache. There were "two categories of artists we have mentioned: those who count on variety of registration for their effectiveness, and those who rely on the interest of the music itself. We shall report below what position Mr. Hesse has adopted with reference to these two approaches; but first, if we had had the time, we would have attempted to describe the theory of interpretation on the organ by inquiring to what extent it is legitimate to follow the fashion that today pervades all branches of music: the fashion of using the novel contrasts that new developments in instrument building have made available to the composer. We would have assessed to what degree this fashion can be reconciled with the organ's chief function, which is liturgical, a factor that must, in our opinion, decide the entire matter.

"One of these special effects, however, has been too lavishly used by today's organ builders, and it makes too great an impression on the public for us not to treat it in greater detail: this is the attempt to make the organ expressive by means of *shutters* that can be controlled at will. Let us first state what genuine resources this ingenious device has added to the organ. It cannot be denied that by allowing certain stops to sound distant as well as restoring all their immediacy, swell shutters significantly increase the variety of which the organ is capable. Since we cannot discuss these effects in detail, we refer back to Tuesday's recital. But that is all the importance we can grant to this innovation, since rather than creating expression as claimed, it produces only a yawn. Expression, after all, comes from feeling: how can it be produced by a mechanism, however sophisticated, since the mechanism remains foreign to the essential nature of the instrument to which it is applied?"

In the year 1844 Morelot won no converts to Danjou's cause by discrediting the Venetian swell. More than seventy years earlier the Englishman Burney had called it "the greatest and most important improvement that ever was made on any keyed instrument." Though this remark is patently inane, the subsequent popularity of the swell had immense influence on 19th century thinking. By Cavaillé-Coll's time it was considered an essential element in the modern organ's dynamic plan, as indispensable as the couplers. Danjou himself would not have forsakeen it, nor any of the other "improvements," such as the Barker lever or the free reed.

Danjou's efforts were directed against the prevailing French taste for world-liness in church music, rather than against inventions designed to modernize the organ's mechanism. He knew that Hesse's severe performing style would impress the connoisseurs, but gave no heed to the fact that it left the crowd unmoved. Not a musician himself, Cavaillé-Coll was not interested in promoting an esoteric move-ment for reform. Intuitively he sought out and cultivated the musicians, such as Lefébure-Wély, who most pleased the clergy and the wealthy class. It would be sev-eral years before Cavaillé-Coll was quite unpredictably won over to the German style of organ playing. By that time the ideological conflict between the two most enterprising French organ builders of the century had been laid to rest.

Not long after the inauguration of the most renowned organ in France since St.-Denis, an accident dealt a fatal blow to Danjou's venture in the competitive world of organ building. On December 16, 1844, when it had been in use only six months, the great Daublaine-Callinet organ in St.-Eustache was completely de-stroyed by fire, through the carelessness of its technical designer, Barker himself. The catastrophe was reported in the *Revue et Gazette Musciale de Paris:* [12]

"Last Monday, the organ in Saint-Eustache was consumed by flames. The ac-cident is doubly unfortunate, for its cause is related to the very preservation of the instrument. As we know, the organ, which was the largest and most magnificent in Europe and was worth 300,000 *francs,* had just been rebuilt by the Daublaine-Callinet firm at a cost of 50,000 *francs.* An original system had been installed, mak-ing the key action as light as that of a piano. The inventor of this system, who is a foreman with Daublaine, had followed the work with all the passion of an artist. He was particularly anxious that the voicing and tuning be perfect for the holiday services. Since Christmas was near he inspected the instrument; noticing an irregu-larity in the action, he entered the very depths of the organ, to a space so cramped that he could work only if he were practically lying down. He had to put his candle down in order to use both hands; and when he pulled on a spring he knocked the candle over, and it fell into the depths of the action. Terrified at the danger, he called the bellows-boy to his aid, but unfortunately, that particular day, there was a substitute, the old man who greeted the parishioners: he was an invalid and could be of no assistance, so in vain was he begged to go fetch some water. Then, unable to secure immediate help, he broke through the part of the action that kept him from reaching the candle, which had already set fire to the backfalls and the trackers. Since he could hardly reach them, he tried in vain to bring the fire under control by covering it for a while with his scarf, despite burns to his hands. The fire soon spread in every direction. Forced to leave for his own safety, he shouted, "Fire!" from the gallery, and immediately went below. When help arrived, the fire had spread rapidly, and no part of the organ could be saved. We may readily imagine the craftsman's despair, watching that magnificent organ perish, an instrument he had contributed much to building. The disaster struck not only the organ: several chapel altars, the rose window, and an arched window containing some stained glass, were destroyed. The pulpit, built after plans by Lebrun, was shattered. Several paintings and statues, as well as the vestibule and the west doors, were also damaged. More than five hundred chairs were smashed or burned. One of the vaults in the north of the nave, and the last one in the lower part, were seriously weakened. The roof timbers are intact."

The fire at St.-Eustache deprived Daublaine-Callinet of its showpiece, and Danjou of his center for musical reform. But yet another mishap soon contributed to the financial ruin of the Daublaine-Callinet enterprise (1845), and ultimately to Danjou's loss of influence. Directly following the inauguration of the organ at St.-Eustache, Callinet had been supervising the "restoration" of the old Cliquot organ at the Church of St.-Sulpice. The extent of his restoration is suggested by a notice dated December, 1844:[13]

"The organ in Saint-Sulpice, which until the new organ in Saint-Eustache was the largest instrument of this kind in the Capital, is going to be enlarged and improved so as to become the finest organ in the world. Among the new stops will be two at 32′ pitch in the *Pédale*, a feature to be found nowhere in France. The Church Council and the Parish Priest have entrusted this work to the firm of Daublaine & Callinet, who built the magnificent organ in Saint-Eustache, and have just installed an excellent choir organ in Saint-Sulpice."

When the work was almost ready for delivery to the church, Callinet, short of funds for the construction of a retirement home, asked his colleagues for loans to cover his debts. No one was willing to help. This provoked such a fit of anger that Callinet stormed about the workshop destroying everything that had been prepared for St.-Sulpice. He was immediately dismissed. Subsequently he took a menial position with Cavaillé-Coll, and died within a year (1846). It was a year before the restoration at St.-Sulpice was once again ready for delivery.

The misfortunes of his competitor did Cavaillé-Coll no harm, but Danjou's efforts to recover from such grave losses were a source of irritation. A few days after the fire, Cavaillé-Coll wrote to Neukomm:[14]

"You have probably heard that the famous Saint-Eustache organ burned, and that Mr. Barker started the fire while inspecting the instrument. This disaster, that could have jeopardized the entire building, is yet another advertisement for the firm whose Director is the notorious Danjou: they say it was the finest organ in Europe and that it was worth 300,000 to 400,000 francs. That's a bit over-done, but it may yet go against them. The Lord's will be done."

Cavaillé-Coll's private viewpoint was vindicated publicly in *La France Musicale,* reporting on the disastrous fire:[15]

". . . We should add that the newspapers have spread a multitude of errors concerning this unfortunate accident, and we must correct them.

"The organ was already old and had recently been repaired by the Daublaine firm for a fee of 25,000 francs, which figure was increased due to some extra work done by the builders. It is also inaccurate to say that the organ was the largest, and that it was worth 300,000 to 400,000 francs, as has been claimed. The Saint-Denis organ, the largest in France and containing all the improvements made in the Saint-Eustache organ, cost only 200,000 francs, all included."

A letter written years later exposes Cavaillé-Coll's personal insight about how the fire at St.-Eustache might have been avoided. Since before the availability of electric light the danger of fire was much greater than it is today, we may observe here one of the reasons for the spaciousness observed inside Cavaillé-Coll's instruments:[16]

". . . One of the most essential measures for protecting the instrument from fire is to arrange all the parts in a rational manner so that everything is easily accessible for maintenance and repair. The disastrous fire in the organ at Saint-Eustache was caused principally by the crowded arrangement of the mechanism, making it difficult to reach the location of breakdowns in that complex machine."

Both competitors sought favor from the critics and patronage from distinguished persons; they arranged for the services of the most popular performers, and probably wrote many of the press notices themselves,[17] for example:

". . . Mr. Danjou, organist of the Archdiocese of Paris, is already one of the directors of this large and useful enterprise, as the public is aware."[18]

"Messrs. Daublaine, Callinet, Girard, and Danjou invited an audience of musicians and music-lovers to inspect and hear an organ built for Saint-Serge in Angers . . . Messrs. Fessy and Séjan, who played it, demonstrated its excellence as well as their genuine talent as organists, a quality that becomes scarcer with every passing day."[19]

On the audition of a Cavaillé-Coll organ destined for St.-Jerôme, Toulouse:

". . . The public is aware of the improvements brought about by Messrs. Cavaillé in organ building, particularly as demonstrated in the great Saint-Denis organ, a truly remarkable instrument and one that we may say has no rival thus far. Thanks to these significant improvements, the organist has at his disposal resources not found in instruments built on the old-fashioned scheme."[20]

A notice of a recital held at Cavaillé-Coll's workshop to demonstrate the organ for St.-Jerôme, Toulouse, mentioned that Lefébure and Cavallo improvised on a theme provided by Rossini. "After the session, Rossini inspected Mr. Cavaillé's extensive workshops, examined several instruments, and expressed his delight to the skillful builders."[21]

In a notice concerning repairs completed by Daublaine-Callinet on the organ of Notre-Dame, Bordeaux: "this organ . . . perfectly demonstrated the superiority of the Daublaine and Callinet firm. According to the inspection and appraisal, this superiority arises from the quality of the materials, the soundness of the workmanship, the attention ot detail, and above all from several most ingenious and original appliances . . . We are indebted to the firm of Daublaine & Callinet for a multitude of improvements and innovations, which were particularly noticed in the organ in Notre-Dame. They are the *Cor anglais, Flûte harmonique, Flûte traversière, Euphone, Salicional,* and *Voix humaine.* Also much commented on was a striking imitation of the harp, whose harmonious arpeggios accompanied a 'cello melody."

When the restoration at St.-Sulpice was finally complete, Henri Blanchard wrote about the formal reception, making no secret of his allegiance to Danjou:[22]

"Mr. Lefébure-Wély dealt in the eclecticism we have just described, namely an *ostinato* imitation on a two- or three-measure subject mixed with modern phraseology, whose only result can be a hybrid kind of religious music . . . So this *artistic* festival went off smoothly, again showing off the finest organ in Paris, and even in Europe . . . the rebuilding does the greatest credit to the skillful builders responsible."

The liquidation of the Daublaine-Callinet enterprise left Cavaillé-Coll in a stronger position relative to his competitors. But Danjou was not ready to concede defeat. Under his initiative the firm was reorganized under the name of Ducroquet, and Danjou moved quickly to generate enough work to keep the new firm solvent. At St.-Roch (Paris), Ducroquet's proposal was rejected in favor of Cavaillé-Coll, who was doubtless supported by the organist, Lefébure-Wély. But in Lorient, where Cavaillé-Coll had built one of his earliest instruments, the organist favored Danjou for modifications and alterations to Cavaillé-Coll's instrument. When Cavaillé-Coll learned that Danjou and Ducroquet (purchaser of the bankrupt Daublaine firm) had actually visited the church, he objected with untypical candor and force:[23]

"Gentlemen, on my last trip to Brittany about two years ago, I had the honor of seeing you, and I learned that the Council intends to make repairs and additions, as requested by the organist, to the organ that we placed in your church. I then asked as a favor that this work be entrusted to us only, for the natural attachment of the craftsman for his work is the best guarantee of his reliability.

"We have just learned through a letter from the parish priest of Saint-Sauveur at Dinan that the new owner of Daublaine & Callinet, accompanied by the founder of that company, Mr. Danjou, organist of the Archdiocese of Paris, went to Lorient to negotiate for the work that the Council proposes to have done on the organ. Knowledge of this fact came to him through the agency of your organist, who is urging him to take advantage of this situation by having that firm make the repairs that the organ in his church requires.

". . . it would be most proper to examine beforehand, in the best interest of the Council, which of the two companies presents the greater assurance of success in performing the work. We do not like to criticize our colleagues, but in this instance we believe that we can ask, without violating the proprieties or the truth, if it is right to entrust work on an organ to an appraiser, who is now the Director of this Company, rather than to a professional organ builder . . . Too often, also, the organist's profession is confused with that of the organ builder. Each demands special training. The science of music teaches nothing of the laws of mechanics or acoustics, nor the application of the mechanical arts, which must be understood in order to build a good instrument. The patronage of Mr. d'Anjou (sic), organist of the Archdiocese of Paris, is therefore not a guarantee, as one might be led to believe . . ."[24]

The following September, Cavaillé-Coll was in Lorient, and presumably, settled the question in his favor.

Soon after the fire at St.-Eustache, the administration of the parish undertook a lottery to raise money for a new organ. This must have been accomplished before May, 1845, when Adrien de La Fage struck out against the suggestion that the proceeds of the lottery should be turned over to the poor. "An organ has been destroyed by an unfortunate accident, and a successful scheme has provided the means to rebuild it. The funds collected for this purpose must not be put to another use."[25]

In August of the same year, Cavaillé-Coll submitted a project for a new organ at St.-Eustache. The covering letter to Father du Guerry shows conclusively with what care and excitement the proposal had been prepared. This would have been Cavaillé-Coll's chance to give France its first 32' facade, such as he had seen and admired in his travels abroad. Convincing as his project was designed to be, Cavaillé-Coll must have known that Danjou would do everything in his power to thwart any hopes for a Cavaillé-Coll organ in the church of St.-Eustache. The plan, nevertheless, yields to Danjou's predilection for free reeds and German string stops, omitting Cavaillé-Coll's characteristic argument for harmonic ranks in great numbers. We give the proposal in its entirety:

August 17, 1845
Detailed Estimate for an Organ
Displaying 32′ Pipes
Designed for the Parish Church of
Saint-Eustache in Paris

This organ will have five keyboards, four manual and one pedal.
The four manual keyboards will have a compass of four and one-half octaves, from C to F, 54 notes.
The pedal keyboard will have a compass of two and one-half octaves, from C to F, 32 notes (sic).

Introduction

N. B. The Introduction which had been composed has been replaced by the covering letter to the Rev. Du Guerry, transcribed below: thus, the letter is not separated from the Specification.

Dear Father Du Guerry,

We respectfully enclose the Detailed Estimate for an organ displaying 32′ pipes, designed for the church of Saint-Eustache. Kindly forgive our delay in forwarding this document to you: we could not draw it up with thoroughness until we had studied the instrument minutely in its relationship to the location of the gallery or loft, and the vast, splendid proportions of the Basilica. In addition, in order to make our work more complete, we were obliged to plan the architectural design of the facade, so that the arrangement of the organ might be reflected in that of the case. Thus, the decorative part of the organ contains large pipes, in our opinion the noblest part of the instrument: these pipes reveal to the eye what the ear is intended to hear.

France doees not yet have a single organ which meets all these conditions. Even the organ at Saint-Denis, which until now and undeniably (is) the largest in the land, displays only 16′ pipes, although it contains 32′ pipes in its disposition.

The organs at Harlem (sic) and Rotterdam in Holland, which we had the opportunity to inspect during a recent trip, are truly impressive with their monumental architecture, containing 32′ display pipes.

In Germany, besides the old organ in the abbey of Weingarthen (sic), illustrated in *The Organ-Builder* by Dom Bedos de Celles, there exist several other organs displaying 32′ pipes.

Even in England, where in general instruments are small, there are two organs with 32′ pipes in the facade: those of York Minster and Birmingham.

The church of Saint-Eustache, with its lofty vaulting and monumental proportions, seem to us perfectly suited to receive an organ of such considerable size. With such a plan in mind, we have drawn up our proposal, of which the enclosed specification is the expression and summary.

This organ, containing *eighty stops:* 4 of 32' pitch, 15 of 16', 30 of 8', 20 of 4', and 4 of 2', with 8 mutation stops only; would be without any doubt the largest and the most complete in existence, by reason of the number of stops and the size of the pipes.

We have included all the families of stops that are known, and we have added that of harmonic stops, our own invention. These have endowed the Saint-Denis organ with an original tone quality, fuller and purer than the tone of conventional stops. They have also enabled us to rid the high ranges of the organ of that thinness of tone which is inevitable in small pipes.

We also include in the specification an extensive use of original mechanical devices recently introduced in organ-building: several of these, of our invention, enrich the instrument with new resources, for the organist's benefit.

1. The use of our new scheme of multi-pressure bellows, ensuring the tonal uniformity of each stop, making the volume of the treble range correspond to that of the bass, as well as avoiding insufficient wind, a shortcoming in every large instrument with conventional bellows.

2. Double pallet-boxes, winding the reeds and mutations separately from the foundation stops, thus avoiding the insufficient wind caused by channels of excessive length, as found in old organs, and the further drawback of never being able to play all the stops in a division together.

3. Combination pedals, also of our invention, allowing the organist to combine the stops as he wishes, putting them on and off as desired, by means of a single pedal for each division.

4. Various devices for coupling manuals by means of pedals: we believe we were the first to use them.

5. Finally, a more extensive use than heretofore of the mechanism devised by Mr. Barcker (sic), for lightening the touch of the keyboards.

We are confident that all these improvements, summarized in the Specification, should endow the new organ in Saint-Eustache with a variety of original effects, and a tonal power in this organ, such as to surpass all instruments presently known.

Such was the goal of our project, and we believe we can state that such would be the result. In the large tasks already entrusted to us, we have given clear proof of the constant improvement we strive to achieve in our craft. These precedents justify the testimonial we presume to make for ourselves, as they show the degree of confidence and the guarantees we believe we can offer: we earnestly request the opportunity to do so for you, Reverend Du Guerry, and the members of the Parish Council.

We are convinced that our Specification is detailed enough to allow a most accurate appraisal of the estimates listed therein. The figure of 109,895 F which is the grand total of these estimates, might seem (less?) considerable if the size of the instrument were not taken into account. We should have wished to include with these figures the drawings and descriptions which would better show their accuracy, but these documents, already drawn up for our own guidance, would require some additional time in order to be made clear enough for use by the Council and the Committee charged with the decision.

We must point out, Reverend Du Guerry, that this large undertaking, which deserves your greatest care, should be the object of a competition before a special Committee, and that the builders of whom you have requested proposals should be required to submit working drawings of the instrument, as was done for the organ in La Madeleine.

With our sincere respect, we are

Your devoted servants,

S.

List of the Stops Playable from Each Keyboard
Pedal Keyboard, 2½ Octaves, C to F, 30 notes

Flûte Family

	Pédale Flue Stops			Pipes	Price
1. *Flûte ouverte*	32′ Wood			30	4,000 F
2. *Flûte*	16′ Wood			30	1,000
3. *Flûte*	8′ Wood			30	400
4. *Flûte double*	4′ Wood			30	300

Montre Family

5. *Contre Basse*	32′	18 treble pipes in display	Tin	30	1,000 F
6. *Violon Basse*	16′	6 treble pipes in display	Tin	30	1,200
7. *Violoncelle*	8′		Tin	30	500
8. *Viole harmonique*	8′	speaks 4′ pitch	Tin	30	550

Bourdon Family

9. *Quintaton*	32′		Wood	30	1,100
10. *Soubasse*	16′		Wood	30	750
11. *Basse*	8′		Wood	30	350
12. *Octave*	8′	speaks 4′ pitch	Metal	30	500

Reed Stops
Wood Stops, Shallots Faced with Leather

13. *Contre Bombarde*	32′		Wood	30	4,000
14. *Basse Contre*	16′		Wood	30	1,000
15. *Basson*	8′		Wood	30	400

Tin Stops, Conventional Construction

16. *Bombarde*	16′		Tin	30	1,400 F
17. *Trompette*	8′		Tin	30	500
18. *Clairon*	4′		Tin	30	350
		Totals		540	19,300

Manual I, *Positif*
Four and one-half Octaves, C to F, 54 notes

				Pipes	Prices
1. *Montre*	8′	12 treble pipes in display	Tin	54	425 F
2. *Prestant*	4′		Tin	54	450
3. *Doublette*	2′		Tin	54	200
4. *Salicional*	8′	12 treble pipes in display	Tin	54	400
5. *Dulciana*	4′		Tin	54	400
6. *Bourdon*	16′		Wood	54	700
7. *Claribella*	4′		Wood	54	450
8. *Quinte*	3′		Tin	54	250
9. *Trompette*	8′		Tin	54	550 (500)
10. *Clairon*	4′		Tin	54	400
11. *Bourdon*	8′		Tin	54	450
12. *Cromorne*	8′		Tin	54	450
				648	5,075
					(5,125)

Manual II, *Grand orgue*
Four and one-half octaves, C to F, 54 notes

Chest 1: *Montre*

1. *Montre*	16′	12 treble pipes in display		54	1,000
2. *Montre*	8′	6 treble pipes in display		54	700
3. *Prestant*	4′			54	450
4. *Viola di Gamba*	16′	12 treble pipes in display	Tin	54	800

5. *Viola di Gamba*	8'	Tin	54	800	
6. *Viola di Gamba*	4'	Tin	54	400	
			324	4,150	

Chest 2: *Grand orgue*

7. *Quintaton*	16'	Wood	54	700	
8. *Bourdon*	8'	Wood	54	450	
9. *Flûte douce*	4'	Wood	54	350	
10. *Flûte conique*	8'	Tin	54	1,000	
11. *Flûte conique*	4'	Tin	54	500	
12. *Super octave*	2'	Tin	54	250	
13. *Quinte*	3'	Tin	54	250	

Plein Jeux

14. *Grande Fourniture* IV Ranke		Tin	216	1,000
15. *Grande Cymbale* V Ranks		Tin	270	1,200
16. *Fourniture* III Ranks		Tin	162	600
17. *Cymbale* IV Ranks		Tin	216	800

Free Reed Stops

18. *Euphone* (no pitch given)		54	1,200
19. *Euphone* ”		54	800
20. *Euphone* ”		54	500
		1,728	13,750

Manual III: *Bombarde*
Four and one-half octaves, C to F, 54 notes

			Pipes	Prices
1. *Soubasse harmonique*	16'	Wood	54	1,000 F
2. *Basse harmonique*	8'	Wood	54	600
3. *Double Flûte*	4'	Wood	54	450
4. *Flautone*	8'	Metal	54	800
5. *Flauto*	4'	Metal	54	500
6. *Piffaro*	2'	Metal	54	250
7. *Principal*	8'	Tin	54	1,000
8. *Quinte harmonique*	8' (sic)	Metal	54	500
9. *Bombarde*	16'	Tin	54	1,500
10. *Trompette*	8'	Tin	54	550
11. *Clairon*	8' (sic)	Tin	54	450
12. *Grand Cornet* VII Ranks		Metal	54 (210?)	700
			804	8,400
				(8,300)

Manual IV: *Récit*
Four and one-half octaves, C to F, 54 notes

Chest 1: *Montre*

1. *Solicional*	8′	12 treble pipes in display	Tin	54	400
2. *Solicet*	4′		Tin	54	400
3. *Unda maris*	8′	12 treble pipes in display	Tin	54	450
4. *Viola d'amour*	4′		Tin	54	400
5. *Aréophone*	16′	Free reed		54	800
6. *Eoline*	8′	Free reed		54	700
				324	3,150

Under Expression

1. *Bourdon*	16′		Wood	54	700
2. *Quintatone*	8′		Metal & Wood	54	450
3. *Galoubet*	4′		Wood	54	400
4. *Flûte traversière*	8′		Wood & Metal	54	800
5. *Flûte octaviante*	4′		Tin	54	500
6. *Octavin*	2′		Tin	54	300
7. *Voix céleste*	8′		Tin	54	1,000
8. *Cor anglais*	16′	Free reeds	Tin	54	1,000
9. *Trompette harmonique*	8′		Tin	54	650
10. *Clairon harmonique*	4′		Tin	54	500
11. *Basson et Hautbois*	8′		Tin	54	500
12. *Voix humaine*	8′		Tin	54	400
				648	7,200

Summary of the Numbers of Stops and Pipes According to Their Pitches

Division	No. of Stops	32	16	8	4	3	2	Cornets Pleins jeux	Pipes	Prices
Pédale	18	4	5	7	3	—	—	—	540	19,300
Positif	12	—	1	5	4	1	1	—	648	9,075
Grand orgue	20	—	4	5	5	1	1	4	1,728	13,750
Bombarde	12	—	2	4	3	1	1	1	804	8,400
Récit 1	12	—	2	6	5	—	1	—	648	7,200
Récit 2	6	—	1	3	2	—	—	—	324	3,150
Totals	80	4	15	30	20 (22)	3	4	5	4,692	56,875 (59,875)

N. B. Display pipes, forming the bass of the various stops listed, are not included in the above estimate. The price of these pipes will be determined subsequently, according to the design selected for the case, at Six Francs per kilogram.

Multi-Pressure Bellows

Multi-pressure bellows of our design shall be built, their dimensions being proportional to the number and size of stops listed above. These bellows will be capable of winding *all eighty stops* in the organ in all the combinations described below, and in the fullest chord the organist can strike on the manuals and pedals together.

In such a case, the wind required may reach the huge figure of 1,000 liters per second.

The various reservoirs shall have a capacity of 20,000 liters of air, and they shall be supplied from a feeder apparatus with a capacity of 500 liters per second.

The bellows, wind-trunks, and accessories shall cost   15,000 F.

Windchests

The following windchests to carry the stops listed, shall be built of choice northern oak, according to good practice and with the improvements that long experience has enabled us to make in this essential part of the organ.

1. Two large chests with eight sliders, to carry the eight foundation stops in the first and third groups of *Pédale* ranks: they shall stand on the chest, with no pipes offset.   2,400
2. Two large chests with four sliders, reserved for the foundation stops in the second group of *Pédale* ranks, whose bass pipes are to stand in the display.   1,200
3. Two large chests with six sliders, for the *Pédale* reed stops.   1,800
4. One chest with twelve sliders, in two sections, for the *Positif* stops   1,800
5. One large chest with six sliders, reserved for the *Montre* and *Viola di Gamba* stops in the *Grand orgue* division.   1,200
6. One large chest with fourteen sliders, with double pallet-boxes, in three sections, for the foundation and reed stops in the *Grand orgue*.   2,800
7. One large chest with double pallet-boxes, with twelve sliders, for the *Bombarde* stops (Manual III).   2,400
8. One chest with twelve sliders and double pallet-boxes, in two sections, for the stops in the *Récit expressif*.   1,800
9. One chest with six sliders, reserved for the stops in *Récit* 2, and directly winding the *Montre* 2.   1,200
   A large *Boîte expressive* shall be built with double walls, equipped with mechanically-operated louvers, to contain the stops in *Récit* 1.   <u>1,000</u>
           17,600

Mechanism

The entire mechanism of the organ shall be made of iron, and not of wood, as is customary. The *rollers,* relaying the key action to the pallets, the *vertical rollers* for the drawstop action, the *squares* and the *levers* shall also be made of iron.

1. All the mechanism connecting the first pedal keyboard to the pallets in the various chests: 1,500
2. All the mechanism connecting the first manual keyboard to the pallets in the *Positif* chest: 550
3. All the mechanism connecting the second *Grand orgue* keyboard with the pallets in the corresponding chests: 1,620
4. All the mechanism connecting the third *Bombarde* keyboard with the pallets in the corresponding chest: 1,100
5. All the mechanism connecting the *Récit* keyboard with the pallets in the various corresponding chests: 1,500
6. All the drawstop mechanism controlling the eighty stops in the organ: 4,000

                                                                                                        10,270

Keyboards

Four manual keyboards shall be made, capped with first quality ivory. The sharps of ebony and the frames of rosewood.   500

The pedal keyboard, German style, shall be made of oak and capped with exotic woods of contrasting colors, the better to distinguish the sharps from the naturals.   150

These keyboards shall be fitted with the pneumatic-lever mechanism devised by Mr. Barker, to lighten the touch. The installation shall be made as follows:

1. A set of 30 pneumatic levers for the pedal keyboard, so that the large pallets controlled by this keyboard may open at the slightest pressure of the foot, thus providing more promptness in the speech of these large pipes.   1,000
2. A second set of 54 pneumatic levers, fitted to the second *Grand orgue* manual, to actuate the three sets of pallets contained in the *Grand orgue* division and the various couplings with the other manuals.   1,500
3. A third set of 54 pneumatic levers, fitted to the third *Bombarde* manual.   1,500
4. A fourth set, also of 54 pneumatic levers fitted to the fourth *Récit* manual.   1,500

                                                                                                        (6,150)

Combination Pedals

To this organ shall be fitted several mechanical devices of our invention, which add to the instrument several quite original resources for the organist to draw upon.

Manual Couplers

1. A mechanism operated by a pedal, coupling the first (*Positif*) manual to the second (*Grand orgue*) manual.
2. A second pedal shall operate a mechanism coupling the third (*Bombairde*) manual to the second (*Grand orgue*) manual.
3. A third pedal shall operate a mechanism coupling the fourth (*Récit*) manual to the second (*Grand orgue*) manual.
4. A fourth pedal shall operate a mechanism coupling the fourth (*Récit*) manual to the third (*Bombarde*) manual.
5. A fifth pedal shall operate a mechanism making the bass range of the manual divisions playable with the pedals, thus augmenting the *Pédale* with the bass range of all the stops in the organ.

These various mechanisms, with their five pedals, complete: 1,000

Reed Combination Pedals

The reed stops in each division, previously selected in any combination by the organist, shall be available as desired to reinforce the foundation stops, by means of various mechanisms operated by the following pedals:

6. The first pedal shall control the reeds in the first (*Positif*) division.
7. The second pedal shall control the reeds in the second (*Grand orgue*) division.
8. The third pedal shall control the reeds in the third (*Bombarde*) division.
9. The fourth pedal shall control the reeds in the fourth (*Récit*) division.
10. The fifth pedal shall control the reeds in the *Pédale* division.

The price of these various mechanisms, with their five pedals: 1,500

Octave Couplers

Various mechanisms shall be built for the purpose of coupling the octaves in a single manual, or from one manual to another, in order to double the tonal resources, in effect doubling the number and power of the stops in the organ. These various mechanisms shall be operated by pedals, as follows:

11. The first pedal shall couple the pedal keyboard to itself, at the octave above.
12. The second pedal shall couple the *Grand orgue* keyboard to itself at the octave below.
13. The third pedal shall couple the *Bombarde* keyboard to itself, likewise at the octave below.

14. The fourth pedal shall couple the *Récit* keyboard to itself, at the octave below.
15. Finally, the fifth pedal shall operate the shutters enclosing the *Récit* stops, to modify the volume of this division throughout all the possible degrees, and play expressively.

This last pedal shall also affect the *Aréophone* and *Eoline* stops (Free reeds) in the *Récit expressif,* by a pneumatic effect.

These various mechanisms, with their five pedals, complete: 1,500

4,000

Summary of Estimate

1.	Eighty stops	56,875
2.	Bellows, regulating reservoirs, wind-trunks, and mechanism	15,000
3.	Windchests for the eighty stops	17,600
4.	Iron actions for all manuals and drawstops	10,270
5.	Four manual keyboards, one pedal keyboard, and four pneumatic Machines for lightening the key action	6,150
6.	Fifteen combination pedals and their mechanisms	4,000
	Grand total	109,895

The contract went to Ducroquet, but nine years and the Revolution of 1848 passed by before the organ was built. By that time the hapless Danjou had given up (1849) and retired to the south. We next hear of the organ for St.-Eustache in 1852:[26]

"The City of Paris, which has undertaken the interior decoration of the church of Saint-Eustache on a grand scale, is also granting a subsidy of 36,000 *francs* for rebuilding the organ, the total cost of which will be 137,133 *francs*. The magnificent case housing it will harmonize with the architectural richness of the church. Judging by the present state of the work, the organ, built by the Ducroquet firm, will be ready for opening about next August." Cavaillé-Coll attended the inauguration in 1854, for which Lemmons, the new champion of the German style, was the chief performer.

CHAPTER FIVE

The Ideological Conflict in the Press

Danjou had not left Paris without doing a great service to Cavaillé-Coll's future admirers. In 1945, he published the first issue of *Revue de la musique religieuse, populaire et classique,* his last and most ambitious undertaking, which became the vehicle for the reform he still cherished dearly. In 1847 there appeared a pair of articles written by Danjou himself,[1] the second of which was a detailed attack on Cavaillé-Coll. So relentless was his assault that Cavaillé-Coll was obliged to respond. Thus Danjou provoked a debate that forced Cavaillé-Coll to formulate his thinking in print.

While admitting that the contract at St.-Denis had, by chance, been awarded to "a true craftsman and an intelligent, hard-working man", Danjou declared Cavaillé-Coll's earlier instruments at Lorient, Pontivy, Dinan and Notre-Dame-de-Lorette to be "not worthy in every detail of the name and talent of this respectable craftsman". Furthermore, said Danjou, Cavaillé-Coll sought only to improve the action, to increase the organ's power, and to imitate orchestral instruments. Harmonic pipes were useful to Cavaillé-Coll only because they were much louder than normal pipes. The main flaw of Cavaillé-Coll's new organ at La Madeleine (1846) was the "noisy brilliance of the trumpets and the harsh tone of the flues. Divine service need not duplicate the miracle that brought down the walls of Jericho."

"As for the imitation of orchestral instruments, sought by Mr. Cavaillé-Coll, if this error were to spread, the results would be disastrous for music." The orchestra, Danjou insisted, is effective for sensuous music, which is inappropriate in the Church. The new "expressive" inventions for the organ (swell, free reeds) are a "fatal gift, considering the uses made of them by the majority of organists." Concluding, Danjou called upon Cavaillé-Coll to renounce his erroneous path, in order to assume a "place in the first rank" to which he would then be entitled. Until he did so, he would remain "inferior to his predecessors like Clicquot". Although mechanical perfection is desirable, Cavaillé-Coll should remember that the organ is first of all a musical instrument. Danjou weakened his position at the conclusion by praising his own work as a director of Daublaine-Callinet.

Cavaillé-Coll was, indeed, driven to defend himself. His responses to Danjou are a masterly profession of his unshakable faith in what he was doing and in the creed that was formulated even before he was thirty years old. Very early he had found conviction, motive, and consistency in what he doubtless looked upon as his mission in life. Thus, he had developed the strength that could carry him beyond the financial crisis caused by the political events of 1848, and the intellectual perseverance to keep his genius alive despite adversity. Clearly the growing irrationality of Danjou's attack left Cavaillé-Coll unmoved, for Danjou had not properly evaluated Cavaillé-Coll's personality.

"Paris, December 26, 1846[2]

"Sir,

I have just read in the eleventh issue (November 1846) of your *Revue* . . . an article on organ-building in the nineteenth century, in which you were kind enough to mention my name several times with praise, and took the pains to evaluate my work and the direction in which my endeavor is leading. I am pleased, Sir, that my work has come to your attention. I thank you for your favorable comments and especially for your criticism, and I should consider myself highly flattered had I deserved them fully.

"I do not boast of having attained perfection in our art; indeed, in the interest of emulation among all my colleagues, I hope perfection will never be reached. My imagination has at times envisioned the goal, but the Creator of all things, keeps it always infinitely remote from us.

"I find it quite natural, Sir, that you should express your opinion on my work: such is your right and, as I am pleased to believe, your conviction. Permit me only to say that you are mistaken in a few points, not as to the goal of my endeavor, but as to the conclusions you draw from it. Kindly devote space in your *Revue* to this explanation: I shall be as brief as possible.

" 'The only tendency plainly shown by Mr. Cavaille's work', you say, 'is improvement in the action, increasing the overall power of the instrument, and giving his stops the tonal character of the orchestral instruments whose names they bear'.

"Such is indeed, Sir, the goal of my endeavor, and you have grasped its meaning perfectly. However, you do not seem to approve of this tendency for you say in another paragraph, 'As for the imitation of orchestral instruments sought by Mr. Cavaille, if this error were to spread, the results would be disastrous for music.' And you add, further on, 'but from the religious point of view, it is no longer an absurdity: it is an impropriety.'

"This opinion does not seem to me to be acceptable. All I aspire to achieve, speaking for myself, is to give the various stops in the organ the tonal character of the orchestral instruments whose names they bear. In my view, strengthening the resemblance between organ stops and the instruments they imitate is improving their quality, not destroying their religious character, if indeed there is religious character in musical tones *per se,* as you seem to believe. In my opinion, religious character is found rather in the composition of the music. The same notes of the scale, after all, can be used to express a religious or a worldly idea, just as the same letters of the alphabet used to write the holy books are used in evil books. In music as in speech, the same voice can express all kinds of feelings, just as organ tones, whatever they may be, will never say aught but what the artist makes them say, by means of the keyboard, always ready to follow his inspiration. Therefore, the organist, not the organ, gives music the religious or worldly character that you seek in vain among the tones of this gigantic but docile instrument.

"Even if we admit for a moment that musical sound *per se* may have a religious character, you will, I think, concede that this character must be found in the instrument whose tone is most perfect.

"Well then, let us compare the various stops of the organ with the corresponding orchestral instruments. Is the sound of a *Trompette,* even one of Clicquot's as perfect as that of a trumpet in the orchestra?

"Is the sound of a *Clairon* as perfect as that of the bugle it imitates?

"Does the sound of the *Basson* have the perfection found in that of the bassoon?

"Does the sound of the *Clarinette* stop equal that of the clarinet?

"Has the *Hautbois* — in my opinion the most closely imitative of organ-stops — reached the perfection of the orchestra's oboe?

"Has the *Cor anglais,* even with free reeds, reached the perfection of the English horn?

"Finally, has the *Voix humaine* ever come near the admirable instrument placed in our larynx by the Creator?

"Obviously not. Therefore, every step towards perfect imitation of these various instruments will lend to the stops of the organ that religious character you seek. Far from being an obstacle, this imitation of orchestral instruments, which you condemn, becomes a resource for the organist to draw upon and heightens the grandeur of liturgical ceremony.

"I shall not speak of the towering ranks which are peculiar to the organ, and whose deep, majestic tones give it an imposing character found in no other instrument. I must limit myself to the instruments of the orchestra that have lent their names to organ-stops.

"The tone of flue stops leaves less to be desired than that of the reed stops we have just listed, but you will surely agree that despite the improvements you have discussed for your readers, we still have far to go before we achieve in our *Flûtes* the tonal perfection that Tulou brings forth from his instrument.

"As for the large-sized stops that give the organists peculiarly imposing, majestic character, I believe that far from spoiling their effect, I have increased it as much as possible, as when I placed in the Saint-Denis organ ranks of 32′ pitch, at the lower limit of audible sound.

"Neither do I think I have detracted from the religious character of the organ by progressively eliminating from our instruments those thickets of *Nazards, Quartes, Tierces,* and *Cornets* that plagued our old organs. Instead, I think I have replaced those snarling stops to good advantage with the new family of *harmonic stops.* They are not simply overblown, as you state; I created them, and I strive to perfect them.

"I hope, Sir, that these brief remarks may improve your estimate of my chosen path, which is to imitate in organ-stops the tone of the instruments they represent.

"Please accept, etc.

A. Cavaillé the younger."

Editor's Response

"If certain of our readers wanted proof of our impartiality in dealing with organbuilding, we could not have produced a more sincere testimonial to our fairness and accuracy than the letter written by Mr. Cavaillé himself. This distinguished craftsman acknowledges that we have correctly appraised his orientation, fairly described his talent, and clearly identified the goal he strives to attain. However, he perseveres in the opinions we have criticized, and with moderation and decorum, he defends them. This is most legitimately his right, as it is our right to refute and oppose ideas we believe to be harmful, as well as principles that lead to no less than a profound subversion of the Catholic tradition in organ design.

"We have said that imitating orchestral effects in the organ is, artistically speaking, *madness.*

"Indeed, in order to produce the orchestra's sound combinations on the organ, and to make orchestral use of the various instruments contained in the organ, we said it would take forty hands, as many keyboards, and an intelligence broad and powerful enough to divide into forty separate wills, controlling diverse instruments and giving each a particular motion, independence, and a separate role, like those they play in the modern orchestra.

"Mr. Cavaillé makes no reply to this first objection, which clearly shows that he understands its full import. In his mind, not just the *effects* but the *sounds* of orchestral instruments are to be imitated, and because he is convinced that these instruments are superior in timbre and quality, he concludes that organ stops such as *Flûte, Trompette, Clairon,* etc. must resemble as closely as possible the instruments whose names they bear. This argument might seem plausible if the organ were merely a collection of instruments borrowed from the orchestra, but Mr. Cavaillé forgets that the organ is several centuries older than the group of instruments we call an orchestra; he forgets that the organ sounded in our churches in the Middle Ages, that its majestic voice intoned our religious chants at a time when orchestras did not exist, and that the organ is therefore a special and original instrument, with its own timbres, qualities, and sounds. Its peculiar effects are independent of the orchestra; they were devised before the orchestra, they were invented by Christian inspiration, consecrated by the Church, and adopted for worship with an entirely different purpose from that of the modern orchestra and the instruments it comprises.

"Therefore, and I regret that I must say these words, the organ is degraded and demeaned, its character is betrayed, and its expression is made sensual when it has grafted onto it instruments from pit and symphony orchestras: they have been improved, if you will, but always with a view to dramatic art. The orchestra's trumpet has a sound that is vigorous, strident, and brilliant: this is because the composer relies on it for a dramatic effect requiring this kind of sound. When Mr. Tulou plays his flute, Mr. Triebert his oboe, or Mr. Batta his 'cello, with all the skill of their fingers, the refinement of their taste, and the charm of their talent — subtle or bold, gentle or lively — I may admire their skill and acknowledge that the instrument each seems to bring to life is suited to all the brilliant, dramatic effects of modern music. But in church and on the organ, this virtuosity, this exquisite sensitivity, this lively yet tender expression are out of place. Calm, dignity, grandeur, majesty, and power are appropriate to the organ in the Catholic church. *Non in commotione Dominus,* say the holy books: the Lord delights not in turmoil or unrest. To find worthy expression, prayer has no need of the flute and its affected graces, the 'cello and its meaning, the trumpet and its warlike tones, the trombone and its bellowing, or the oboe and its thin, quavering sounds.

There, contrary to the opinion of Mr. Cavaillé, we maintain that the organ, being older than the modern orchestra, must retain its special character, borrowing none of the effects or sounds of instruments invented or developed for theaters and modern music. The organists in Mr. Cavaillé's entourage may not share our opinion, because they have not sufficiently considered the requirements of religious art; but organists come and go, while the laws of beauty are eternal. They may be overlooked for a time, but sooner or later they reassert themselves.

"It is quite noteworthy, considering the ideas he puts into practice, that Mr. Cavaillé was the very builder chosen for installations in churches where religious art suffers from the effects of poor taste: Saint-Denis, notoriously redecorated by Mr. Debret; Saint-Roch, where sensuous music is favored; Notre-Dame-de-Lorette, that tawdry boudoir so improperly turned into a church; and finally la Madeleine, that pagan Greek temple originally dedicated to Victory or some ancient god.

"Surely Mr. Cavaillé's genuine merit fully deserves the preference given to him, and surely no other organbuilder working today is as painstaking or as advanced; however, it cannot be denied that when this craftsman tries to imitate orchestral instruments, does away with most of the mutation stops, and uses ever more harmonic stops, he debases the organ's character and puts his talent to poor use: if he persists in following the path he seems to have chosen he will eventually incur the wrath of Christian artists."

"Paris, February 26, 1847[3]

"Sir,

Thank you for publishing my first letter. I hope that you will see fit to grant the same indulgence to a few more remarks occasioned by your article on organ-building in the nineteenth century.

"These remarks concern the mechanism.

"According to you, Sir, 'what is expected of the organ is beauty of sound, majesty and propriety: mechanical perfection comes only after these essential qualities; and although an important feature, it is not indispensable'.

"This comment would be perfectly accurate if it were possible to conceive of tonal perfection apart from the mechanism, but this cannot be: if the tone is modified by the shape and proportions of the pipes, its very life depends upon the mechanical elements. For this reason, I first set about perfecting the mechanism. I went back to the source of the tone, seeking by improving the mechanism to secure the tonal advantages which you point out yourself in modern instruments, as compared to earlier organs.

"Until the present time no builder, in my opinion, made better pipes, flue or reed, than the famous Clicquot, whose work you rightly praise. But just as a good instrument played by a person without talent does not produce beautiful sounds, so the best pipes fitted to an imperfect mechanism will never produce all the tonal beauty of which they are capable. Thus, for example, not long ago the bellows was an imperfect device, as you know: those fine pipes, sounded by unsteady wind, were of necessity unstable in pitch; in combinations, they suffered from shockingly insufficient wind. The causes were not only faults in the design of the bellows *per se*, but also pood windsupply through *trunks, chests, pallets,* and key-action. Therefore, in order to improve the sound of our old organs, it was essential to perfect these various parts, or risk standing still and considering the work of our predecessors as the limit of perfection.

"Moreover, Sir, you attacked your own opinion of the mechanism as a secondary factor, when you spoke of Mr. Barker's *pneumatic lever*. Indeed, although this invention belongs to the action alone, this fact did not keep you from admitting that it tends to improve *the speaking parts of the instrument*. You go even further, saying, 'This discovery is surely the most important in centuries for improving the organ.' However, you add, 'Such are the indifference and the ignorance that surround everything concerning this beautiful instrument that no one in the clergy or in parish councils has taken an interest in it.'

"No one before me recognized the admirable discovery you mention, and no one has encouraged its development more than I. As you say, I had attempted to find a solution for the problem that Mr. Barker was fortunate enough to solve first, when in 1839 he came to France to patent the invention that he had been unable to promote among builders in his homeland. The friendly welcome and the enlightened assistance that Mr. Barker found with our firm were, I think, of no small help to the success of his invention: several of our Parisian colleagues were making every effort to prove the appliance useless. And stranger yet, one organist, when faced with this discovery and the new strength it afforded him in demonstrating the resources of his art, highly disapproved of making the keyboards easy to play. As a faithful defender of the religious character of the organ, he averred that organists were already in the habit of playing too many notes on the august instrument: now they would play even faster, and the organ would thereby lose all its dignity.

"I do not doubt that you recognize by now how unfounded these objections were. Nevertheless, they moved the organ committee of the Saint-Roch parish council to ask a certain question of us and of the Daublaine firm: at that time, you were the Director of Daublaine, and the firm did not yet have the right to use the *pneumatic lever*. The council was considering the restoration of the organ at Saint-Roch, and the terms of the question were as follows:

"'Since church organs are dignified instruments, and since echoes in the nave become blurred when they occur in too-rapid succession, is Mr. Barker's scheme really necessary in the organ at Saint-Roch?'

"I do not know with what arguments Daublaine supported its opinion, but mine is the opposite. I quote it exactly:

Reply

"'Organ music must certainly have a dignified character, considering the nature of the instrument and the majesty of its setting.

"'It is also true that echoes in the nave become blurred when they occur in too-rapid succession. We may even add that fast playing, currently the custom on the piano, shows the worst of taste when transferred to the organ. The latter instrument possesses broader resources and should inspire loftier ideas. However, although the organist must consider these points, they do not justify the objection against light key action.

"'The organist's technique must be guided not by the resistance of the keys but by the understanding and the artistry that govern his inspiration. Organ playing requires too serious a study and too broad a knowledge for us to allow physical demands to be placed upon the organist, in addition to those made upon his intellect. Quite the contrary: we think that if it were possible to design the organ in such a way that it might respond to the organist's inspiration alone, the effect would be more sublime, and organ music would attain its perfection.

" 'Since it makes the keyboard action lighter, Mr. Barker's invention can only be welcomed by organists and all those who are interested in improving the instrument.'

"These simple arguments were sufficient, as you know, to convince the clergy and the council-members of Saint-Roch that this invention is sound and effective, just as other equally simple arguments demonstrated the superiority of harmonic stops, our multiple-pressure wind system, and several other improvements mentioned in our restoration proposal and favored by those concerned.

"So you see that *ignorance* and *indifference* on the part of the clergy and the councils are not so great an obstacle to useful inventions as you say they are. For my part, I have encountered only good will and encouragement, and whenever I have been obliged to explain or demonstrate an improvement or a new idea, I have found without exception that it was easier to overcome the preconceptions of those whose principles are cut and dried, and who through conviction or self-interest oppose progress of any kind.

"I shall close here, Sir, as my purpose was not to set forth in detail everything I have done to improve the mechanism of the organ. I simply wished to acknowledge the importance of the mechanical parts of the organ, as I believe your November article fails to do. I refer to your readers the task of judging the merits of our respective comments.

"Please accept, etc.

A. Cavaillé the younger."

Danjou's response was brief:

"Our readers will welcome with interest this second letter from Mr. Cavaillé, in which the talented builder emphasized the importance of the mechanism in organ building. We have never denied this importance, and Mr. Cavaillé himself proves as much, once again. We can but agree with his remarks, pointing out nevertheless that they in no way relate to our own comments on Mr. Cavaillé's trend as concerns the pipework of his instruments. We have once again made our position clear concerning Mr. Cavaillé's endeavors, in our reply last issue, and this time he has felt obliged not to bring the matter up.

(the Director)"

Cavaillé-Coll's last encounter with Danjou seems to have been in 1856, when Danjou, as editor of *Le Messager du Midi*, reported erroneously on awards conferred at the Exposition of 1855. Cavaillé-Coll was justifiably irritated, and wrote a letter protesting the slight:

"Letter on the Exposition, addressed to Mr. Danjou, Editor of *Le Message(r) du Midi*

"In last Dec. 25th's issue of your paper, I find an article entitled, 'Letters on the Universal Exposition;' this is a review, signed by Leymarie, concerning instrument building. This review contains a few erroneous judgements, which I feel obligated to correct.

"'The Exposition Jury,' says Mr. Leymarie, 'recognized the merits of our two leading organ builders, by giving the Cross to Mr. Barker, foreman with Ducroquet, and a Medal of Honor to Mr. Cavaillé.'

"There are several errors in these lines, as follows: the Jury has never been empowered to *award Crosses*. It has merely brought to the attention of the Chief of State those manufacturers whose reputation is acknowledged, and has requested an honorary reward if no such award had been granted at previous Expositions. I recognize Mr. Barker's merits, and I believe he is very deserving of the Legion of Honor. He knows that it was I who opened the door for him, leading to a career as a craftsman here in France, and through a chance opportunity that I promptly seized, I was the first to have the pleasure of pinning on his breast the Cross that the Emperor had just given him. However, this distinction has nothing to do with the awards granted by the Jury to exhibitors, especially Mr. Ducroquet, and his foreman Mr. Barker, who was also an exhibitor. (Four categories of medals, the *Grand Medal of Honor, Medals of Honor, First-class Medals, Second-Class Medals,* and then Honorable Mentions. These are the distinctions granted *to exhibitors by the international Jury.*

"In which category were Messrs. Ducroquet and Barker placed? Your correspondent fails to inform your readers. Did they receive Grand Medals of Honor, or was it merely Medals of Honor, like that awarded to me? Mr. Leymarie does not make this clear; or rather, his terms cannot fail to mislead the public. For this was the only way to show true basis for comparison and to inform the public how the Jury had just recognized the merits of our leading organ builders. The Grand Medal of Honor was awarded to *five* instrument makers: Boehm, of Munich; A. Cavaillé-Coll, of Paris; the Paris Chamber of Commerce; and Sax and Vuillaume, of Paris. I am the only organ builder in this first group. *Five* instrument makers received the Medal of Honor: Alexandre, Erard, Hertz, Pleyel, and (Triebert): none of them is an organ builder. *Sixty six* received the First-Class Medal, and this is the category in which we find Messrs. Ducroquet and Barker, with several other organ building concerns, French and foreign, such as Bovington of London, Suret of Paris, Lorenzi of Vienna, etc. This information is found in the official roster of awards, published in *Le Moniteur* of Dec. 8.

"I am not surprised, Sir, that your correspondent shows strong sympathy for the firm you founded, nor that he voices numerous criticisms of the improvements I have introduced in organ building. But you will not be surprised either if I point out that several improvements which he condemns, for example, the use of harmonic stops, are mentioned officially among the grounds for awarding me the Grand Medal of Honor: 'excellence of Mr. A. Cavaillé-Coll's pipe organs, improvements in the

wind supply, and harmonic stops.' Such are the terms of the Jury's decision, record-
ed in *Le Moniteur* of Nov. 16. Secondly, I ask you why the firm you endorse is
trying to copy the very improvements that your paper criticizes.

"'Respected artists,' continues Mr. Leymarie, 'judge that Mr. Cavaillé has made
excessive use of combination pedals.' This criticism is too bizarre to be anything but
a completely unintentional error. I do not know a single 'respected' organist in Paris
who would accept an organ which did not possess these new pedals. I could list the
names not only of organists, but of composers and builders, who are authorities, and
who have an entirely different opinion of the improvements I have made in organ
building.

"It would be pointless to discuss at greater length a topic on which the music
world has been enlightened for some time. Moreover, your paper furnishes me the
best reply to its own criticisms. Indeed, now that I have correctly reported the way
'the Jury of the Exposition recognized the merits of our two leading organ builders,'
I can do no better than quote your correspondent's own words:

"'We may state that at the Universal Exposition of 1855, as at the national
Expositions, musical instrument manufacturers were judged with the strictest impartiality. As for individual opinions, we clearly see how incomplete and risky they
must be, if not enlightened by those of the jury. Insofar as they are not influenced
by the Jury, they must be considered as isolated impressions.'

"I expect you, in a spirit of impartiality, to print my reply in the next issue of
the *Messager du Midi*. Yours, &"

Cavaillé-Coll need not have troubled to respond. Danjou's career in organ
building had already come to an end. In 1855, after the Exhibition, the firm of
Ducroquet, with two hundred workers, was acquired by Merklin of Belgium, under
the title *Société anonyme pour la fabrication des orgues, établissement Merklin-
Schutze.*[4] Barker remained only until 1858, when he left to found a new firm with
Verschneider.

CHAPTER SIX

The Organ at La Madeleine

Although loud instruments were the order of the day, Cavaillé-Coll's new organ at La Madeleine in Paris was severely criticized by Danjou because of its great power: "... a horrible din ... is in store for the parishioners of La Madeleine, and this new suffering is added to the pain they must feel at the sight of that worldly pagan temple".[1] Later, Abbé Ply cited the instrument at La Madeleine for its lack of mutation stops:[2]

"Indeed, when Mr. Cavaillé-Coll completed the organ for La Madeleine in 1846, the music world was astonished to see that this 48-stop instrument contained only one mutation, a *Quinte* 3'. Some hailed this innovation, and Berlioz was surely not among the last to do so; but most enlightened artists criticized the builder for doing away with those stops: used sparingly in judicious registrations, they give the organ a unique character and distinguish it from all other instruments."

The stop list follows:[3]

Pédale, 25 notes C to C
Jeux de Fond

1.	Quintaton	32
2.	Contre-Basse	16
3.	Violoncelle	8
4.	Grosse Flûte	8

Jeux de combinaison

5.	Bombarde	16
6.	Basse-Contre	16
7.	Trompette	8
8.	Clairon	4

Grand Orgue, 54 notes, C to F
Jeux de Fond

1.	Montre	16
2.	Violon-Basse	16
3.	Montre	8
4.	Salicional	8
5.	Flûte harmonique	8
6.	Bourdon	8
7.	Prestant	4

Jeux de combinaison

8.	Quinte	3
9.	Doublette	2
10.	Plein-jeu	X
11.	Trompette	8
12.	Cor anglais	8

Positif, 54 notes, C to F
    Jeux de Fond

1.	Montre	8
2.	Viola di Gamba	8
3.	Flûte douce	8
4.	Voix-celestes	8
5.	Prestant	4

    Jeux de combinaison

6.	Dulciana	4
7.	Octavin	2
8.	Trompette	8
9.	Basson et Hautbois	8
10.	Clairon	4

Bombardes, 54 notes, C to F
    Jeux de Fond

1.	Sous-Basse	16
2.	Basse	8
3.	Flûte harmonique	8
4.	Flûte traversière	8
5.	Flûte octaviante	4

    Jeux de combinaison

6.	Octavin	2
7.	Bombarde	16
8.	Trompette harmonique	8
9.	Deuxième Trompette	8
10.	Clairon	4

Récit expressif, 54 notes, C to F
    Jeux de Fond

1.	Flûte harmonique	8
2.	Bourdon	8
3.	Muzette	8
4.	Voix humaine	8

    Jeux de combinaison

5.	Flûte octaviante	4
6.	Octavin	2
7.	Trompette harmonique	8
8.	Clairon harmonique	4

48 stops, 2882 pipes

Pédales de combinaison
1. Tirasse: coupler, manuals to pedal.
2. Reeds, *Pédale.*
3. Super octave coupler, *Pédale.*
4. Sub octave coupler, Grand Orgue.
5. Sub octave coupler, Bombardes.
6. Jeux de combinaison, Positif.
7. Jeux de combinaison, Grand Orgue.
8. Jeux de combinaison, Bombardes.
9. Jeux de combinaison, Récit.
10. Coupler, Positif to Grand Orgue.
11. Coupler, Grand Orgue to Bombardes.
12. Coupler, Bombardes to Récit.
13. Tremolo, Récit and Positif.
14. Expression, Récit.

Barker machines were installed on the *Grand Orgue* and *Bombardes.*[4]

As for Cavaillé-Coll, there is little doubt that he was pleased with the instrument, which had been voiced by his brother, Vincent.[5] The original design had prevailed almost intact, despite suggestions for extensive changes made by Hamel,[6] secretary for the commission named to examine and approve the organ. Hamel's proposal and Cavaillé-Coll's rebuttal have survived. We quote them here because they demonstrate Cavaillé-Coll's firm stand on a number of issues, such as pitch, order of manuals, and free reeds:[7]

8 June 1842

"The Replies of Messrs. Cavaillé

to the Observations of Mr. Hamel Concerning

his Suggested Modifications to their

Design for an Organ in the Church of La Madeleine.

"Mr. Hamel's Observation No. 1

"None of the proposed designs has specified the pitch of the organ, although this is a very important point. Since concert pitch is nearly one tone higher than liturgical pitch, adopting the former would involve omitting from each stop the two lowest pipes: since the large pipes are the most costly, this omission would have a rather noticeable influence on the price. In order to reconcile the daily needs of the choir with the occasional necessity for playing together with orchestral instruments, I believe the organ should be *one-half* or a *whole* tone lower than concert pitch, and it should have *transposing keyboards.* This would be facilitated by the fact that Mr. Cavaillé's keyboards are not directly connected to trackers.

Messrs. Cavaillé's Reply

"The pitch of the organ is specified in our design, and it conforms to the most widespread practice today in France, as well as to long-established practice in England and Germany, where organ-building has been taken the most seriously. The lengths of the pipes shown in our drawings correspond to concert pitch. The organ cannot therefore be lowered to the old liturgical pitch without adding two large pipes to each rank. This would entail a rather substantial increase in price, since as Mr. Hamel himself points out, these large pipes are the most costly.

"We should point out, moreover, that these pipes cannot be added without upsetting the plan of our design and cluttering the interior of the organ with a hundred or so large pipes that would impair the effectiveness of the other parts. The present pipes already fit all too nicely within the case as planned. Therefore, more large pipes would simply compound the difficulty, detracting from the organ more than they would add.

"We should add that the organ at Saint-Denis is at concert pitch, as directed by the Fine-Arts Commission of the Institute. The organ at Saint-Roch has also been raised to concert pitch, as are all new organs and old ones that have been rebuilt.

"Mr. Neukomm's opinion, cited by Mr. Hamel, could also be taken into account when making a decision concerning the pitch of the organ. According to Mr. Neukomm, the works of the great masters, J. S. Bach or Handel, lose their character when played on organs that are not at concert pitch. A further consequence is that music [arranged] for organ and orchestra becomes unrecognizable because of the keys implicit in these compositions and reflected in the tuning of the organ.

"As for transposing keyboards, we do not think they would be practical either. However simple this device may appear when applied to a piano or a small, single manual organ, it would involve such a complex mechanism that it would detract considerably from the organ's durability and be a constant source of trouble.

"Mr. Hamel's Observation No. 2

"It would have been preferable to include in the specification for the organ some genuine *expressif* stops, with a bellows operated by the organist himself. I believe such a division could be used to good advantage, as my experience and Mr. Neukomm's opinion confirm.

"Messrs. Cavaillé's Response

"We have not included any *expressif* stops, *i. e.* free reeds, in the stoplist for this organ. Nevertheless, we believe we can obtain similar and even better effects as to volume and dynamic range with the new device called the *boîte expressive*: the originality of this appliance may be observed in our organs at Saint-Denis and Saint-Roch. The inclusion of free reeds in pipe organs creates problems that have yet to find satisfactory solutions: tuning, limited dynamic range, and limited wind pressure as generated by the organist himself. We have been seeking solutions to these problems for some time, and if, as we hope, we arrive at a satisfactory result, we shall not fail to include free reeds at la Madeleine.[8]

"The second point, which we welcome, should nevertheless be left to our discretion in the contract: we undertake to do all we can to find a satisfactory solution.

"Mr. Hamel's Observation No. 3

"Instead of a *Gros Nazard* in the *Pédale*, I should prefer a *Quinte* (10⅔′), since from the combined frequencies of a 16′ stop and its fifth we obtain a 32′ effect: the Germans never fail to take good advantage of this in their organs.

"Messrs. Cavaillé's Reply

"The *Gros Nazard* in the *Pédale* can be replaced by a *Quinte* (10⅔′), as Mr. Hamel requests. However, because of the wide scale of this stop, it may be necessary to omit also the 4′ *Flûte* or another *Pédale* stop deemed less important, in order to make room for the requested stop.

"Mr. Hamel's Observation No. 4

"Far from considering the special effects obtained from the organ as the instrument's chief distinction, I do think we ought not to overlook the advantage to be taken of the location. The space that will be left between the ceiling of the vestibule and the floor of the organ could be used to produce effects similar to the ones admired in the organ at Fribourg.

"Messrs. Cavaillé's Reply

"As for special effects to be obtained from the location, we do not think any can be derived from the space that will be left between the vestibule ceiling and the floor of the organ. This space will exist only to either side of the vestibule, and the stairwell already occupies one side. The other side would be extremely inaccessible, not to mention the complex action required for such an addition to the organ. From another standpoint, we do not think the conditions are the same here is in F., where according to Mr. Hamel, the sound can exit from the rear of the organ and, passing beneath it, reach the nave.

"Mr. Hamel's Observation No. 5

"Such a skillful mechanic as Mr. Cavaillé should have no trouble making a tremulant to be controlled by a pedal and whose beating can be accelerated or slowed by varying the wind-pressure. I am convinced that in this manner we could obtain effects far superior to the steady beating of a tremulant, which remains constant so long as the stop is drawn.

"Messrs. Cavaillé's Reply

"The tremulant can be controlled by a pedal, and we have built several of this type. However, to vary the rhythm as requested poses a problem in mechanics: we undertake to look into the matter and to install such a device if it proves to be practical.

"Mr. Hamel's Observation No. 6

"In the organ at Frankfurt, the most powerful stops are played from the lowest manual: it can control the other manuals by means of couplers. The next manual contains less powerful stops, and the third contains the solo stops. I merely point out this arrangement: it may have its advantages but it conflicts with our established customs. This point should be discussed with the organists before a decision is made.

"Messrs. Cavaillé's Reply

"The distribution of the stops among the manuals arranged as they are at Frankfurt is quite unimportant to the tonal effect of the organ, in our opinion. The result would be to alter the arrangement generally used in organs in France, and it would involve the preparation of an entirely new design (for la Madeleine).

"In drawing up our specification, we have taken pains to give each manual its function and its traditional location. However, thanks to new mechanical accessories made available to the organist, the second or third manual may be made to control all the others, and thus all the stops in the organ may be played together, separately, or in any combination. These possibilities are as yet unique, and in our opinion they are at least as significant as the arrangement of the manuals in the organ at Frankfurt.

"Mr. Hamel's Observation No. 7

"Finally, the greatest charm of the good organs I have heard results from the tonal variety of their stops, and especially from the use of *Gambes* and *Violons* in both the manuals and the pedals. Therefore, I recommend the greatest care in placing these stops and in voicing them. The *Quintadène,* when well made, produces a delightful effect. The combination of these various stops produces tone qualities unknown in our French organs.

"Messrs. Cavaillé's Reply

"We are well aware of the fact that the greatest charm of good organs results from the tonal variety of their stops. Our purpose in creating the harmonic stops which figure so prominently in our design was to introduce new tonal qualities. The harmonic stops give the instrument a variety of timbres hitherto unknown, and they give the upper ranges of the organ a fullness that makes them proportional to the bass ranges: this uniformity of volume has always been lacking. Nor have we failed to introduce the *Gambe* and *Contrebasse* stops found in German organs. However, since German instruments have nowhere near as many reed stops, the builders have been able to increase the number of flues, and thus of strings. Now we believe that in the limited space afforded by the organ-case in La Madeleine, as compared to the size of the building, the more powerful reed stops would replace to good advantage the weaker flues such as the numerous strings in the organ at Frankfurt.

"The *Quintadène* requested by Mr. Hamel could easily be installed instead of a *Bourdon,* since the two stops have the same dimensions.

"In summary, it is our considered opinion that not only our own interest, but that of the Parish Council and that of quality in the organ would best be served as follows:

1) Keep the organ at concert pitch, as provided in our design.
2) Include free-reed stops: we undertake to do so.
3) Install a *Quinte* (10⅔') in the *Pédale.*
4) Abandon as impractical the idea of adding special effects.
5) Install a variable-rhythm tremulant, provided we solve the mechanical problems successfully.
6) Retain the order of the manuals specified in our design.
7) Finally, retain the *Gambes* and *Violoncelles* specified in our design, and install a *Quintadène* instead of a *Bourdon* of the same pitch."

Hamel and the other members of the commission proclaimed the finished organ a "masterpiece". Cavaillé-Coll was so pleased that he made up a pamphlet including the report and the inaugural programs, not forgetting to list a newly-acquired title on the cover:

A. Cavaillé-Coll, père et fils
Facteurs d'Orgues du Roi[9]

The members of the commission signing the report were:

Baron Séguier, President, member of the *Académie des Sciences*
Baron Cagniard de la Tour, member of the *Académie des Sciences*
Savart, member of the *Académie des Sciences*
Ad. Adam, member of the *Académie des Beaux-Arts*
Ambroise Thomas, composer
Huvé, architect of La Madeleine, member of the *Académie des Beaux-Arts*
Hamel, judge of the civil court, Beauvais, amateur organ builder
P. Érard, *Facteur de pianos du Roi*
Marloye, professor of acoustics
Davrainville, organ builder
Simon, organist at St.-Denis
Séjan, organist at St.-Sulpice
Lefébure-Wély, organist at St.-Roch
Fessy, organist at La Madeleine

The inaugural concert featured three of the four organists who were members of the commission: Fessy of La Madeleine, Lefébure-Wély of St.-Roch, and Séjan of St.-Sulpice. Improvisations alternated with vocal solos and choral selections: not one previously-composed organ work was performed. When a second concert was organized two weeks later, Séjan had been dropped, thus making of the program a competition between the two most popular organists of the day. Lefébure-Wély, clearly triumphant, was awarded the cross of the Legion of Honor and given Fessy's post as organist at La Madeleine, while the latter replaced Lefébure-Wély at St. Roch.

Thus continued the rise to celebrity of Lefébure-Wély, chief among French organists as promoter of Cavaillé-Coll organs. But what of the improvisations that brought Lefébure-Wély such a rich reward? The following note by Louis Roger appeared in *L'Indépendant littéraire*:[10]

"One of Lefébure's biographers relates the following incident: When the organ in La Madeleine had been inaugurated, a second recital was given for the benefit of flood victims in the Loire valley. The great musician took as his inspiration the various episodes of the disaster, and depicted them in music. The river overflowed its banks; the rampaging waters roared onward, spreading death and destruction everywhere. The victims could be heard moaning and shouting in desperation. Suddenly, the organist halted his improvisation and intoned a faraway *De profundis* on the *Voix humaine*. A deathly shudder ran through the audience, and their tear-filled eyes bore witness to both the triumph of a distinguished artist and the infinite resources of his instrument."

CHAPTER SEVEN

Lefébure-Wély and Lemmens

During the 1840's Louis-James-Alfred Lefébure-Wély (1817-69) was unquestionably Cavaillé-Coll's favorite organist. Indeed, during a period of twenty years or more, he did more than any other musician to publicize Cavaillé-Coll's organs. These were critical years for the organ builder, a fact that sealed his friendship with Lefébure-Wély. The organist sought and obtained the most coveted posts in Paris. We have noted that in 1846 he left St.-Roch, where his father had preceded him, for La Madeleine; then, in 1863, through the influence of Cavaillé-Coll, he was appointed to St.-Sulpice, where he played the greatest organ in France. At eighteen, Lefébure-Wély had won first prize at the *Conservatoire* under Benoît; the very next year (1836) he made the news by playing a recital on Cavaillé-Colls Poïkilorgue.[1] During the *Exposition de l'Industrie* of 1839, Lefébure-Wély demonstrated the Poïkilorgue two hours a day, four days per week.[2] In 1840, Cavaillé-Coll included a free copy of Lefébure's *Méthode* with the delivery of each Poïkilorgue.[3]

In 1842, it was Lefébure's friendship with the brother of the Curé at the Cathedral of St.-Brieuc that won an organ contract there for Cavaillé-Coll. The next year, Rossini attended a concert at Cavaillé-Coll's shop, where the new organ for St.-Jerôme, Toulouse, was heard for the first time. The *Revue et Gazette* took note of Lefébure's and Cavallo's improvisations on a theme provided by Rossini, who, like many people in high places, spoke approvingly of Lefébure-Wély's playing. He was heard, as well, at the inauguration of a Daublaine-Callinet instrument at Gisors (1844), a concert shared by Cavaillé-Coll's rivals, Dietsch and Danjou; then again, on June 18, 1844, at the opening ceremonies of the ill-fated organ at St.-Eustache.

Stephen Morelot, commenting on the inaugural concert at St.-Eustache,[4] damned Lefébure-Wély and Fessy with faint praise: "Coy grace in ornamentation, thematic distinction, and variety in registration characterize this school, which seems to scorn the dignified canons of musical discipline." Words like these only served to strengthen the growing friendship between Cavaillé-Coll and Lefébure-Wély, since Morelot left his readers in no doubt about his preference for Boëly or Benoît over Lefébure, and for the relatively severe style of playing introduced by Adolphe Hesse, "inheritor of the traditions of the Bach school." Nevertheless,

Morelot concluded that "the easy, elegant playing of Messrs. Lefébure-Wély and Fessy was greeted with the usual enthusiasm".

The critic, Henri Blanchard, commented a few days earlier on Hesse's demonstration of a Daublaine-Callinet organ at the *Exposition des Produits de l'Industrie*.[5] For that occasion, perhaps Hesse's first appearance in France, the artist had chosen to play a fantasy in fugal style, a fugue in G minor by Bach, and Variations on "God Save the King" by Spohr. Scarcely mentioning Hesse's "pure" style and his "marvellous" pedal technique, he spoke at length about the instrument that had been played. Blanchard, unwilling to give wholehearted endorsement to Hesse, also had reservations concerning Lefébure-Wély's style. At the "reception solennelle" for the organ at St.-Sulpice, early in 1846,[6] several hundred people forced the doors and joined the official aristocracy who had been invited to attend:

"Mr. Lefébure-Wély indulged in the eclecticism we have just described, offering an *ostinato* imitation based on a two- or three-measure theme, mingled with modern phrases, resulting inevitably in a sort of bastardized religious genre."[7]

In Mme. Lapresté's dossier there are two documents side-by-side apparently written for the same purpose, both unsigned and undated but addressed alike to "Monsieur le Président et Messiers les Membres du Conseil de Fabrique de l'Eglise St.-Roch à Paris". One, in Cavaillé-Coll's hand, seems to be the draft of a request for an increase in Lefébure's salary as organist at St.-Roch. The other, not in Lefébure-Wély's hand, is less formal and stronger, pleading for the same. We may conclude that Lefébure-Wély sent his version to the man he most trusted, Cavaillé-Coll. Then, when Lefébure-Wély was subsequently offered Fessy's job at La Madeleine (see chap. 6), possibly through Cavaillé-Coll's intervention on his behalf, there would have been no need to send either version of the letter to St.-Roch. Letter in Cavaillé-Coll's hand, no date:

"To: The Chairman and Members

      Council of Saint-Roch

      Paris

Sir:

"In my letter of (   ), I asked for a raise in salary. The Chairman advised me that the Council could not take action on my request until its next meeting.

"I now write to request the Council to grant a moment's consideration to the following statement of the reasons for my action, in hopes that you will grant to the various points raised in my letter the honor of your serious discussion.

"When I resolved to end my career as organist, for the reasons I set forth in my first letter to you, in order to take up a profession which, if not more prestigious, would at least be more profitable, as required by my situation and that of my family, several of my benefactors, whom I count as my friends, advised me not to leave the post in which I was brought up, convinced that the Council of Saint-Roch, in a spirit of kindly concern, would be so generous and fair as to afford me the means of pursuing the art which I have chosen, and which I should be most reluctant to abandon.

"Under these circumstances, Geentlemen, I write to inquire whether it would be possible for you to grant me a regular salary of 4,000 francs. For my part, I am convinced that I deserve as much, and I assure you that I shall strive ever more diligently to prove worthy, not only through my talents as an organist but by discharging faithfully the duties incumbent upon me.

"I enclose testimonials kindly furnished by outstanding musicians and generous friends. I hope the Council may find their professional and personal regard for me sufficient grounds for granting me the salary I respectfully request."

Undated letter in unknown hand:

"To: The Chairman and Members
    Council of Saint-Roch
    Paris

Gentlemen:

"Since childhood, I have devoted my life to organ study, hoping to show by diligent effort that if my benefactors at Saint-Roch took me under their protection when I was still quite young, they might one day be proud of their organist's accomplishments. No man should sing his own praises, but if I dare to do so you have only yourselves to blame, for I think you have rather neglected opportunities to demonstrate your satisfaction.

"My recent success at the inauguration of the organ in La Madeleine has made me so bold as to write you explaining the awkward, nay distressing position in which I find myself. My organ studies have greatly hindered the work I should have liked to pursue on the piano. You are also aware, Gentlemen, that an unavoidable prejudice plagues the existence of the pianist-organist: students of the piano select a pianist for their teacher and not an organist. As a result, I give only a very limited number of piano lessons. As for organ pupils, they are very hard to come by, since few take up that instrument for the simple reason that after a few years of study a pianist can earn five or six thousand francs per year. This is true of a pianist with *no reputation*, while Litz, Thalberg, Grudent (?), Dohler, Choppin, Kontsky, the brothers Herz, Rosselen, Ravina, Goria, *etc.*, almost all of whom were classmates of mine at the Conservatory, are making between twenty and forty thousand francs a year. Organ study enables a man to live on bread and water: such is the life of an organist, and so is mine.

"In the interest of art in general, and on behalf of my colleagues and myself in particular, I appeal to the sense of justice of the Saint-Roch Council members, asking whether the 2,000 francs granted to me as a salary is really enough to pay the rent, expenses, and meals for my wife and children! You will decide whether this sum is adequate, and I ask whether such an income enables me to meet the obligations of my position. It pains me to make this confession, but if you do not grant me a salary which allows me to specialize in the organ, I shall be forced to give up my career as an organist and accept a more rewarding position.

"Looking forward to your reply, I remain your humble and obedient servant."

In September, 1849, Cavaillé-Coll organized a petition to the Minister of the Interior to grant Lefébure-Wély the Legion of Honor:

(final draft)   To the Minister of the Interior

Your Excellency,

"May we bring to your gracious and equitable attention the merits of an artist whose name, in our opinion, deserved inclusion among those honored at the close of the last Industrial Exhibition.

"Numerous precedents, based on Ministerial Directives, show that the Jury's attention may turn even towards artists whose work cannot take the form of exhibited products, bearing their name.

"However that may be, your Excellency, we feel we are discharging an obligation in hereby requesting of you the Legion of Honor for Mr. Lefébure-Wély, organist of La Madeleine, whose talent and learning have rendered genuine services to instrument-making and made significant contributions to progress in that industry. In particular, the organ builders whose instruments Mr. Lefébure-Wély has often played take the liberty of recommending him to your attention.

"Indeed, your Excellency, without the searching study of the characteristics of the organ made by this learned artist, and without the admirable talent which enables him to combine the resources found in the organ, many improvements would not have been attempted by builders: this organist has often revealed to them the possibility of further improvements.

"His excellent compositions, so well suited to the character of each instrument, and his masterful, varied improvisations have allowed musicians and amateurs to realize the wealth of resources to be found in small reed organs: this has created a new industry that already supports many workmen in Paris, and is destined to grow further.

"In addition to these impeccable credentials, we believe it no less convincing, your Excellency, that Mr. Lefébure was initiated by his father, the organist at Saint-Roch, to the difficult art of organ playing, and could substitute for his father by the age of eight. When he was orphaned at eleven, the post of organist for this prominent parish became his as a rightful inheritance.

"An outstanding student at the Conservatory, he won first prizes in organ and piano at the age of fourteen. Having since become one of France's leading organists, Mr. Lefébure-Wély has never failed to contribute his talent to instrument-building.

"His unflagging zeal and the thorough study he made of the new instruments he has introduced, as well as of the inventions and improvements realized in pipe organ building in our day, have greatly contributed to the expansion and progress of an industry that a few years ago was all but abandoned in France, but today ranks high among other nations.

"Finally, your Excellency, allow us to point our further that in every Exhibition since 1834, the Jury has called upon this skilled artist to demonstrate the features of the instruments being examined.

"May we then hope, your Excellency, that you will see fit to consider the request the undersigned respectfully submit to you, by decorating Mr. Lefébure-Wély with the Legion of Honor, for services rendered to musical art and the making of instruments.

4 copies of the above letter to . . .

Annotations to . . .

Signers . . ."

(letterhead)   "Paris, Sept. 20, 1849
"to Baron Charles Dupin, President, Exhibition Jury
"My Lord,

"I respectfully enclose the petition addressed by the musical-instrument makers to the Jury, on behalf of an artist who has contributed to the progress of our industry: Mr. Lefébure-Wély, organist of La Madeleine.

"The members of the Music Division of the Institute have been kind enough to add their comments to this request and recommend to your favorable attention the artist therein named.

"Allow me, my Lord, to seize this opportunity to reiterate my sincere respect.
                                    Your most humble servant.
                                    A. Cavaillé the younger"

Lefébure-Wély's success was phenomenal. He was the only organist in France who participated in all the important inaugural concerts. Danjou abhorred his flamboyant style but knew the crowd would love whatever Lefébure-Wély's fingers played; Cavaillé-Coll adored his playing and indulged Lefébure-Wely's demands for attention as the two became inseparable friends. Inseparable, that is, until Lefébure-Wély discovered that there was another organist whose playing touched Cavaillé-Coll more deeply than his own. That rival was Jacques-Nicolas Lemmens from Belgium, a pupil of Hesse and already a professor at the Brussels Conservatory.

It was Fétis, Director of the Royal Conservatory at Brussels, who wrote to Cavaillé-Coll introducing the young professor before Lemmens' first trip to Paris in the spring of 1850. Accordingly, Cavaillé-Coll scheduled his visit, chose the organs he would play, and selected the audiences who would hear him, for there was no public recital.

Lemmens played at least six organs, four by Cavaillé-Coll and two that had recently been restored by Ducroquet: St.-Sulpice (1846) and the instrument destined for the Cathedral of Clermont-Ferrand (1850) which happened to be set up and playable in the Ducroquet workshop in Paris. Because Cavaillé-Coll wished Lemmens to see his best work, he enlisted the cooperation of his friend, Lefébure-Wély, who obliged several times by making available the organ at La Madeleine. Lefébure-Wély even invited him to perform in a private recital before a distinguished gathering at his home.

Unquestionably, Lefébure-Wély was threatened by Lemmens, who was educated in the polyphonic tradition quite unfamiliar to Lefébure. Lemmens could play all the Bach Trio Sonatas from memory: his fame did not rest on pleasing the crowd with portrayals of storms, or the woeful cries of victims of flood and shipwreck.

As for Cavaillé-Coll, Lemmens' playing raised him to a new level in the understanding of organ music. At the same time, Cavaillé-Coll realized that he was first of all a businessman. He had just survived the most severe financial crisis of his life during the Revolution of 1848 and its aftermath, when his men were out of work for more than six months.[8] What would be his response to the artistic conflict within him? On the one hand, he knew that his old friend, Lefébure-Wély, had done more than any other musician since Rossini to ensure his success. Lefébure-Wély was, indeed, France's "most skillful" organist and a staunch ally.

On the other hand, Cavaillé-Coll had been carried away with Lemmens' performances, especially when he heard the music of J. S. Bach. The 27-year-old virtuoso had actually opened for him a new world of musical expression, and this music seemed perfectly suited to the instruments of his making. Cavaillé-Coll and Lemmens both knew the instruments of Walcker in Ludwigsburg, Mooser in Fribourg, Bätz in Utrecht, and Hill in London. Thus, through Lemmens' genuine enthusiasm for Cavaillé-Coll's organs, Cavaillé-Coll could at last view himself as a leader on the international level. It had, after all, been only two or three years since he had sustained the blistering attacks of Danjou, the self-appointed standard bearer for early music, who detested Cavaillé-Coll's organs. The appreciation of Lemmens, the foreign celebrity, gave something to Cavaillé-Coll that his old associate, Lefébure-Wély, could not do.

It must have been a painful predicament. Cavaillé-Coll elected, typically, to deal with the two virtuosi as honestly as he could. Thus, he continued to promote

Lefébure-Wély as his first choice for inaugurations of new instruments because he could always be sure of a warm public reception; and, at the same time, he sought still closer ties with Lemmens, because he knew that the future of serious organ playing lay, to a large extent in his hands. The policy was successful, for a time. Cavaillé-Coll felt obliged to seek for Lefébure-Wély the most prestigious post in Paris, that of organist at his new 100-stop organ at St.-Sulpice (1863), but he confided privately to Lemmens in that same year: "I had dreamed of the possibility of seeing you in that position." Lefébure-Wély continued to demonstrate his organs for potentates and royalty, as, for instance, when he played Franck's organ at Ste.-Clotilde for the Duchess of Albi more than two months before the inaugural program. But, Cavaillé-Coll persuaded the young Widor and Guilmant to enroll with Lemmens in order to learn the new legato style, apparently sensing that Lemmens, and not Lefébure-Wély, would set the standard of French performance on the organ for generations to come.

After Lemmens' earliest visit in May, 1850, Cavaillé-Coll wrote long letters to him and to Fétis, indicating how deeply committed he already was to assisting Lemmens' career in Paris. These we give in full:[9]

"Mr. Fétis, Director
Royal Conservatory, Brussels
"Sir: Thank you for sending Mr. Lemmens to us, and for the opportunity of submitting our work to the judgment of the learned professor.

"I lost no time in doing what I could to further your plans, securing access for Mr. Lemmens to the organs in Saint-Denis, La Madeleine, and Panthémont, which we built; and in Saint-Roch, which we restored. We also enabled him to visit the work of our colleagues, in particular the great organ in Saint-Sulpice, the masterpiece of Clicquot just recently restored by Daublaine and Callinet; and the new organ that firm has just built for the Cathedral of Clermont, at present set up in their workshops.

"Mr. Lemmens will report to you on the various instruments he played and examined: whatever his opinion, I am no less delighted to have been able to assist you on this occasion. I am entirely at your disposal whenever you may condescend to call upon me.

"Permit me also to thank you for the token of interest you deigned to show for us in your Report to the Academy of Fine Arts: Mr. Lemmens brought it to my attention, and as you comment on the progress made in France where our industry is concerned, you bring our name to the attention of the Government. I am most appreciative for this word of encouragement from you, and whichever builder is called upon to build the organ you have caused to be created, yours will always be the honor of having made a useful gesture on behalf of the country whose musical education you direct, as well as organ building and music, which are international.

"What you seek for music in Belgium would be no less useful in France: a great organ for use on public occasions, on which organists of all nations could play the works of the great masters, which are not in their place in church. This is done in Germany and England, and it would be a great boon to music in general, as well as a powerful stimulus for our young organists.

"Although Mr. Lemmens spent only a short time in Paris, he did not go unnoticed. Our most skillful organists, Mr. Lefébure-Wély of La Madeleine, Mr. Neumann of Panthémont, and Mr. Simon of Saint-Denis all hastened to place their instruments at the disposal of this professor from your Conservatory, and they acknowledge the eminently distinguished talents that he possesses as composer and organist.

"I should have liked to arrange a public recital by Mr. Lemmens, but the same obstacle that prevents this sort of performance in Belgium is encountered in Paris as well. However, I must add that thanks to the kindness of Mr. Lefébure-Wély, we were able to hear him four times at the organ of La Madeleine: at three weddings and at high mass on Whitsunday; also in several other recitals arranged for him by Mr. Neumann at the church of Panthémont, and finally at a small party given by Mr. Lefébure at his home. On this occasion, Messrs. Ambroise Thomas, Adolphe Adam, Stamati, L. Lacombe, D'ortigues, and H. Prévost, plus Mr. Danjou, who happened to be in Paris, heard this learned musician and were no less delighted than we were to compliment Mr. Lemmens on the crystalline, prodigious interpretations he gave of the great masters, as well as on the scientific originality of his splendid compositions.

"I reiterate my sincerest thanks for the opportunity of meeting Mr. Lemmens and admiring his great talent. I shall be no less delighted to show you our work when you come to Paris.

"Until then, etc—

"P. S. Mr. Lemmens will surely tell you of a magnificent Erard piano with pedal keyboard, which he tried in the shop of that distinguished builder. Mr. Érard was no less honored than we to hear his instrument resound under the skillful hands and no less skillful feet of the organ professor. Mr. Érard spoke to Mr. Lemmens of his intention of sending to Brussels one of these fine instruments, so that it may be heard to such good advantage. He also charged Mr. Lemmens with presenting his compliments to you."

"Mr. Lemmens, Professor of Organ[10]
Royal Conservatory of Music, Brussels
"My dear Mr. Lemmens,

"I was pleased to receive your letter of June 23, for Mr. Neumann, Mr. Lefébure and I were impatiently awaiting word from you. A few days after you left Paris, I received the tuning-forks from Mr. Fétis, and I have compared them with the one by Father Jansens that you left me, whose pitch seemed extremely inaccurate.

"My business has not allowed me time or learning enough to engage in a polemic over the pitch of Father Jansens' fork, which seemed extremely inaccurate.

"My business has not left me time to analyze carefully all the errors in his pretentious and arrogant system. I have merely written down the attached notes, which I ask you to give to Mr. Fétis, so that the great master may use them if he finds them to his liking. For my part, I have neither the time nor the learning to engage in a polemic on Mr. Jansens' pitch.

"I have seen Mr. Bourges several times, and he said he had not found your *Journal* at Brandus': Mr. Brandus himself did not have the honor of seeing you. I assured him that you had gone there several times but did not meet him, and that I was present when you left the issue of your *Journal*. Finally he was found, but he excused himself saying he hadn't been able to write anything, first because of other work, and then because it was too late: he promised he would make good, since you are to return in August.

"As for Mr. D'Ortigues, I did not have the opportunity of seeing him again: I suppose that because I failed to remind him of his promise, he forgot about you completely.

"I have seen Mr. Erard but once since then, and I spoke to him of your desire to acquaint others in Brussels with his magnificent instruments. I believe he wants to wait until he has lengthened the pedals to accommodate your foot. He has already asked my Neumann whether I lengthened the pedals at Panthémont. Moreover, when I gave him your letter yesterday, Mr. Neumann promised to write you himself on this matter and on some points concerning the tuning-fork you sounded when you returned to Brussels.

"Finally, I have promised several persons a visit from you in August. I hope you have not changed your mind, and we shall beat the big bass drum to announce your arrival.

"You said you would send the first three issues of your *Journal* to Messrs. Lefébure, Neumann, and D'Ortigues, as well as to the *Gazette musicale*. Remember that I too wish to subscribe, not to play your compositions, but to have them played, and to secure new subscribers.

"Meanwhile, please send your first three issues to Mr. Collin, organist at the Cathedral of Saint-Brieuc (Côtes-du-Nord). He is a pupil of Mr. Lefébure's and a friend of mine. I am anxious to present him with a year's subscription, so you may bill me for it.

"Now I must make another comment, in your interest. Mr. Bourges, with whom I chatted about your intention to give your publication to Mr. Brandus, told me you had acted quite irresponsibly in this matter, leaving Paris without conferring with Mr. Brandus. He added that as a Belgian, you must know that pirated publications, so skillfully made in Belgium, could also be made in France, and that you might thus lose the reward for your work. I pass this comment on to you so that you may further consider the situation.

"Farewell, my dear Mr. Lemmens. Please relay to Mr. Fétis my renewed and sincere gratitude for the tokens of interest he is kind enough to give me. I am as anxious as you to find an opportunity for proving myself worthy.

Sincerely, etc."

Lemmens returned to Paris in August, and Cavaillé-Coll had indeed "beaten the big bass drum" by seeing that Henri Blanchard heard him play at the Panthémont. The reward was abundant; while introducing Lemmens,[11] Blanchard used the occasion to discuss the true style of organ playing:

". . . Mr. Lemmens, who is professor of organ at the Brussels Conservatory and publishes a periodical devoted to the organ, . . . [is] an artist who has before him a fine career as a composer of religious music, in a pure, classical style.

"Thanks to our operatic composers and our leading builders — first among whom is Mr. Cavaillé-Coll — the organ has begun to progress. Its mechanical and tonal resources are being improved, and its stops and composition pedals are now extremely varied. Since Meyerbeer's *Robert le Diable* and Halévy's *La Juive* made such dramatic use of the instrument, the organ has become secular. Many music-lovers go to church as much for the lofty, solemn tones of this noble, many-voiced instrument, as for prayer. The defenders of sacred-style music wonder if this is indeed progress. The clergy, with its ascetic frame of mind, says no. But since very few clergymen are really musicians, they let the trend continue. The scope and appeal of the services are increased, and in the clergy's opinion this is the main thing: they know that services without music, hymns, or organ are not religion.

"The chief question for professional musicians, who have exacting tastes and standards, is determining what genuine organ style should be. Most French organists, with the exception of Mr. Boëly, who plays at St.-Germain-l'Auxerrois, favor 'fantasias' that are more or less clever, smooth, and Rossini-like. They improvise pretty exercises in harmony, with 'suspensions' such as have been lying around for years in every textbook on composition, or they play some wistful love-song at the Élévation, all because they either hate fugues or never adequately studied their possibilities. Their scorn for classical ideas is fostered by self-styled critics who cannot conceive that fugue is the source of unity, clarity of ideas and economy of harmonic means. They cannot understand that no rule of harmony requires a fugue subject to be gothic, periwigged, or rococo, or that it can be a vigorous or graceful melody, quite in a modern style, even a waltz, if you want to avoid packing it with canons, imitations, or *stretti!* On the other hand, used with taste, discernment, and moderation these features give any musical composition an aura of learning that attracts and pleases every discriminating mind schooled in musical quality and beauty. This is what the *Gazette musicale* has been saying for over ten years, and we shall never tire of repeating it, because such is the true, the useful, the inevitable result that must be sought by any man endowed with a genuine feeling for music, and any young composer confident in his true mission. Mr. Lemmens is a man of this temper. After studying with the distinguished organist of Breslau, he soon became an organist himself and professor of organ in Brussels, his native city. There, as in France, the vagaries of officialdom encourage the production of composers and send one to Rome every year, after which he may become a guitar-teacher, a wine-dealer, or anything he likes except a composer, for all his prizes. So it is that the Belgian government paid for the musical education of a young man who was sent to Germany. He came back an excellent organist, and he trains excellent pupils, who win prizes at the Brussels Conservatory, but they can hardly demonstrate their skill to their fellow Belgians: there are as few organs in the churches of Brussels as there are opera-houses in our national and artistic capital, Paris; and the throngs of native and foreign composers find here every opportunity for starving.

"More resourceful than the chef who required a rabbit in order to make a rabbit stew, Mr. Lemmens produces excellent organists without an organ. And so, to reward himself for his exhausting, unrewarding labors, he recently came to play upon the fine instrument built by the Cavaillé-Coll firm for the Protestant church of Panthémont. The young Belgian organist gave a recital whose length went unnoticed by the audience, proving that an austere style need not preclude grace or melodic and harmonic refinement. After he had read us some of J. S. Bach's beautiful fugues, he played us a few of his own: the style was good, and the manner was modern, like the one we discussed above. If the wealth of composition pedals on the fine instrument seemed at times to astonish and perplex our young Belgian virtuoso, it was not to the detriment of refinement, for his ideas were always stated with purity, elegance, and clarity. His Prayers, which we are tempted to call charming mystical nocturnes, make you dream of religion, science, and we might almost say love, all at the same time; but this love is pure and tranquil, midway between sensuous ideas and the profound feeling of noble friendship. This is also without doubt the result of his *legato* style of playing and his finger-substitutions, that we might almost call slick. This technique is carefully analyzed in Mr. Lemmens' organ magazine. It will, we are sure, be instrumental in producing good organists and awakening broader interest in this beautiful instrument. The organ's ethereal, powerful voice will one day join with the substantial voices of the orchestra, in concerts which will achieve new sounds and enlarge the domain of music."

Despite his admiration for Lemmens, Cavaillé-Coll could not abandon his old friend, Lefébure-Wély. It was Lefébure-Wély who was named organist in 1863 at St.-Sulpice, the most coveted post in France after Cavaillé-Coll had enlarged the instrument. The letter below was written after that appointment, and before that long association was finally ended:

"Pierrefonds, Monday the 31st
 Hotel des Bains

". . . I trust, dear friend, that you are seeing to my organ. During my last service, the sound suddenly died under my fingers, in an important piece. I questioned my blowers and they swore they had not stopped pumping. Look into that, dear friend. There is obviously a serious upheaval in that organ, caused by high temperatures. The octave couplers hardly work, or not at all, and *the entire action needs* regulating.

"If it were possible to make the *Voix humaine less effective,* maybe it would be *better.* The *tremblant* is too lively, that much is certain. Are you also thinking about our rain and hail? You *absolutely must attract attention to that masterpiece,* dear friend. When a smart performer wants to fill the house, he shows off his skill at the door: trumpets, bass drums, etc. As for us, we have to attempt imitating our worthy colleagues. Let's pack them in, using thunderstorms, bells, bird songs, tambourines, bagpipes, and 'human voices'. Then we'll slip into the ears of those uninitiates the entrancing, tender tones of the organ in Saint-Sulpice, which after all is the most beautiful organ ever known.

"Overlook nothing, dear friend, and if you back me up, I give you my word of honor that you will be pleased with me.

"When they return, the seminary students must jump up and dance on their choir stalls, all books must be closed, and all ears open. We must attempt a revelation, to win a victory. Let us also think of the importance of our gathering of the distinguished Rossini, Auber, Ambroise Thomas, etc.

"Above all, keep this between us. Be not indiscreet . . .

Lefébure-Wély

Illustrations

Fig. 1. Cavaillé-Coll at age 25 (from E. and C. Cavaillé-Coll, *Aristide Cavaillé-Coll: Ses origines, sa vie, ses oeuvres*. Paris, 1929).

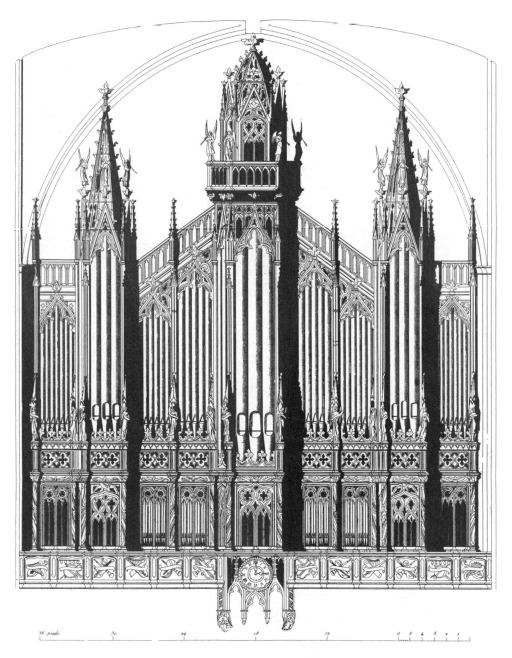

C.^D ORGUE DE L'ÉGLISE ROYALE DE S.^T DENIS.
construit par MM CAVAILLÉ-COLL père et fils, facteurs d'Orgues du Roi.
inauguré le 21 Septembre 1841
Dessin de M.F DEBRET architecte de l'Église royale

Fig. 2. St.-Denis: Façade (from J. Adrien de la Fage, *Orgue de l'eglise royale de Saint-Denis*. Paris, 1841).

Fig. 3. St.-Denis: The bellows (photograph by J.L. Coignet).

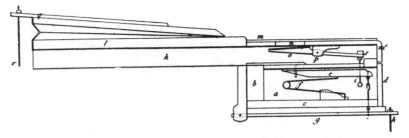

Levier pneumatique, d'après le dessin original de Barker.

Fig. 4. The Barker machine (Plate 25 from *Nouveau manuel complet de l'organiste*. Paris, 1905).

Dessin de **M. HUVÉ**,
ARCHITECTE DU MONUMENT.

Gravure publiée par le journal
L'ILLUSTRATION.

GRAND ORGUE DE L'ÉGLISE DE LA MADELEINE
A PARIS
Construit par **A. CAVAILLÉ-COLL**, père et fils,
FACTEURS D'ORGUES DU ROI,

Inauguré le 29 Octobre 1846.

MENUISERIE EXÉCUTÉE PAR
M. LINDEMBERG.

Sculptures par M. MARNEUF.

Fig. 5. La Madeleine: Façade (from *Rapport . . . du Grand Orgue de l'eglise de la Madeleine*. Paris, 1846).

Buffet d'orgue de l'église Saint-Vincent-de-Paul, construit par M. Aristide Cavaillé-Coll, d'après les dessins de Hittof, architecte de cette église.

Fig. 6. St.-Vincent-de-Paul: (from Calla, *Rapport sur la construction et la facture des grandes orgues de M. Aristide Cavaillé-Coll*. Paris, 1854).

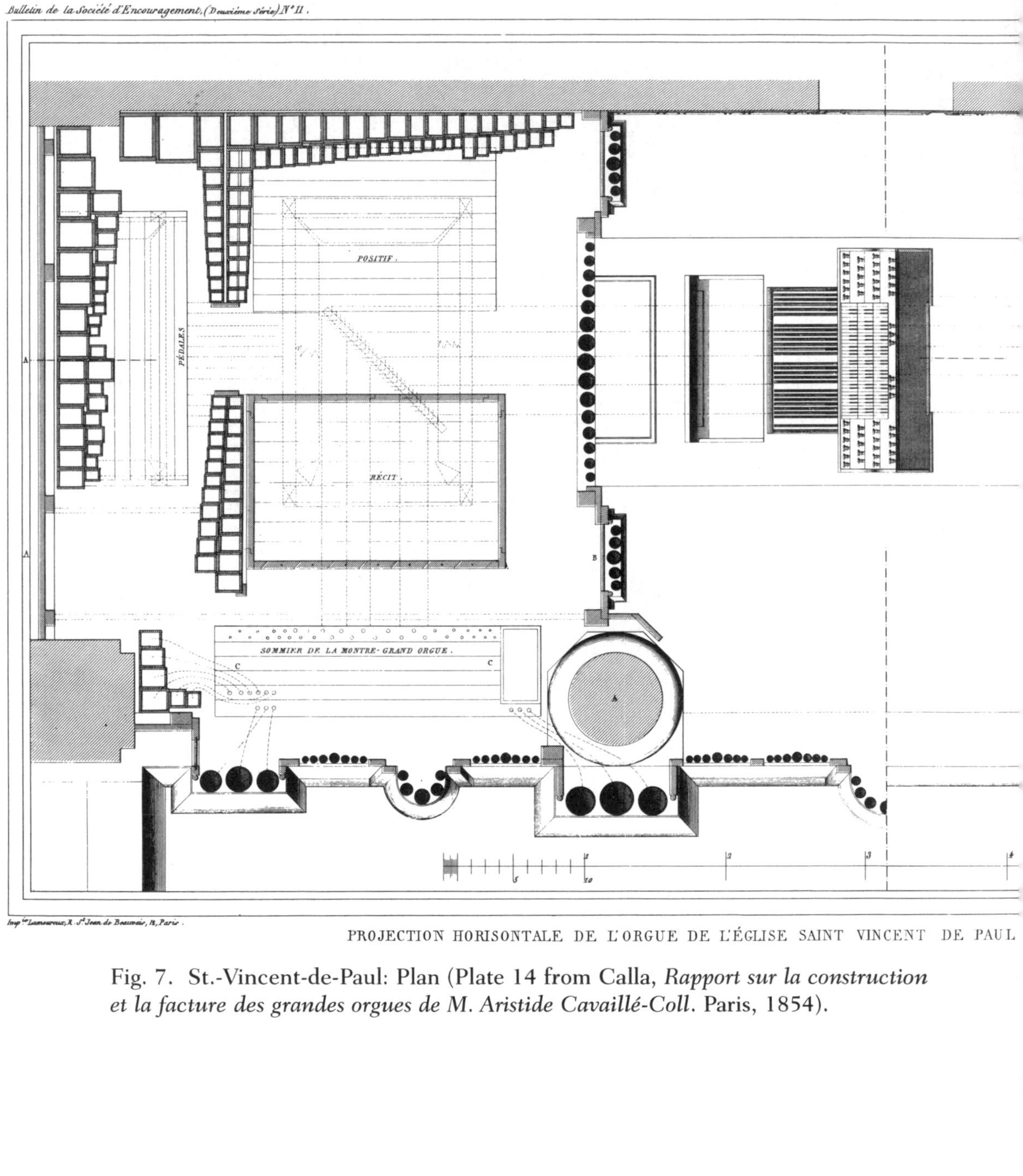

PROJECTION HORISONTALE DE L'ORGUE DE L'ÉGLISE SAINT VINCENT DE PAUL

Fig. 7. St.-Vincent-de-Paul: Plan (Plate 14 from Calla, *Rapport sur la construction et la facture des grandes orgues de M. Aristide Cavaillé-Coll.* Paris, 1854).

Pl. 14

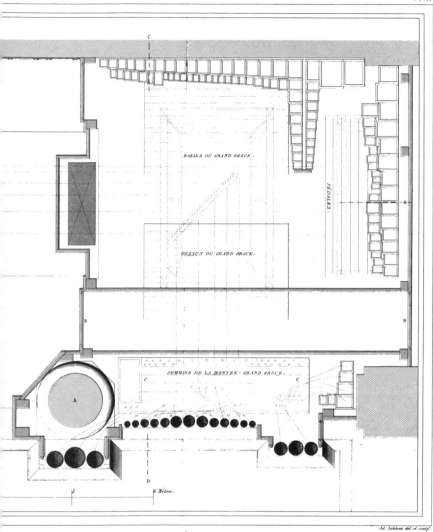

BASSES DU GRAND ORGUE.

PÉDALES.

DESSUS DU GRAND ORGUE.

SOMMIER DE LA MONTRE - GRAND ORGUE.

A

6 Mètres.

CONSTRUIT PAR Mᵉ ARISTIDE CAVAILLÉ COLL.

Ad. Leblanc del. et sculp.ᵗ

SECTION LONGITUDINALE ET VERTICALE DE L'ORGUE DE L'ÉGLISE SAINT

Fig. 8. St.-Vincent-de-Paul: Longitudinal section (Calla, Plate 15).

Pl. 15.

Fig. 3.

VINCENT DE PAUL, PAR M.ᴿ A. CAVAILLÉ COLL.

Ad. Leblanc del. et sculp.ᵗ

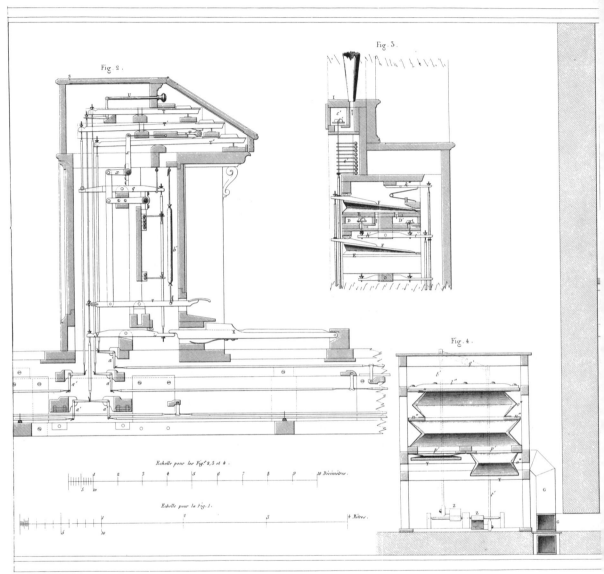

Fig. 9. St.-Vincent-de-Paul: Transverse section (Calla, Plate 16).

Pl. 16.

Fig. 1.

Ad. Leblanc del. et sculp.

DE L'ORGUE DE L'ÉGLISE SAINT VINCENT DE PAUL, PAR M. A. CAVAILLÉ COLL.

Fig. 10. Ste.-Clotilde: Façade (Coignet).

Fig. 11. César Franck.

Fig. 12. St.-Sulpice: Façade (from Lissajous, . . . *Grand orgue de Saint-Sulpice à Paris*. Paris, 1865).

COMPOSITION DES JEUX, DES REGISTRES ET DES PÉDALES DE COMBINAISON.

CLAVIER DE PÉDALE ou pédalier d'Ut à Fa, 30 notes.	PREMIER CLAVIER grand-chœur, d'Ut à Sol, 56 notes.	DEUXIÈME CLAVIER grand-orgue, d'Ut à Sol, 56 notes.	TROISIÈME CLAVIER bombarde, d'Ut à Sol, 56 notes.	QUATRIÈME CLAVIER positif, d'Ut à Sol, 56 notes.	CINQUIÈME CLAVIER récit exp., d'Ut à Sol, 56 notes.
1 Principal-Basse. 32	1 Salicional. 8	1 Principal-harm. 32-16	1 Soubasse. 16	1 Violon Basse. 16	1 Quintaton. 16
2 Contre-Basse. 16	2 Octave. 4	2 Montre. 16	2 Flûte conique. 16	2 Quintaton. 16	2 Bourdon. 8
3 Soubasse. 16	3 Grosse Fourniture 4 r	3 Bourdon. 16	3 Principal. 8	3 Quintaton. 8	3 Violoncelle. 8
4 Flûte. 8	4 Grosse Cymbale. 6 r	4 Flûte conique. 16	4 Flûte harmonique. 8	4 Flûte Traversière. 8	4 Prestant. 4
5 Violoncelle. 8	5 Plein-jeu. 4 r	5 Flûte harmonique. 8	5 Bourdon. 8	5 Salicional. 8	5 Doublette. 2
6 Flûte. 4	6 Cornet. 5 r	6 Flûte Traversière. 8	6 Gambe. 8	6 Viole de Gambe. 8	6 Fourniture. 4 R
Jeux de Combinaison.	7 1re Trompette. 8	7 Montre. 8	7 Violoncelle. 8	7 Unda Maris. 8	7 Cymbale. 5 R
7 Clairon. 4	8 2e Trompette. 8	8 Bourdon. 8	8 Kéraulophone. 8	8 Flûte douce. 4	8 Basson et Hautbois. 8
8 Ophicléide. 8	9 Clairon. 4	9 Diapason. 8	9 Flûte Octaviante. 4	9 Flûte Octaviante. 4	9 Voix humaine. 8
9 Trompette. 8	10 Clairon-Doublette. 2	10 Flûte à Pavillon. 8	10 Prestant. 4	10 Dulciana. 4	10 Cromorne. 8
10 Basson. 16	11 Basson. 8	11 Prestant. 4	*Jeux de Combinaison.*	*Jeux de Combinaison.*	11 Cor Anglais. 16
11 Bombarde. 16	12 Basson. 16	12 Grosse Quinte. 5 1/3	11 Grosse Quinte. 5 1/3	11 Quinte. 2 2/3	12 Voix Céleste. 8
12 Contre-Bombarde. 32	13 Bombarde. 16	13 Doublette. 2	12 Grosse Tierce. 3 1/5	12 Doublette. 2	*Jeux de Combinaison.*
			13 Quinte. 2 2/3	13 Plein jeu harm. 3-6	13 Flûte harmonique. 8
			14 Octave. 4	14 Tierce. 1.3/5	14 Flûte Octaviante. 4
			15 Octavin. 2	15 Larigot. 1.1/3	15 Dulciana. 4
			16 Cornet. 5 R	16 Picolo. 1	16 Nazard. 2.2/3
			17 Trompette. 8	17 Trompette. 8	17 Octavin. 2
			18 Clairon. 4	18 Clarinette. 8	18 Cornet 5 Rangs. 8
			19 Baryton. 8	19 Clairon. 4	19 Trompette. 8
			20 Bombarde. 16	20 Euphone. 16	20 Trompette harm. 8
					21 Bombarde. 16
					22 Clairon. 4

PÉDALES DE COMBINAISON.

1 Orage.	11 Anches Bombardes.	
2 Tirasse Grand-Chœur.	12 Anches Positif.	
3 Tirasse Grand-Orgue.	13 Anches Récit.	
4 Anches Pédale.	14 Copula Grand-Chœur.	
5 Octaves Grand-Chœur.	15 Copula Grand-Orgue	
6 Octaves Grand-Orgue.	16 Copula Bombardes.	
7 Octaves Bombardes.	17 Copula Positif	
8 Octaves Positif.	18 Copula Récit.	
9 Octaves Récit.	19 Tremblant.	
10 Anches Grand-Orgue.	20 Expression.	

REGISTRES DE COMBIN.

1 Combinaison Pédale. G.
2 — Grand-Orgue. G.
3 — Bombardes. G.
4 — Positif. G.
5 — Récit. G.
6 Combinaison Pédale. D.
7 — Grand-Orgue. D.
8 — Bombarde. D.
9 — Positif. D.
10 — Récit. D.

REGISTRES ACCESSOIRES.

1 Sonnette du Haut. G.	3 Sonnette du Haut. D.
2 Sonnette du Bas. G.	4 Sonnette du Bas. D.

RÉSUMÉ.

100 jeux. — 118 registres. — 20 pédales de combinaison et 6,706 tuyaux.

Fig. 13. St.-Sulpice: Console (from Lissajous).

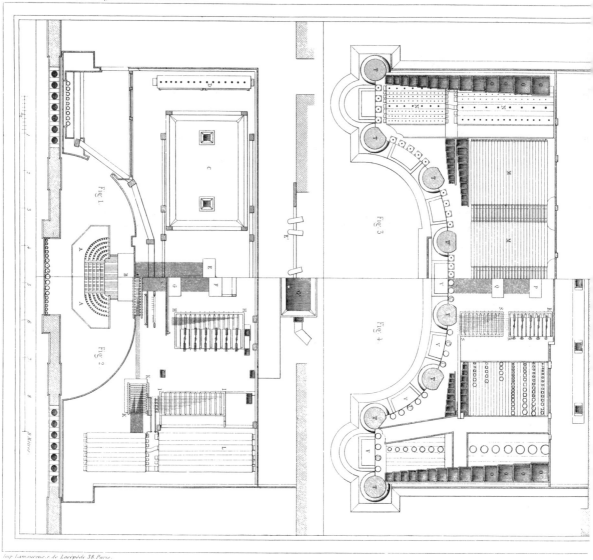

PLANS DES DIFFÉRENTS ÉTAGES DU GRAND ORGUE DE SAINT SULPICE. A

Fig. 14. St.-Sulpice: Plan at various levels (from Lissajous, Plate 310).

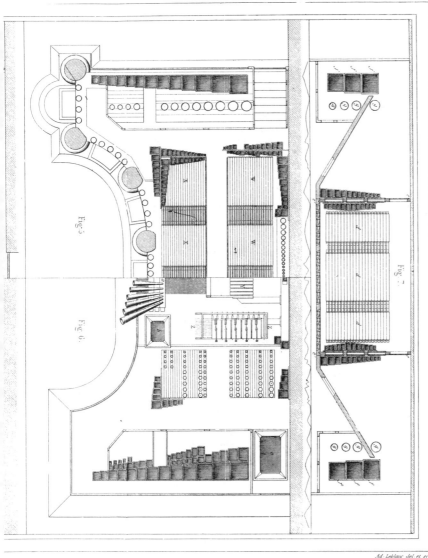

Pl. 310.

Fig. 5

Fig. 6

Fig. 7

PARIS, RECONSTRUIT PAR M. A. CAVAILLÉ-COLL.

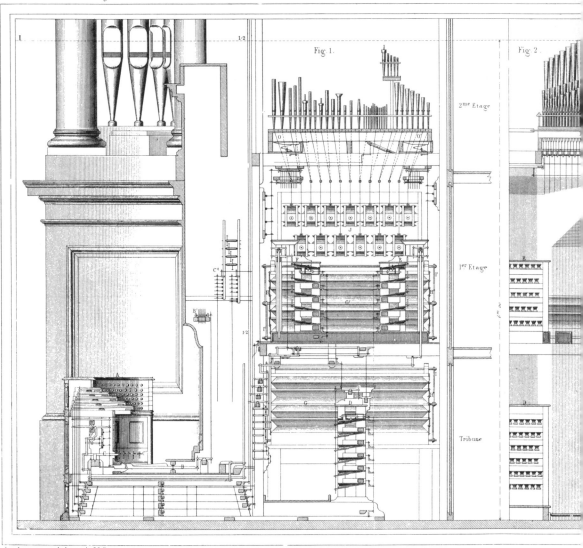

SECTIONS VERTICALES DE LA TRIBUNE ET DES IER ET 2ME ÉTAGES DU GRAND ORGUE D

Fig. 15. St.-Sulpice: Section of the first three levels (Lissajous, Plate 311).

II

Ad Leblanc del. et sc.

Sᵀ SULPICE A PARIS, RECONSTRUIT PAR M. A. CAVAILLÉ - COLL.

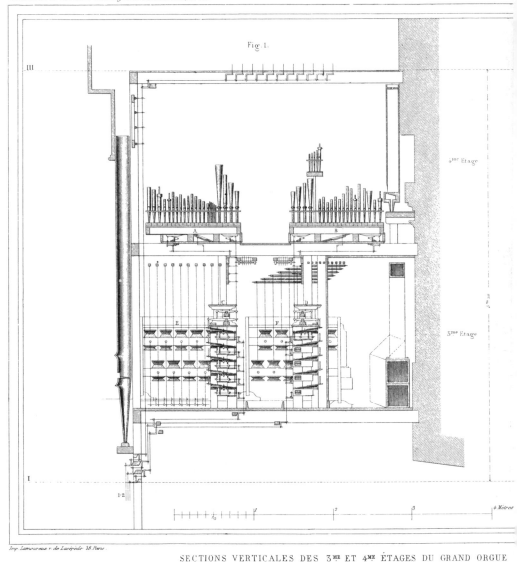

SECTIONS VERTICALES DES 3ME ET 4ME ÉTAGES DU GRAND ORGUE

Fig. 16. St.-Sulpice: Section of the fourth and fifth levels (Lissajous, Plate 312).

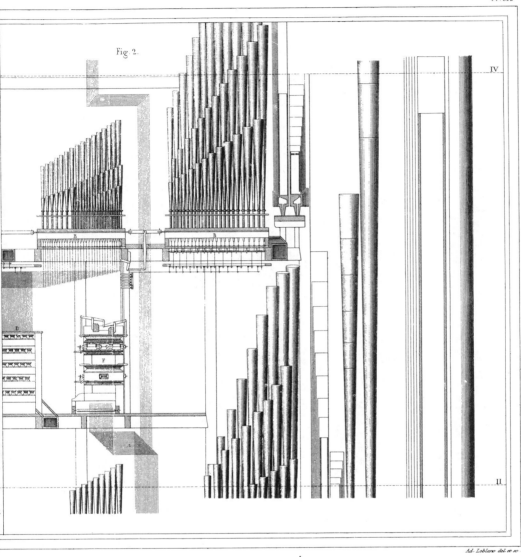

Pl. 312

Fig. 2.

IV

II

B

B

D

F

Ad. Leblanc del. et sc.

DE S.T SULPICE A PARIS, RECONSTRUIT PAR M. A. CAVAILLÉ- COLL.

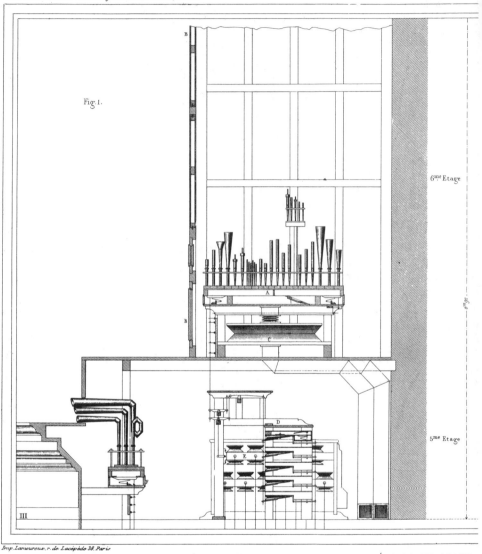

Fig. 1.

6.me Etage

5.me Etage

III

SECTIONS VERTICALES DES 5.ME ET 6.ME ÉTAGES DU GRAND

Fig. 17. St.-Sulpice: Section of the sixth and seventh levels (Lissajous, Plate 313).

Pl. 313

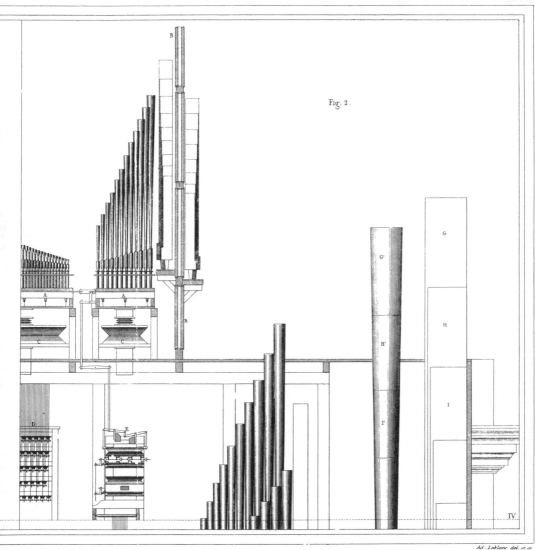

Fig. 2.

Ad. Leblanc del. et sc.

RGUE DE Sᵗ SULPICE A PARIS, RECONSTRUIT PAR M. A. CAVAILLÉ-COLL.

CHAPTER EIGHT

The Organ at the Church of Saint-Vincent-De-Paul

After La Madeleine, Cavaillé-Coll's next major Parisian installation was the 46-stop organ for the new church of St.-Vincent-de-Paul, inaugurated January 26, 1852. The original contract and several related documents will be found in the appendices. Below, we reprint *in extenso* a remarkable 16-page pamphlet and accompanying plates in which the new organ was studied in detail to demonstrate Cavaillé-Coll's innovative procedures in organ building. There are concise explanations of Coll's wind supply, including the *soufflerie à diverses pressions,* the system of *sommiers à doubles laies,* the improved Barker machine installed at St-Vincent-de-Paul, and the harmonic pipes, that were, of course, used freely in that instrument. The publication of the pamphlet by the *Société d'Encouragement pour l'Industrie Nationale* commemorated the award of the *grand médaille d'or* to Cavaillé-Coll on May 17, 1854.

"Society for the Advancement
of French Industry
Founded 1802

Recognized as a Public Service Organization by Official Order Dated April 21, 1824

Offices: 44 rue Bonaparte, Paris

Report
by Mr. Calla
On Behalf of the Committee
on Mechanical Arts
on
The Manufacture and Building of Pipe Organs
By Mr. Aristide Cavaillé-Coll
94-96 rue de Vaugirard

Gentlemen:

The Committee on Mechanical Arts and the Commission on Fine Arts have charged us with reporting to you on their inspection of the pipe organ built by Mr. Aristide Cavaillé-Coll for the church of Saint-Vincent-de-Paul.

The instrument has 46 stops, 12 composition pedals, and 2,576 pipes.

The organ-case, designed by the architect for the building, Mr. Hittorff, is decorated with 161 display pipes, 111 in the facade and 50 in the sides.

The keyboards are located in a separate cabinet in the center of the gallery, under the vault which divides the case into two parts.

The stoplist is as follows:

Pédale Division

25 notes, C to C

1. Bourdon	32'	5. Basse-contre (free reed)	16'
2. Contre-basse or Flûte	16'	6. Bombarde	16'
3. Basse or Flûte	8'	7. Trompette	8'
4. Octave or Flûte	4'	8. Clairon	4'
Reeds			

Grand orgue Division

54 notes, 4½ octaves, C to F

Group 1: Bass pipes in display

1. Montre	16'	4. Gambe	8'
2. Gambe	16'	5. Montre	4'
3. Montre	8'	6. Voix céleste	8'

Group 2: Stops located inside the organ

7. Bourdon	16'	11. Salcional (sic)	8'
8. Bourdon	8'	12. Prestant	4'
9. Flûte harmonique	8'	13. Doublette	2'
10. Flûte octaviante	4'		

Group 3: Reeds and Mutations

14. Quinte	3'	18. Trompette	8'
15. Fourniture	IV Ranks	19. Basson / Hautbois	8'
16. Cymbale	III Ranks	20. Clairon	4'
17. Bombarde	16'		

Positif Division

54 notes, 4½ octaves, C to F

1. Salcional (sic)	8'	Reeds and Mutations	
2. Flûte harmonique	8'	7. Doublette	2'
3. Bourdon	16'	8. Trompette	8'
4. Bourdon	8'	9. Cromorne	8'
5. Flûte octaviante	4'	10. Clairon	4'
6. Dulciana	4'		

Manual III: *Récit expressif*

54 notes, 4½ octaves, C to F

1. Voix humaine	8'	Reeds and Mutations	
2. Cor anglais	8'	6. Quinte	3'
3. Bourdon	8'	7. Doublette	2'
4. Flûte harmonique	8'	8. Trompette harmonique	8'
5. Flûte octaviante	4'	9. Clairon harmonique	4'

Summary of Stops and Pipes at the Various Pitches

Division	32'	16'	8'	4'	3'	2'	Pleins jeux	Stops	Pipes
1. *Pédale*	1	3	2	2	0	0	0	8	200
2. *Positif*	0	1	5	3	0	1	0	10	540
3. *Grand orgue,* Group 1	0	2	3	1	0	0	0	6	324
4. *Grand orgue,* Group 2	0	1	3	2	0	1	0	7	378
5. *Grand orgue,* Group 3	0	1	2	1	1	0	2	7	648
6. *Récit expressif*	0	0	5	2	1	1	0	9	486
Totals	1	8	20	11	2	3	2	47	2576

On first examining this ensemble, we observe as its peculiar characteristic a perfectly rational design, which bespeaks a learned and skillful craftsman.

May we here recall that in 1834 our esteemed colleague Mr. Mallet reported to you on an ingenious circular saw which Mr. Cavaillé had just submitted for your judgment, and for which you awarded him a bronze medal the following year. Mr. Mallet concluded his report in the following terms:

All have been prompt in paying tribute to the intelligence, industry, and ingenuity with which Mr. Cavaillé seems to be endowed . . . This young craftsman is settling in Paris, there joining the ranks of those distinguished men who each year vie for the awards which you take such pleasure in bestowing upon true merit. He will surely not be long in proving his worth.

Nineteen years have passed since then, and most of you have followed with interest the remarkable achievements through which Mr. Cavaillé has proven the accuracy of our colleague's prediction.

Your Committee on Mechanical Arts and Commission on Fine Arts have examined the great organ in the church of Saint-Vincent-de-Paul, the most recent example of the improvements which Mr. Cavaillé is constantly making in the construction of those noble instruments. In it they have found as it were the epitome of the achievements towards which this skillful builder has striven ever since you first rewarded him with a prize.

At the risk of repeating what has often been said of Mr. Cavaillé's work, we observe with pleasure that there is no aspect of organ-building in which he has not demonstrated such care and precision in workmanship as were unknown before him and are still rare among other builders today.

The organs in Notre-Dame-de-Lorette, the Basilica of Saint-Denis, La Madeleine, and Saint-Vincent-de-Paul, not to mention several smaller instruments, reveal in every part that character of diligence, understanding, inventiveness, and sound judgment that you were pleased to recognize in his earliest instruments.

We cannot summarize for you all the improvements Mr. Cavaillé has made in the building of organs.

The Jury reports from the Exhibitions held in 1839, 1844, and 1849, and the special reports made on the great instruments built for Saint-Denis, La Madeleine, Saint-Vincent-de-Paul, etc., fill entire volumes. Merely to summarize them would be a greater task than the regular work of our executive board. We shall simply point out some of the chief features of Mr. Cavaillé's instruments, in particular the improvements he has incorporated in the organ for Saint-Vincent-de-Paul.

Bellows. The feeder bellows are located in a chamber next to the gallery. They supply wind to six large reservoirs housed in the base of the organ. Capt. Piobert has shown that the most efficient way to use human energy is to raise the weight of the body. In other words, a man produces the greatest amount of work by using the leg muscles. In order to take advantage of that information, Mr. Cavaillé devised the following arrangement which we shall describe.

He replaced the lever, operated by the hands and arms, with two pedals, one for each foot. The man's entire weight, therefore, rests on the pedals; and if he raises one foot, his full weight bears on the opposite pedal, which descends as the other one rises. Shifting the weight to the first pedal produces the opposite effect. Any hand-hold within reach would have enabled the man to keep his balance, but such an arrangement would have facilitated the operation only at the expense of the work done. In order to turn the support furnished the man to the benefit of the instrument, Mr. Cavaillé provided two vertical rods, connected at their upper ends to a walking-beam and at their lower ends to the two pedals. In this way, each stroke of the legs is followed and strengthened by the arms, and the muscles are used to their capacity.

Turning from the bellows to the reservoirs, we find features which are just as remarkable, by reason of the alert mind that designed them and the simplicity of their construction. The wind-supply or reservoir for a pipe-organ, as is well known, consists of two large rectangular boards forming the top and bottom, and several wooden frames to which are attached the folds which enclose the reservoir.

Inverting the folds, or fitting inward and outward folds in alternation so as to compensate for the respective action of each fold, was a common practice and did not escape Mr. Cavaillé's attention. However, it was necessary to avoid having certain folds remain closed or only part way open, while others were almost always open and closed but slowly. The effect striven for was true compensation, in the form of a uniform angle in each fold. To achieve this effect, Mr. Cavaillé has simply connected the various frames between the folds with a pantograph linkage that relays to the lazy folds the excess motion of the active folds. Mr. Cavaillé thus obtains not only a genuine balance among all the folds, but also precise uniformity in the angles of all the folds regardless of the height to which the top board rises.

Between the bellows proper and the organ pipes, the wind is stored in regulating reservoirs located near the pipes they supply: these regulators create the pressure appropriate to the stops for which the wind is intended.

Windchests.   As in all organs, the lower ends of the pipes stand on wooden assemblies known as *windchests*. In these chests are provided the passages which channel the wind supplied by the conduits or wind-trunks to the pipes, and provide the necessary connection among these various channels. Under the [upper portion of the] chests are the pallets, which admit wind to the pipes: they are enclosed in *pallet-boxes*. It will readily be seen that because of this rather complicated construction, while the organ is being played the wind must undergo weakening and noticeable variations in pressure, and these must compromise the accuracy of pitch and the blending of the organ's voices.

In order to steady the wind pressure at the very point where it is about to enter the pipes, Mr. Cavaillé has replaced one of the rigid walls of the pallet-boxes with an elastic sheet of rubber having a thin board at its center and light springs bearing against it. The wind pressure is thus steadied when in the course of a performance wind is used suddenly and in short bursts.

In addition, the use of various stops in combinations has led the builder to place on the same chest several sets of pipes that the organist may play separately or together.

In conventional organs, a single pallet controls the wind supplied to all the pipes corresponding to a given key. However, since these pipes are of different dimensions, and since the wind follows a single channel, it must enter the various pipes at different pressures. This is a natural consequence of different sizes for pipe-holes, and the length of the channels, some of which are quite long.

In his complicated wind-chests, which Mr. Cavaillé calls *double-pallet-box* chests, he has fitted two sets of pallets and divided the box enclosing them into two parts. In this manner he groups together the low-pitched pipes, and similarly for the higher-pitched stops. He has even succeeded in supplying these two divisions with wind at different pressures, thus achieving a definite improvement in the precision and stability of the pitch, and in the power of the tone.

This improvement has broadened the range of stop combinations, by eliminating the obstacles we have just mentioned. Thus Mr. Cavaillé's new organs afford a variety and richness of tonal effects previously unattainable.

The windchests for the six stops in the Saint-Vincent-de-Paul organ, whose pipes are displayed in the case are designed according to entirely original principles. Each pipe has its own pallet, and the advantage of direct wind-supply is so obvious as to need no justification. The greater number of pallets might have given rise to a greater number of leaks, but the pallets are made in such a way that when the stop they control is not playing, they make any wind loss impossible.

In these chests, the registers or sliding strips that open and close the stops whose pipes are in the display are replaced with ventils: these are much easier to operate than sliders, so by means of a single pedal which is very easy to operate the organist can put on the six *montre* stops all at once or in any combination, as required by the piece of music he wishes to perform.

Here is the list of composition pedals in the organ in Saint-Vincent-de-Paul.

Arrangement of the composition pedals, from the right of the player.

1. *Expression*　　opens and closes the swell-box enclosing the *Récit* division.
2. *Trémolo*　　controls the tremulant mechanism.
3. **Copula**　　controls the mechanism coupling the *Récit* division to the *Positif*.
4. *Copula*　　couples the *Positif* division to the *Grand orgue*.
5. *Appel*　　adds the reeds and mutations in the *Récit* division to the foundation stops in the same division.
6. *Appel*　　adds the reeds and mutations in the *Positif* division to the foundation stops in the same division.
7. *Appel*　　adds the reeds and mutations in the *Grand orgue* division to the foundation stops in the same division.
8. *Accouplement*　controls a mechanism coupling the octaves in the *Positif* manual.
9. *Accouplement*　controls a mechanism coupling the octaves in the *Grand orgue* manual.
10. *Appel*　　controls a mechanism putting on the six *montre* stops, in whatever combination the organist desires.
11. *Appel*　　puts on the *Pédale* reed stops.
12. *Accouplement*　couples the bass range of the *Grand orgue* division to the *Pédale*, enabling the player to increase at will the volume of accompaniment in the bass.

We must cut short this summary and merely point out some of the other improvements Mr. Cavaillé has made in organ-building, particularly in the Saint-Vincent-de-Paul organ. Examples are the best choice of materials, the most painstaking workmanship, the new composition pedals, and double glass walls for the swell-box. Neither can we describe for you the successful way in which he has resolved problems arising from the overall construction of the case. We must, however, make special mention of the application ot his instruments of a new device known as the *pneumatic lever*.

In old organs, the various keys in a single manual offered different degrees of resistance to the organist's fingers, depending on the size of the pipes to be sounded, the remoteness of the pipes, or often both these factors. One result was fatigue for the organist, and another was slowness and uncertainty in the speech of certain pipes. An Englishman, Mr. Barker, undertook to remedy this fundamental defect.

The possibilities of the steam engine are such that by operating a small valve, a child can move and control weights of several thousand kilograms. From this Mr. Barker concluded that since a reservoir of air under pressure is always available for sounding the pipes, this energy, like steam, could easily be used for operating the action.

Finger-pressure need only open a small pallet, and wind, rushing through this little opening and pressing against a surface proportional to the resistance to be overcome, would conquer all the inertia of the action. Reasoning thus, he set about adding to the organ, already so complicated an instrument, a steam piston for each key that controls a large pipe. In Mr. Barker's view, the principle was simple, the results were useful, and the application was easy. It seemed to him that he need only publicize the idea, and it would be welcomed without delay.

However, a brilliant idea usually needs another genius in order to be understood and appreciated, and he left his country, having found not a single builder who would listen to him.

In Paris also, a few doors closed to him, but he met Mr. Cavaillé, who not only was able to understand and appreciate the implications of his discovery, but cooperated effectively in its practical application. Thanks to his pains and knowledge, the venture was a success.

We have yet to speak of a significant improvement introduced long ago by Mr. Cavaillé: the first application was in the great Saint-Denis organ. This refinement has enabled him to include in his new organs a family of new stops which are called *harmonic stops*. Everyone knows that wind instruments without fingerholes, like the French horn and the trumpet, produce the various pitches through adjustments made by the player in the wind pressure. In the light of this fact, Mr. Cavaillé took the greatest care in maintaining a steady wind-pressure, in order to ensure precision of pitch in the stops of his organs. Moreover, Mr. Cavaillé's experiments in this connection led him to the noteworthy results which we must report to you.

We know that a stopped pipe of a given length speaks the same pitch as an open pipe of twice the length. However, as concerns volume, the open pipe produces nearly twice the sound of the stopped pipe.

Furthermore, experiments proved to Mr. Cavaillé a fact related to the previous one: by increasing in the desired proportion both the length of the pipe and the pressure of the wind, it is possible to attain the pitch of a pipe made to the usual dimensions and wind-pressure, but with an intensity, volume, and tone quality far superior to those achieved by customary methods.

Such, in brief, is the principle of Mr. Cavaillé's harmonic stops, which he has incorporated in all the organs that have left his workshop since the Saint-Denis instrument, and of which there are eight in the Saint-Vincent-de-Paul organ.

Persons desiring fuller information concerning this significant improvement will find extensive details in the scholarly report on the Saint-Denis organ, published in 1845 by Mr. Adrien De LaFage.

We have on several occasions heard the organ which Mr. Cavaillé has submitted for your examination, and we are impressed with its remarkably effective tone and power. Played by the skillful and modest parish organist, Mr. Cavallo, the instrument produced the greatest variety of effects and the most pleasing tones. It fully measures up to what we expected from Mr. Cavaillé's latest work.

In conclusion, Gentlemen, we request 1) that you congratulate Mr. Aristide Cavaillé-Coll on the noteworthy progress he has made in organ-building, and 2) that you insert the present report in the *Bulletin* together with the engraving of the Saint-Vincent-de-Paul organ.

Signed, Calla, secretary

Adopted in the meeting on January 25, 1854.

Explanatory legend for the figures in plates 14, 15 and 16, showing the pipe organ in the church of Saint-Vincent-de-Paul.

Plate 14 shows the plan of the gallery and the overall layout of the organ.

Plate 15 is a vertical lengthwise section along line AB (pl. 14) of the action and pipes.
> Fig. 1 in this plate is a vertical section of the console located at the center of the gallery. Figs. 2 and 3 show two pneumatic machines, the first connected to the *Positif*, and the second to the *Grand orgue*. Wires leading from the console (Fig. 1) operate the pallets and sliders in the various chests.

Plate 16, Fig. 1 is a cross-section of the organ along line CD (pl. 14).
> Fig. 2 is a vertical section of the console, showing the rods connected to the keys operating the pallets and sliders [sic].
> Fig 3 is a vertical section of the pneumatic levers, and
> Fig. 4 is a cross-section of main feeder bellows.
> Figs. 2 and 3 are drawn to larger scale.
> The identifying letters are uniform in all three plates.

The gallery is divided into three sections by columns AA (pl. 14). The center section, beneath the rose-window that lights the nave, is reserved for the organ console. To the right are the *Grand orgue* and part of the *Pédale*, and to the left are the *Positif*, the *Récit*, and the rest of the *Pédale*.

The display pipes, with walkboards BB between them and the rest of the organ, stand on separate chests CC, which thus wind the large case-pipes directly.

These chests are mounted in either side of the case at the level of the pipe toes, and they carry six stops, the bass notes of which are borrowed from the façade.

Separate chests, I, are mounted over the pneumatic machines (pl. 15, Figs. 2 and 3), and supply wind directly to the two sets of display pipes.

K through K''''' are six regulator reservoirs filled by the bellows located in a chamber off the gallery. They regulate the pressure of the wind supplied to the various stops, and they are located near the chests which distribute the wind to the pipes.

L through L''' are ducts connecting one reservoir to another.

M, N, M', and N' are the *Pédale* chests.

a, a', b, and b', are the bottom boards of reservoirs K''' and K'''' (pl. 15).

c, c', d, and d' are the top boards of the same reservoirs.

e indicates flexible conduits connecting the reservoirs.

f indicates regulating valves located in the foot of the conduits.

g indicates iron arms mounted on the top boards; the forked lower ends rest on valves f.

i, k, i' and k' (pl. 15) are the backfalls connecting the pneumatic levers to the roller-boards controlling the *Grand orgue* and the *Positif*.

l, m, l', and m' are other backfalls operating the roller-boards for the *Positif* and *montre*.

n, o, n', and o' are diagonal levers for the octave coupler.

OP (pl. 16, Fig. 1) is a section of the treble pallet-box for the chest carrying the bass pipes of the *Grand orgue*.

O' P' is another view of the double-pallet-box chests carrying the treble pipes of the *Grand orgue*.

QQ' are the bass pallet-boxes.

R is the sliderless chest for the display-pipes, in cross-section.

s indicates the stop-channels through which wind enters chests R.

t is a *roller* controlling pallets u opening from these stop-channels.

r through r''' are pallets enclosed in the pallet-boxes under chests O, P, O', and P', and connected to the manuals.

p indicates partitions separating channels O, P, O', and P'.

s' and s'' are ventils for allowing communication between the two palletboxes under the chests (pl. 16, Fig. 1).

H (Fig. 1) indicates iron rollers relaying motion from the manual to the *Grand orgue* chest.

h (pl. 16) is a pantograph device for keeping the reservoir top-boards level and the fold angles uniform. The pantographs are connected by link j.

S (Fig. 2) is the organ console.

T through T″ are three banks of keys one above the other, to wit: T, *Récit* manual; T′, *Grand orgue* manual, to which all the others are coupled; and T″, *Positif* manual, to which the *Récit* may be coupled at will.

U is a drawstop for the new *Montre* chests controlling ventils.

V indicates couplers and composition pedals.

X is one key of the German-style pedal keyboard.

v (Fig. 2) is a drumstick controlled through square *xx* by a pedal, for coupling the *Positif* to the *Grand orgue* when desired.

y z is a backfall operated by pedal X connected at *y* to the *Pédale* chests, and at *z* to the manual coupler.

a′ indicates brass squares relaying the motion of the various keyboards to the pallets in their respective divisions.

b′ is a rubber spring for regulating the stiffness of the composition-pedal action.

q (pl. 16, Fig. 2) is a backfall whose pivot may be raised by means of a pedal, coupling the pedals to the manuals.

G (Fig. 4) is the main wind-trunk carrying wind from the feeder bellows to the regulators placed inside the organ.

Y (Fig. 4) indicates feeders generating wind for the reservoirs.

Z indicates pedals which the blower operates with his weight and the muscles of his legs.

l′ [should be *l″*] (pl. 16, Fig. 4) indicates cast-iron weights mounted on the top boards of the reservoirs to keep the boards from warping and provide the correct weight for the wind-pressure.

m′ [*m″*] is the top board of the reservoir.

n′ [*n″*] indicates frames for maintaining uniform angles in the inverted folds, *o′o′*.

p′ indicates the bottom board of the reservoir, where feeders YY are mounted.

q′ is a walking-beam connected to pedals V by wooden rods *t′t′*: by grasping the rods, the blower exerts useful effort on the bellows.

D (pl. 16, Fig. 3) is a wind channel of the Barker machine, receiving the wind that inflates the pneumatic. D′ is another channel, for exhausting the wind.

E is a section of the bellows constituting the pneumatic lever.

FF indicates the movable boards of these pneumatics.

f′ is the valve admitting air to the pneumatics.

g′ is the exhaust valve.

h′ i″ is a backfall connected at *i″* to the corresponding manual.

k″ is a small lever fitted with a spring, for regulating the resistance of the keyboard controlling the pneumatic machine.

c′ (Fig. 3) is the stop-channel in the separate windchest for the *montre* pipes.

d' indicates separate pallets for the individual pipes.

e' is the roller-board relaying the action of the pneumatic levers to the *montre* chest.

Description of the chief parts of the Saint-Vincent-de-Paul organ and their function.
1) *Multiple-pressure bellows.* This new design consists of a series of superimposed reservoirs, as many as there are pressures to be obtained, connected by means of flexible conduits and regulating valves. The bottom boards of these reservoirs, *a a'*, *b b'* (pl. 15) rest on their supports, while the top boards, *c c'*, *d d'*, move up and down as air is forced into the reservoirs. Each board is weighted as required to compress the air. Since the lower reservoir is more heavily weighted than the upper one, it would appear that the air in the former should easily enter the latter. If the regulating valves always remained closed, there would be no communication; but arm rod *g h*, mounted on the top board, rests on the valves and opens them, and wind flows into the upper reservoir and expands, to balance the pressure exerted by the weight on the top board. It will be seen that as the wind in this reservoir is exhausted, it is replaced from the lower reservoir, while the distance between the two movable boards is kept constant.

When the feeders fill the lower reservoir, the upper reservoir is also filled, in such a way that as soon as a small amount of wind enters the first, the one above it also receives its share. Thus each reservoir instantly receives wind at the predetermined pressure.

Assuming an indefinite number of reservoirs thus placed one atop another and communicating through flexible conduits and regulating valves, each can be adjusted to furnish wind at a different pressure, although all are supplied from the same feeders.

Multiple-pressure regulating reservoirs are intended, as Mr. Calla has reported, to wind the bass, tenor, and treble ranges of organ stops at different pressures appropriate to the intensity of the tone, give more uniform tone to the stops, and avoid insufficient wind and therefore weak tone.

2) *Double pallet-boxes and new composition pedals.* The wind chest design shown in pl. 16, Fig. 1 contributes to a better wind supply for the stops, and it gives rise to new combinations which afford the organist numerous resources for varying as he desires the volume of sound.

The pallet-box, containing the pallets controlled by the keys, receives wind from the reservoirs. In addition to the pallet-box traditionally placed along one edge of the chest, Mr. Cavaillé has added a second at the opposite edge. The channels extending between the two are blocked by a partition, so that each pallet need supply wind for only half the number of stops. The foundation stops are winded from one pallet-box; and the mutations, mixtures, and reeds, from the other. As a result, the two series of stops may speak simultaneously with no possibility of insufficient wind, and the tone and power of the organ are enhanced.

In addition to this advantage deriving from double pallet boxes, their use has made possible another significant improvement which affords the organist new resources for registration, in the form of *composition* pedals, shown in pl. 16, Fig. 2, V. These pedals have as their function connecting the two pallet- boxes at will, by means of ventils *s′ s″* (Fig. 1).

Here is the operation: first observe that both pallets *r r′* (pl. 16, Fig. 1) open simultaneously when a key is depressed. Pallet *r* has admitted wind to the channel from O to *p*; and pallet *r′*, from P to *p*. However, the wind can enter the double pallet-boxes only through ventils *s′ s″*, operated by the composition pedals. The result of this arrangement is that all the stops winded from the second pallet-box, *r′* and *r″*, may be drawn all together or in any combination, and they will be put on instantly by means of the pedals we have just described.

Thus, by operating a single ventil, the new pedals respond as promptly as the keys, and they control as many stop combinations as are allowed by the number of stops winded from the second pallet-box. With only eight stops, 255 combinations could be obtained with a single pedal.

3. *Sliderless chests built for the display pipes.* In the chests illustrated as R (pl. 15, Fig. 1) each stop is put on by a single ventil which admits wind to channels *s s*; and each key controls as many pallets as there are stops on the chest, by means of roller *t*. Each ventil opens into a channel which winds the pipes belonging to a stop.

If ventils *u u*, which take the place of sliders, admit wind to two channels only, then when the key opens the six pallets by means of roller *t*, only the two pipes standing on those two channels will speak. The same would be true for all the other pipes: wind can be admitted or closed off at each stop, so that the pipes may speak or be silent.

This windchest design simplifies the action considerably, replacing the sliders with ventils that respond to the slightest pull. It has made possible new composition pedals, enabling the player to add the stops in the various combinations allowed by the stops in the division: the six *montre* stops mentioned above give 63 different combinations.

4. *New pneumatic levers, simpler than Mr. Barker's original device.*

The pneumatic appliances, shown in cross-section (pl. 16, Fig. 3) are located below the separate chests for the display pipes facing the gallery, where the console stands.

Lever *h′ i″* is connected at *i″* to a manual key, and it operates pallets *f′* and *g′*. Wind from the reservoir is supplied to wind channel D. When the key depresses lever *h′ i″*, pallet *f′* opens and wind immediately fills pneumatic E: board F operates the trackers and rollers, opening the corresponding pallets in the windchest. When the key is released, inlet valve f' closes and exhaust valve g' opens, the wind in the pneumatic escaping through channel D'. Board F falls immediately, and the pallets connected to it close in like manner. The small lever, k', provides the amount of resistance desired in the keyboard.

It will be seen that the motion of lever h' i'', controlled by the key, is relayed to board F. The latter exerts a force proportional to the area of the pneumatic and the pressure of the wind. These two factors must be adjusted in such a way as to achieve sufficient force, at the point where the action connects to the pneumatic, to overcome all resistance.

It will also be seen that since the manual key need only operate the two small valves, f' and g', its action will be very light.

5. *Harmonic stops.* Organ stops, as designed until the present time, are made up of pipes speaking the fundamental pitch. In these stops, the bass notes possess suitable volume, while the higher notes become progressively weaker and thinner. This defect appears to be inherent in the design of the stops used until now.

We know that each stop contains a pipe for each key, and that each pipe speaks the pitch of its key. We also know that the dimensions of the pipes are in roughly inverse proportion to the frequency of the sound vibrations.

Taking low C on the manual as our standard, we find the following progression:

Pitch	CC	C	c	c'	c''
Cycles	1	2	4	8	16
Dimensions	1	1/2	1/4	1/8	1/16
Volume	1	1/8	1/64	1/516	1/4096

Assuming that the volume produced by a pipe is proportional to the volume of air it contains, the preceding table will show how rapidly volume decreases from bass to treble, and it will not be surprising that high pitches in the organ are weak compared to the bass.

The harmonic pitches of pipes had never before been used in the organ. We know that these sounds have a power and fullness unobtainable from pipes which produce only the fundamental. The air column in a pipe that speaks a harmonic is divided into two, three, four, or more portions vibrating independently. The air column modifies the tone, giving it improved quality and greater power without shrillness.

As a general rule, the sounds acquire fullness and volume in proportion to the size of the air columns modifying them.

We said earlier that the bass notes of the various organ stops produce a suitable volume of sound by means of a pipe's fundamental pitch, while the remaining notes lose fullness and volume as they progress upwards. In order to correct this deficiency, Mr. Cavaillé has built several stops in which the lowest octave of pipes speaks the fundamental; the second octave, the first harmonic; etc. In this manner, the higher the pitch, the greater the size of the air column in relation to the pitch; and the tone quality is rendered uniform throughout the stop.

It should be noted that harmonic pitches require higher wind-pressures the more vibrating portions are present in the air column. Especially in reed pipes, this increased pressure is necessary in order to give the tones all the fullness and power they can achieve.

The new multiple-pressure reservoirs are a valuable resource in giving harmonic stops the best possible tone quality, quite apart from their beneficial effect on conventional stops.

List of Awards Bestowed
on Mr. Aristide Cavaillé-Coll for Improvements Made by Him
in the Building of Pipe Organs for Churches.

1. Society for the Advancement of French Industry, Regular Meeting, March 19, 1834, Bronze Medal.

2. Jury, Arras Exhibition, 1838, Silver Medal.

3. Jury, 1839 Exhibition, on Report by Mr. Félix Savart, Bronze Medal.

4. Independent Society for the Fine Arts, Meeting, May 7, 1844, Silver Medal (highest award), for improvements incorporated in the great organ for Saint-Denis.

5. Jury, 1844 Exhibition, Gold Medal.

6. Jury, 1849 Exhibition, Gold Medal, as a result of which Mr. Cavaillé was decorated with the *Légion d'Honneur*.

7. Finally, the Society for the Advancement of French Industry, in its regular meeting on May 17, 1854, awarded its Grand Gold Medal to Mr. Aristide Cavaillé-Coll, in consideration of the reasons set forth in the above report.

CHAPTER NINE

Cavaillé-Coll's Favorite Organists in the Fifties

Maurice Bourges reported that the inauguration of the new organ at St.-Vincent-de-Paul was "truly a splendid spectacle."[1]

". . . The lofty church was ablaze with light. An impatient crowd filled the nave, the galleries, the side aisles, and the chapels. And what a distinguished multitude! Musicians, prominent music-lovers, ladies covered with dazzling jewelry, the most gifted journalists and men of letters; in short, a legion of luminaries had gathered to hear the first tones of the new instrument that Aristide Cavaillé-Coll was unveiling to the Public.

"First of all it was a feast for the eyes. The organ-case was fascinating by virtue of its original design, quite in contrast to the usual forms. Mr. Hittorff, the architect of the church, has divided the organ façade into two parts, with a lofty arch between. This spacious opening allows the gaze to travel deep into a square gallery, whose sides are decorated with carved woodwork and symmetrical groupings of metal pipes. This gallery is intended for the organist and, on occasion, for vocal soloists. During the day, this space is generously lighted by a rose-window containing but few colored portions; and at night, the brilliant lamp-light makes the polished pipes sparkle, giving the gallery a singularly dramatic appearance.

"We may add, to the credit of the worthy organ-builder, that he was faced with enormous difficulties due to the placement of the instrument. The demands of architecture (and she insists on having her way) forced the builder to install his instrument one level higher than it should be placed. As a result, the powerful sounds are blocked by the nearby vaulting of the church (which vaulting is itself detrimental to the acoustics) and do not fill the building as they could otherwise. Another chance occurrence was the temporary drapery covering the murals by Messrs. Picot and Flandin: they absorbed a certain amount of sound. We must, therefore, make allowance for these obstacles. In order to overcome them brilliantly, as it did, the new organ had to possess in the highest degree all the qualities of an excellent instrument."

The new organist at St.-Vincent-de-Paul, Cavallo, shared the program with Lefébure-Wély and the usual singers. But it was Lefébure-Wély and his wife, a singer, who made the evening a success:

"There was in particular a pastoral scene, highlighted with a storm, terror, and prayer, in which Mr. Lefébure-Wély made excellent use of the *Viola di gamba* stops, whose timbre is a surprisingly faithful imitation of bowed strings. Elsewhere, he used to the best advantage the *Cor anglais* and the *Flûtes,* and then the *Voix humaine* — all these stops being of outstanding quality and excellently voiced — when accompanying Cherubini's *Ave Maria* and Lesueur's Blessed Sacrament motet, which were sung with exquisite taste by Alexis Dupond. For their part, the Misses Landry and Montigny, and Mrs. Lefébure-Wély, she of the charming voice and pure style, beautifully sang a few religious compositions. Here we have a kind of *Voix angélique* that Aristide Cavaillé may well imitate in some future organ, the plans for which his alert mind is even now developing."

Cavaillé-Coll had arrived at the pinnacle of success, being credited with a musical triumph over the acoustical obstacles created by the architect. Nor was he criticized, if indeed anyone cared, for dividing the organ on two sides of the gallery, or placing the organ behind a veritable façade rather than within a free-standing case, for restricting the pedal compass to two octaves, for detaching the console, or for any other aspects of the design that in another age might have been described as defects. What, then, had kept Lemmens at home in Belgium on the evening of the opening concert? Did Cavaillé-Coll fear a chauvinistic reaction from the press, or was his apparent preference for Lefébure-Wély guided by his unerring instinct for public response and approval? It seems he did not dare risk unfavorable criticism, for we know that a Paris appearance for Lemmens was very much on Cavaillé-Coll's mind.

If Lemmens had played at St.-Vincent-de-Paul that evening, as he did later in a private recital,[2] he would have chosen very carefully among the works of Bach because of the organ's limited pedal compass. Though Cavaillé-Coll had travelled widely in Europe, he had not yet reached a decision about this matter; it was a question that hinged upon the performance of German music with which he was unfamiliar. As to the French requirements, Lefébure-Wély could doubtless adjust to anything, because he seldom played composed music. Had Lefébure-Wély provided the incentive for doing so, Cavaillé-Coll could easily have imposed a standard compass on the *Pédale* and, for that matter, on the *Récit.* He had shown himself willing enough to include whatever was required to sell organs abroad, even to the point of specifying mixtures in the *Pédale:* this was a practice never known in France.[3] But until he met Lemmens, none of his closest associates among the organists seemed to have definite opinions about pedal compass. It would be some years before the man who had fought long and hard for standard pitch would settle on a consistent approach to the problem of pedal compass.

We list below some representative pedal compasses in order to illustrate Cavaillé-Coll's inconsistency during the 1850's and earlier. All data come from instruments by Cavaillé-Coll, unless noted otherwise.

Date	Place	Pedal compass	Sources
1836	Paris, N.-D.-de-Lorette	25 notes, F to F	Devis I, #1
1837	Dinan	29 notes, F to C	Devis I, #8
1841	St.-Denis	25 notes, F to F	see above, p. 27
1844	Paris, St.-Eustache	28 notes, A to C	Roret. p. 103[4] (Daublaine-Call.)
1845	Paris, St.-Eustache	30 notes, C to F	see above, p. 45
1845	Paris, Oratoire	27 notes, C to D	Devis I, #170[5]
1845	Paris, St.-Jean-St.-François	20 notes, C to G	Roret, p. 127
1846	Paris, La Madeleine	25 notes, C to C	see above, p. 63
1846	Paris, Panthémont	27 notes, C to D	Roret, p. 125
1847	Liverpool, Cathedral	31 notes, C to (F#?)	Devis I, #298
1847	Tournai, Cathedral	20 notes, C to G	Devis I, #276
1848	Quimper, Cathedral	25 notes, C to C	Devis III, #225
1849	Lyon (Petit Séminaire)	25 notes, C to C	Devis I, #354
1852	Mortain	30 notes, C to F	Lettres IV, #2349[6]
1852	Paris, Oratoire	30 notes, C to F	Devis IV, #539
1853	Paris, Ste.-Clotilde	25 notes, C to C	Devis IV, #584
1854	Paris, St.-Eustache	30 notes, C to F	Roret, p. 134 (Ducroquet)
1855	St. Omer, Cathedral	27 notes, C to D	Etats, p. 259
1856	Doncaster	30 notes, C to F	Devis V, #733
1857	Paris, St.-Sulpice	30 notes, C to F	Devis V, #731
1857	Paris, Ste.-Clotilde	27 notes, C to D	Lettres VI, #4086
1859	Vouvry (Switzerland)	30 notes, C to F	Lettres VI, #4086[7]

Throughout the 1850's, Cavaillé-Coll acted as an impresario for Lefébure-Wely when it came to inaugural concerts. The popular virtuoso responded with warm friendship and praise:

May 29, 1852

Dear old friend,

"As you requested, I hasten to answer your letter.

"I intended, in case I were asked to play the dedication recital on your organ, not to make the trip for less than *1,500* francs. True, for dedicating the Dalbade organ, I only got 1,200 francs, but . . .

". . . in short, I want to show them that there's only one builder who puts his heart and soul into his instruments, and his name is Cavaillé-Coll. We two grew up together, and I want that brotherly association to end only in death.

"Do as you think best, to wit: either at least 1,000 francs paid by the council; or a recital in exchange for *chair rentals* and *collection*; or else 1,000 francs for a first recital, with the chairs and collection for the Council, plus a second whose proceeds will be shared equally by the church and myself.

"La Madeleine is constantly full of foreigners come to admire your instrument. My dear friend, keep on building those heavenly organs and let them prepare a place for you in Heaven one day: may you be granted that grace, *Amen.*   A L-W."

We have clear proof of Lefébure-Wély's intense jealousy of Lemmens in a letter of June, 1852. Knowing how his friend felt about Lemmens, Cavaillé-Coll did not dare to introduce Lemmens publicly at the inauguration of his new instrument at St. Vincent-de-Paul.

Lefébure-Wély to Cavaillé-Coll
Thursday, June 10, 1852
(Answered June 15, 1852)

"Dear friend,
    . . . Do you know, my friend, what I have just found out from someone just in from *Brussels?* Your protégé, *my friend* and colleague, Lemmens, is telling all and sundry that he hopes to be engaged at La Madeleine, replacing M. Lefébure-Wély. What do you say to that, old friend?

"I mentioned it to Dietch, and he had a good laugh from it. I confess that I should like him to fill my position for a year. This would be the way I hadn't yet found to return to the Madeleine (after him) with a salary of 6,000 francs. According to another person I saw recently at Massart's, Lemmens' success in Paris has made him unbelievably arrogant. Here's how generous I am: I leave Paris for two months, giving my rival the chance to take my place. What luck if he did! I've been yearning for so long to be *free*. And we'd see how the congregations at the Madeleine would react to the great man . . .
                                    Sincerely yours,
                                    A. Lefébure-Wély"

On February 5, 1853, Cavaillé-Coll wrote to Lemmens: "I know the priest, and a word would suffice to give you preference over all the small-time organ grinders who are applying for that job." He referred to St.-Eustache.

It had been more than eight years since the fire at St.-Eustache, and the magnificent church was about to receive a monumental new organ, built by Ducroquet. Cavaillé-Coll saw this as a golden opportunity to attract Lemmens to Paris, and he set about using his influence in order to bring this to pass. A logical first step would have been to persuade the priest to secure Lemmens for the inaugural concert, which would thus be a musical event of major importance. This much he accomplished, but apparently the priest had no interest in pursuing the matter further, for Batiste became organist at St.-Eustache.

Seven thousand people packed the church for the concert on May 26, 1854; it was the first such occasion in some time when Lefébure-Wély was not featured. In addition to Lemmens, there were three Parisian organists on the program, Cavallo, Bazille, and César Franck, whose participation was noted with scant enthusiasm:[8]

"The day had finally come when one of the most beautiful and most musical of Paris churches was again to have a pipe organ, after being tragically struck by fire ten years ago. The ceremony took place last Friday before a huge crowd, and the work of the famous builder, Mr. Ducroquet, gave the measure of its quality. The Musicians' Association organized the ceremony, planned the program, and supervised the performance. Once again, they acquitted themselves well, and distinguished artists eagerly heeded their call to the seat of honor, to vie for recognition of their talents.

"Mr. Lemmens, First Organist to His Majesty the King of the Belgians, had traveled to Paris for the occasion. He was the first to seat himself at the console, and he returned twice. Mr. Cavallo, of St.-Vincent-de-Paul, Mr. Bazille, of Ste.-Elisabeth; and Mr. Franck, of St.-Jean-St.-François each took a turn at the keyboards. Under their masterful fingers, the magnificent instrument revealed all its treasures one after the other, and we admired its pure tone and the remarkable variety in the timbres of its stops. We have already reported that the organ built by Mr. Ducroquet has four manuals, each with a compass of 54 notes.

"First, Mr. Lemmens played his Introduction and Fugue on *Laudate Dominum*, then a Prayer in E, also his own composition, and the Finale from the First Sonata by Mendelssohn. Later in the program, he played an Offertory in G, a Prayer in C, and a Fugue in C. minor. For his third appearance, he played a Prelude and Fugue in E. minor by Bach, a Prayer in F, and an improvisation. His share of the program was extensive and demanding, and Mr. Lemmens demonstrated the qualities we observed when he played at St.-Vincent-de-Paul. His distinctive traits, as compared to his rivals, are chiefly the strength and austerity of his style: he strives for classicism first and foremost. He is a direct descendant of Bach, and he would consider it an affront to the dignity of his instrument if he made the slightest concession to today's secular tastes.

"Mr. Cavallo needs no introduction. He distinguished himself in two improvisations, the first of which we consider to be a masterpiece of inspiration and development, both overall and in its details. If we had to award a prize for the best performance of the day, we should unhesitatingly bestow it upon this perfect piece, and we wish it could have been taken down by some musical stenographer.

"Mr. Bazille gave two improvisations as well. His performances were marked by youthful facility, and were perhaps a bit frivolous for the setting of a Christian church.

"Mr. Franck performed a carefully composed Fantasia, interpreting it with great vigor . . ."

Lefébure-Wély was nettled, and others resented his being neglected. As for Cavaillé-Coll, he was disapointed, when he wrote:

"Mr. Albert Legrand, Saint-Omer[9]

". . . As for the dedication of the Saint-Eustache organ, I do not think anyone was pleased with the results, the audience, the recitalists, or I think even the builders. The program was long and boring, and the gigantic instrument failed to come up to the public's expectations.

"The organ case, designed and built by Mr. Baltard, architect of the building, is without doubt the most handsome of its kind ever built, and it does great credit to the architect and the craftsmen who worked together to construct it."

It is not easy to understand why César Franck would have been included among the performers at St.-Eustache. At thirty-one, he was organist at St.-Jean-St.-François in the *Marais,* where he played a two-manual organ of eighteen stops, built by Cavaillé-Coll. The public had not heard from Franck for years, since he had thrown off the domination of his self-seeking father, who wished to make him a concert pianist. Joseph, César's younger brother, organist at St.-Thomas d'Aquin, was better known as a pianist, organist, composer, violinist, and teacher. Since César-Auguste had done no more than dabble in organ composition, there was no clear reason for the invitation to St.-Eustache, unless his friend, Cavaillé-Coll, had suggested it to the priest. That the Francks were among Cavaillé-Coll's close friends was shown by the report of Cecile Cavaillé-Coll that they were among the dinner guests at Aristide's wedding on February 4, 1854.[10]

If Cavaillé-Coll had planned to bring Franck into the limelight, he could have done no better than to expose him to Lemmens. Franck had never heard such organ playing. In 1844, when Lemmens' teacher, Hesse, played in Paris, Franck almost certainly would not have attended; nor was he invited to any of Lemmens' private recitals in Paris from 1850 to 1852. Like almost everyone else in France, Franck was accustomed to the gaudy style of Lefébure-Wély and the dry performances of his professor from the *Conservatoire,* Benoît. To understand how little inspiration Franck must have drawn from Benoît, one need only refer to Benoît's flabby little Preludes. At St.-Eustache Franck was introduced to Lemmens, and he heard the master of baroque counterpoint play Bach's magnificent Prelude and Fugue in E minor. This was probably the first time the work had been played in France. For Franck it was an experience of profound importance.

The poorly-trained Franck, who learned more from his ears than from his teachers, was introduced that evening to the famous legato of Professor Lemmens, whose new style of finger substitution on the organ was still unknown in France. Franck resolved to improve himself, but in January 1858, when he went to Ste.-Clotilde, there was no organ in the church. A month later, he bought a dummy pedalboard for practice. Finally, in 1859, he was ready to perform a great work of Bach at the inauguration of his own organ at Ste.-Clotilde. As for the work chosen, of course, it was Bach's great Prelude and Fugue in E minor.

While Franck was practicing, teaching, and composing, the battle raged between the "sensualists" and the "classicists" among organ players. The sharp-tongued Blanchard issued another pronouncement, entitled:

"The Organ and Organists:[11]

"Several pretenders vie for the crown of King of Instruments. The violin long reigned supreme. The piano claims first place by virtue of its usefulness, its flexibility, and even its ambition of singing as a brilliant solo instrument. And now the organ, with its many voices — resonant, grandiose, and diverse — is becoming worldly, and is even promising to become the King of Instruments.

"The French clergy, who are quite unmusical, encouraged our organists to perform what is called light, popular music in church. The Lord was praised to the sensuous strains of Rossini, revolutionary hymns, and street-ballads; and people were wondering just what sacred, austere, religious style was when Mr. Hesse, the organist of Breslau, came and showed us what church music ought to be. His pupil, Mr. Lemmens, has carried on the German musician's crusade here in Paris.

"Mr. Lefébure-Wély, the eclectic organist, has not seen fit to follow the classical path of the old organ masters, in part because he has been captivated by the wealth of new tonal resources placed at the disposal of organists by modern builders, especially Mr. Cavaillé-Coll . . ."

The banter between Lefébure-Wély and Cavaillé-Coll continued as though there were, indeed, no controversy about loyalty or taste:
No date (after 1854, before 1858)

"How about my *Voix Humaine*, you vile scoundrel? I had a wedding yesterday, and I couldn't use the stop, even though that's *all* I'm paid for.

"Tomorrow is the feast of St. Mary Magdalene: the whole Récit is out of tune and my *Tremblant* doesn't work. You would have done much better, my friend, not to spend your time fixing Érard's Canary-organ but taking care of ours. Your reputation would be the better for it.

Lefébure-Wély

My respects to Mrs. Cavaillé-Coll."

Finally, Cavaillé-Coll made a false step: he tried to include the rival virtuosi, Lefébure-Wély and Lemmens, on the same inaugural program, first at St.-Omer and then at Ghent. The correspondence given below shows that in both places Lemmens was eventually shunned, while at Ghent Cavaillé-Coll's blunder cost him dearly by arousing the anger of the influential Fétis.

February 14, 1855 to Mr. Legrand, Treasurer, Council of the Cathedral, St.-Omer[12]
". . . I assume the council will elect to ask an organist from Paris to inaugurate the organ. If so, I should like to be informed so that I may agree on the date with him. Since the dedication is separate from the examination and approval of the instrument, I take the liberty of naming the organists who are best acquainted with our design and show off our instruments to best advantage. They are Mr. Lefébure-Wély, organist at La Madeleine, Mr. Simon of Saint-Denis, Mr. Fessy of Saint-Roch, Mr. Cavallo of Saint-Vincent-de-Paul, and Mr. Durand of Sainte-Geneviève. In Brussels there is the learned organist, Mr. Lemmens, who has already played our instruments and makes good use of them. However, this organist plays in the manner of the great masters, and would perhaps be less successful in the opinion of the audience. Nevertheless, if the council could have the privilege of calling on Mr. Lemmens, professor at the Brussels Conservatory, and Mr. Lefébure-Wély, organist at La Madeleine, in Paris, you would have, in my opinion, the two best organists I know . . ."

April 27, 1855 to Mr. Legrand, Treasurer, Council of the Cathedral, St. Omer[13]
". . . I had hoped that Mr. Lefébure, whom I have seen since, would reduce his fee to 600 f, and I wrote to Mr. Lemmens saying that the council expected a more moderate price than Mr. Lefébure's . . .

"From their replies you will see that both men are equally demanding, and I think the reason is the rivalry of two talents the council wishes to bring together. Confidentially, Mr. Lefébure told me that if he hadn't already quoted the figure of 600 f, he would not have gone to Saint-Omer for less than 1,000, pointing out that precisely because of Mr. Lemmens, he could not risk playing the organ without having tried it a day in advance . . . I pleaded in vain on the council's behalf and my own, but Mr. Lefébure persisted, and consequently Mr. Lemmens insists on 600 f.

". . . I must add that I believe either one would prefer to do the job alone . . ."

June 5, 1855 to Mr. Legrand, Treasurer, Council of the Cathedral, St.-Omer[14]
". . . We are truly dogged by misfortune . . . Mr. Lefébure is to leave for Grasse on the 17th, where he is receiving 1,800 f. for an inaugural organ recital

on the 24th. He offered to give me the Curé's letter to show why he declined Saint-Omer . . ."

June 6, 1855 to Mr. Legrand, Treasurer, Cathedral Council, St.-Omer[15]
". . . I hasten to advise you that we can count on Mr. Lefébure . . . I see we shall be luckier than I dared hope."

March 6, 1856 to Mr. Fétis, Director, Royal Conservatory of Music, Brussels[16]
"Dear Sir:

I am most disappointed to learn that you decline to serve as Chairman of the Examining Committee for our organ in Ghent. I was already distressed at the news that Mr. Lemmens was not approached, but I hoped things would work out and that I would have the good fortune to submit for your judgment an instrument on which we have lavished great care.

"I am all the more provoked by this unfortunate state of affairs because it was your suggestion that led to the building of this organ: I have striven to make it as complete and perfect as possible, so as to merit the esteem you expressed in your learned Report to the Belgian Royal Academy concerning our work.

"I confess, Sir, that I was far from expecting this result, since the council and the builder were unanimously in favor of submitting this large instrument for your appraisal. I am perhaps partly to blame, and I have been chastised. I had brought Mr. Lefébure-Wély to the attention of the Dean as being the organist who was best acquainted with the resources of our instruments, and at the same time I mentioned Mr. Lemmens, as being the most learned and skillful organist of our time.

"Unfortunately, a financial matter changed all the plans: the council intended to call on both these artists, but faced with the rather excessive demands of Mr. Lefébure, the council seems to have shrunk from assuming the expense involved in paying the fees of both organists, hoping to call on Mr. Lemmens for a recital to be scheduled after Easter. To my great consternation, all my hopes were dashed when you declined. I understand your reasons, however, and I can only convey to you my regrets.

"I hope, Sir, that this unfortunate situation will not impair the good will you have consistently shown me, and with my regrets, I remain . . ."

A month after Cavaillé-Coll's letter of apology for the unintended exclusion of Lemmens at the Ghent inauguration, Fétis submitted an acrimonious harangue to the *Revue et Gazette de Paris,* entitled "Worldly Organs and Erotic Music in Church".[17] He quoted *Le Messager de Gand* reporting on Lefébure-Wély's performance at the inaugural concert at the church of Saint-Nicolas: "In a word, he aims to please, and he succeeds. We saw proof of this in *the enthusiastic applause and repeated bravos* that greeted his Offertory in C♯ *minor, and especially his storm scene.* The organizers of the recital deserve mention here, *for their clever idea of dimming the gaslights in the middle of the storm."* Fétis complained of the degraded taste of French organists who appealed to the sensual, then proceeded to praise the work of Lemmens, ". . . brought up on a knowledge of finger-substitution, without which legato organ-playing is impossible. . . . The essential inferiority of French organists is precisely the result of their obsession with what they call *improvisation.* . . . Not one of them has what may be called an *organist's training.* Not one of them could master the great compositions of Bach. All their attention is turned towards special effects, tonal contrasts, . . . and ways to arouse and gratify sensual instincts. This situation is far from new, for men like Marchand, Calvière, Daquin, Balbâtre, and Charpentier were tending in this direction. There have been no distinguished organists in France since the seventeenth century: Couperin was the last. . . . The *storm* has been a standard ever since. When I was young, a certain *Mr. Miroir* enjoyed a great reputation for that kind of wizardry . . . The audience was terrified, but Mr. Miroir had enough good taste to calm the excitement of his audience with little solos on the *Musette, Petite Flûte, Voix humaine* with tremulant, or *Cromorne en taille."*

A few weeks later,[18] there appeared a carefully worded response, submitted by Abbé Lamazou, Vicar of St.-Sulpice, and champion of Cavaillé-Coll's work. Can the Abbé have seen Cavaillé-Coll's correspondence over the inauguration at Ghent? "We need not explain why Mr. Lefébure-Wély was chosen. His reputation as a giver of dedication recitals is beyond dispute. The Council of St.-Nicolas in Ghent is therefore to be praised for its discernment in inviting the organist of La Madeleine in Paris to dedicate the new instrument. Nevertheless, would it not have been proper and more in keeping with the demands of patriotic sentiment, to invite Mr. Lemmens as well? This eminent professor at the Brussels Conservatory plays the organ with great purity of style and great skill.

"Let us recall that not quite two years ago, on the occasion of a similar recital held in Paris, a similar mistake was made: Mr. Lemmens was invited, and not Mr. Lefébure. What was the outcome? Mr. Lefébure's absence was as good as a triumph; and the praise given to Mr. Lemmens, as well as to his fellow *virtuosi,* was noticeably dampened by a unanimous regret that the Franch organist was not present.

". . . We are sorry that so distinguished a mind should have used such inconclusive data as the basis for his strictures on French music, which deserved more objectivity and fairness. We also regret that he should have summed up his condemnation with the extravagant title, *Worldly Organs and Erotic Music in Church.* Such strange terms are easy to remember, but they are not worth debating. For their very excess is the best rebuttal. Religious style, whether in music, architecture, or rhetoric, is apparently the one that lifts the soul up to God and inclines the faithful to prayer and meditation. From this standpoint, Mr. Lefébure's style is religious in its very essence."

CHAPTER TEN

Lefébure-Wély and César Franck

For some time before the fall of 1856, delivery of Cavaillé-Coll's organ for the Cathedral of Carcassonne was delayed because of restoration work in the building. The instrument was set up in the workshop, and several concerts were held there. On July 13, there was a recital featuring Cavallo. Henri Blanchard, reporting for the *Revue et Gazette*, pointed out that Cavallo demonstrated the instrument's rich tonal resources by "imitating the wind, thunder, and even rain." A few weeks later, Cavaillé-Coll invited César Franck to give a demonstration of the same instrument, a gesture to help Franck gain some recognition. The notice was brief and to the point, probably written by Cavaillé-Coll himself:[1]

"Before he delivered to the Bishop of Carcassonne the fine organ he has built for the Cathedral in that city, Mr. Cavaillé-Coll decided to have it played one more time for the many admirers of that admirable instrument. The player, the excellent organist Mr. César Franck, displayed all its rich tonal resources, first in a scholarly performance of his excellent austere compositions, and then in brilliant improvisations."

The next item on the page was the following, which in context seems ironic with regard to both Cavaillé-Coll and Lefébure-Wély:

"And speaking of miniature organs, we must mention a recital given in Mr. Debain's new showrooms, *place* Lafayette, to demonstrate his 'Harmonicorde'. This ingenious instrument, a piano-organ under expression, is a whole orchestra. Mr. Debain selected Mr. Lefébure-Wély to show off his 'harmonicorde', and he could not have made a better choice . . . 'The Pilgrimage' and 'The Return of the Bride and Groom', . . . 'March of the Guards', . . . 'The Night Watch'."

We are told that in the 1850's, after Franck's appointment at St.-Jean-St.-François, he was considered one of Cavaillé-Coll's "artistic representatives". This is not true. Only after his appointment at Ste.-Clotilde in 1858 did Franck emerge as one of the leading organists. And not long afterwards the young Widor and Guilmant took over the leadership where Lefébure-Wély had left it. Whenever Cavaillé-Coll suggested performers for the inauguration of his instruments in the 50's, Franck's name was conspicuously missing. As an example, for the church of La Madeleine in Tarare, after Lefébure-Wély as the first choice, Cavaillé-Coll listed in order:

1. Cavallo, of St.-Vincent-de-Paul
2. Simon, of Saint-Denis
3. Durand, of Saint-Roch
4. Camille Saint-Saëns, of Saint-Merry

The fee Cavaillé-Coll mentioned was 500 f. Can he have known that from 1855 to 1862, Franck was traveling to Orléans annually to work as an accompanist in concerts, for only a small fraction of that customary fee for dedications? Franck was not, in Cavaillé-Coll's opinion, one of the most attractive artists for such events. In the letters, there is not one word of praise for Franck, while comments such as the following are not at all rare:[2]

"To Mr. Mercaux, Music Teacher and Man of Letters, Roncq
. . . "P. S. Yesterday, I attended funeral services for the Minister of Justice at La Madeleine. Our Mr. Lefébure played a prelude and a postlude which lasted nearly one half hour each, and I can assure you that rarely has a modern (I almost said "model") organist risen to such heights. The prelude was a genuine funeral symphony, and it held the large and distinguished audience in a solemn meditation. The postlude was a great, beautiful funeral march that deeply affected the august gathering: their eyes turned upwards to the majectic instrument. Lefébure-Wély shows how great an artist he is, on these solemn occasions. All the orchestras in the world cannot equal, for liturgical purposes, a symphony played by Mr. Lefébure on the organ at La Madeleine."

Like all great organ builders, Cavaillé-Coll admired most the organists who admired his organs. In the 1850's Lefébure-Wély and Lemmens were unquestionably the favorites. But what of his relationship to César Franck, whose nature was diametrically opposed to Lefébure-Wély and whose virtuosity would never measure up to that of the younger Belgian?

Because of Cavaillé-Coll's success in endearing himself to the élite of musical society and particularly to the clergy, he frequently found himself in a position to influence appointments. In the 1840's he helped Lefébure-Wély at La Madeleine, and possibly Cavallo at St.-Vincent-de-Paul. In 1853 he offered to intercede on behalf of Lemmens by using his freindship with the priest at St.-Eustache, even though the rival firm of Ducroquet had built the organ there; and in 1858, there is little doubt that he suggested Franck for the new church of Ste-Clotilde. In the biography of her father, Cecile Cavaillé-Coll points with pride to his influence in these matters.[3] Referring to the coveted position at St.-Sulpice, left vacant in 1869 by the death of Lefébure-Wély, she states that her father was free to choose between two leading candidates. This was the very post Cavaillé-Coll sought six years earlier for Lemmens; but by 1869 the contest was between César Franck, then forty seven years old, and Charles-Marie Widor, who was only twenty four. According to Cecile, Cavaillé-

Coll chose Widor because he was planning that Franck would soon succeed Benoît (1798-1878) as professor at the *Conservatoire*. With this explanation Cecile seems to excuse her father for passing over Franck for the most important organ position in France. We doubt that this is correct.[4] Widor was chosen because he was the most promising young virtuoso in Paris, who was, significantly enough, a pupil of Lemmens. We are left to speculate: if Franck had moved up to St.-Sulpice in 1869, how that choice might have altered the course of history!

On the subject of Franck's organ at Ste.-Clotilde, one of his biographers states that "the specification of this new instrument was so original as to cause endless discussion among the experts."[5] The statement has no basis in fact. Cavaillé-Coll's letters show that he rarely listed the Ste.-Clotilde organ among his most important instruments. Furthermore, the record reveals that the specification was in no way original, being an exact copy of a proposal of Cavaillé-Coll drawn up in 1849, for the Cathedral of Bayonne. (See below, Chapter XI). Thus, the specification was ten years old by the time of the inaugural concert. Franck could not have taken part in planning it; indeed, he may have been dissatisfied with certain details from the start.

As the organ neared completion, toward the summer of 1858, Cavaillé-Coll asked Lefébure-Wély to share the inaugural concert with Franck, the organist of the church. This is precisely what had happened in 1852 at St.-Vincent-de-Paul. Cavaillé-Coll wanted to be sure that the clergy and the public would receive the instrument enthusiastically and that the final bill would be paid. Note, in the following letter, that Lefébure-Wély even controlled the order of the program, reserving for himself the most favorable position:

Letter from Lefébure-Wély to Cavaillé-Coll (late 1858 or early 1859)

"Tuesday morning

"Dear Friend,

My devilish opera is keeping me so busy that I'm not sleeping, eating, or even taking care of our little human weaknesses. But don't worry, dear friend: I'm still drinking, and I gladly accept that certain bottle you invite me to enjoy at Dijon. If it's all right with you, we'll leave *Monday* on the 11 a.m. train. Do write a note to *Poligny* ahead of time, so we don't get Siberian-type rooms: I don't intend to skate on my basin.

As for the Ste.-Clotilde dedication, just tell me what you want me to do, so long as I don't *begin* or *end the program*. If you want a storm piece, make it *the last one I play*. A new registration, devised by yours truly, will give me a chance to put into the *obbligato* pastoral piece a new number, entitled 'The Flea Dance', and 'Chirpings of Bedbugs in Labor'. (This time I hope Simon won't beat me to it, and my luck will improve.) After that, "Awakening of the Toads and Festival of the Frogs, Stagnant-Water Music in Two Parts".

> Yours,
> Lefébure de Wailee
> Organist Without Position [*Place*]
> (unless it be Under the
> Guillotine, or Flat Broke)."[6]

If Cavaillé-Coll had wanted a novel approach to the conventional storm, Lefébure-Wély might have "improvised" at Ste.-Clotilde on his new plan for a "Voyage at Sea", found among his letters to Cavaillé-Coll:

"Organ piece: *Ocean Voyage*
The Ship Sets Out
   Imitation of Waves   Sailor's Song
All Foundations   *Voix humaine* stop
except *Prestant.*

Start *forte* and diminish gradually. When *pianissimo* has been reached and imitates the distant ship, *play the wind*: 16′ *Pédale* stops. Increase the volume, and imitate the waves breaking and crashing. The thunder, lightning, rain, and storm increase. *Imitation of the signal cannon, sailors' shouts, invocation, sailors' prayers*; soft, reverent melody: *Voix humaine.* The roaring tempest seems to yield to the sailors' prayers. The crew resumes the voyage and enters port, to the noise of the *military band*: *grand choeur.*"

Cavaillé-Coll must have vetoed the storm, as Lefébure-Wely chose the conservative approach by improvising on well-known Christmas tunes. But almost three months before that cold December 19 when the inaugural concert finally took place, we note that the organ at Ste.-Clotilde was used for at least two events at which Lefébure-Wély, rather than César Franck, performed for distinguished gatherings:[7]

To Mr. Amyon, Music Director and Organist at Poligny:

". . . Recently, the Duchess of Albi, sister of the Empress, and other great ladies came to Sainte-Clotilde to hear Mr. Lefébure play our organ. Next Thursday there will be a big wedding in the same church, performed by Monsignor de la Bouillin, Bishop of Carcassonne, and Mr. Lefébure will again play our new organ. I am sure there will be a large audience to hear the noted organist, and you must come . . .".

A notice in *Le Ménestrel*[8] calls attention to Lefébure-Wely's first performance at Ste.-Clotilde and it must have amused César Franck:

"A music that is by far too dry and abstract, and a volume that is scarcely varied or restrained, at length deaden the ears instead of delighting them. In most religious ceremonies, the faithful need not do penance to that extent."

After the official inauguration,[9] December 19, 1859, Franck was rewarded for his patience and hard work. Adrien de LaFage's review of his performance at the inauguration elaborated at some length about Franck's superb command of Bach's fugue in E minor, a satisfactory tribute to the best student Lemmens ever had. But of course, the warmest and lengthiest praise was reserved for Lefébure-Wély:

"Dedication of the Organ at Sainte-Clotilde

"The great instrument built by Mr. Aristide Cavaillé-Coll for the new church of Sainte-Clotilde was dedicated on December 19. A huge audience braved a cold so bitter and a fog so dense that Parisians and visitors alike could have thought they were anywhere but in France. The audience, numbering many famous artists, did not regret having accepted the invitation of Mr. Cavaillé. In another article I shall speak of the organ and touch on certain serious topics, but for now I shall limit myself to the dedication recital.

"The parish organist, Mr. Franck senior, began with a broad composition whose vigorous style created an impression on the audience. Mr. Franck was no less admired when, setting aside his role as composer, he called forth the genius of J. S. Bach. Playing this composer in public is always a great risk, and in a certain sense organists are right indeed to play their own music rather than Bach's. In my opinion, the difficulty lies not so much in conveying Bach's ideas without making mistakes, as in drawing upon that mighty fund of music in such a way as to render all that the music can yield. When performing Bach in public, we must first clearly understand that in those complex harmonies lies something beside notes, fingering problems, difficult passages, and other hurdles that practice can overcome. Beyond the precision and regularity that are so hard to attain, lies the necessity for giving the performance color and character, in a word to reveal the *soul* of that great music. Only thus can it be interesting, and even moving. How (we may ask) can we sense that color, how can we express it on the organ, that inexpressive instrument? How? That is the secret of the great organists, and they can no more reveal it than I can, for it is a kind of intuition. They can recognize it, but they cannot comprehend it, and even less explain it to others. Such seems to be the goal of Mr. Franck, and the way he acquitted himself of the E minor Fugue showed that he does not strive in vain. Study as profound as the work he must have done testifies to his perseverance and earns for him, today, a place among organists of the first rank. He again gave a most favorable account of himself when he returned to the console with his own composition, played on the *grand choeur*. This finale showed the thought and technique of a true master.

"What can I say now of Lefébure-Wély? What can I say of the charming improvisations of this most pleasant of organists, this true representative of our French school? On hearing him, should not the French school think about renewal and regeneration, rediscovering as he has done formal elegance, musical grace, felicitous registrations, piquant special effects? His perfect knowledge of the instrument tells him immediately which stop is appropriate to which idea and vice versa, and he manages to create a marvelous whole with a multitude of details.

"The qualities of his admirable talent were plainly to be observed in the first two improvisations: he showed off all the resources of the organ, revealing a different aspect each time. We heard the most characteristic stops one by one, and their tones charmed every ear.

"But he was most fully himself, and he truly carried his audience away with the symphonic improvisation: mindful of the approaching season, he seemed to seek his entire inspiration in the Christmas Gospel, striving for a dramatic portrayal of the birth of Jesus. In this mighty piece he used the hymn *Adeste Fideles*, rather modern but most engaging: played upon the *Voix humaine* and with all the expressive resources devised by modern organ-building, it produced the sweetest feeling. Finally, he closed with an elaborate *grand choeur* on the rather familiar tune of "Il est né le divin enfant". We never tire of hearing those old French melodies, justly admired for their simple, straightforward character. Under Lefébure's skillful, learned fingers, this tune gained fresh charm with each passing moment.

"I say 'skillful, *learned* fingers', because some have been foolish enough to criticize the very essence of his talent and its chief trait, namely his graceful ideas, the often light harmony he prefers, and his habit of improvising almost always, and never playing from a score.

"In this last respect, and despite the scant attention owed to such critics, we cannot imagine them to be so simpleminded as to think that Mr. Lefébure does not play from a score because he cannot read well enough to perform correctly the music of the great masters who have gone before him. By the way, our improviser has replied recently and excellently to the partisans of that cerebral music who are so uncerebral themselves. Mr. Lefébure has published in Mr. Heugel's *Maîtrise* all too few organ pieces in legato style: here is where true learning appears in its most elegant form; here is where ideas, perfectly organized and chastely developed, unfold with just enough harmonic richness but without the slightest heaviness. Observing the limits of good taste and that right reason which the finest imaginations obey effortlessly, he and those like him show that these trifling consessions increase their strength and secure for them priceless advantages.

Adrien de LaFage"

CHAPTER ELEVEN

Franck and the Organ at Ste.-Clotilde

The contract for the organ at the new church of Ste.-Clotilde in Paris was, as we have said, a duplicate of a proposal, dated in 1849 for the Cathedral of Bayonne. Consequently there is no likelihood that Cavaillé-Coll consulted César Franck about the stoplist, nor can he have had any idea that one day Franck would occupy the post at Ste-Clotilde. The earliest evidence of contact between the two men appears in 1848, three years after Franck had been appointed assistant organist at Notre-Dame-de-Lorette. Cavaillé-Coll had met Franck when the organist was twenty three years old. The letter of 1848 is simply a formal response to an inquiry from Franck:[1]

Mr. César-Augte Franck

69, rue Blanche, Paris

"Enclosed please find the specifications of the three organs you inspected in our workshop, together with the prices at which we could install [one of] these organs in the chapel of a convent in the city of Langres, as you have indicated.

Yours truly,

Specifications

1. No. 1, p. 327 of the list	3,500 f.
2. No. 2, p. 328 of the list	4,000 f.
3. No. 3, p. 263 of Volume 2	3,000 f.
Together	10,500 f.

Aside from the cross-reference in Devis I for this letter, the contracts and letters contain no other correspondence between the two men. We conclude, then, that Franck had no part in drawing up the stoplist for Bayonne or Ste.-Clotilde. This may be a crucial point as we examine conflicting evidence. In the following pages all the documents relevant to the construction of the Cavaillé-Coll organ at Ste.-Clotilde are given fully in chronological order, from 1849 to 1859.

[The estimates for Bayonne and Ste.-Clotilde are printed on facing pages so that the reader can more readily compare them.]

Devis I, #357, April 20, 1849
Itemized Estimate for a 16′ *Grand Orgue* with Three Manuals
and Pedals for Said Cathedral (Bayonne)[2]

List of Stops
Pédale Division
25 Notes, C to C

Foundation Stops

1. *Contrebasse* or *Flûte ouverte*		16′	25 pipes	1,000
2. *Basse* or *Flûte ouverte*		8′	25 pipes	400
3. *Octave* or *Flûte ouverte*		4′	25 pipes	300

Reed Stops

4. *Bombarde*		16′	25 pipes	1,300
5. *Trompette*		8′	25 pipes	500
6. *Clairon*		4′	25 pipes	300
	Totals		150 pipes	3,800

Positif Division
54 Notes (4½ Octaves), C to F

1. *Montre*	Tin,	8′	54 pipes	500
2. *Prestant*	Tin,	4′	54 pipes	400
3. *Bourdon*	Tin,	8′	54 pipes	450
4. *Flûte douce*	Tin,	4′	54 pipes	350
5. *Salicional*	Tin,	8′	54 pipes	500
6. *Quinte*	Tin,	3′	54 pipes	250
7. *Doublette*	Tin,	2′	54 pipes	200
8. *Plein-jeu*	V Ranks Tin,		270 pipes	750
9. *Trompette*	Tin,	8′	54 pipes	550
10. *Cromorne*	Tin,	8′	54 pipes	400
			756 pipes	4,350

[Bayonne continues on p. 116].

Devis IV, #584, January 21, 1853

Text of Proposal for the Church of Ste.-Clotilde, Paris

Itemized estimate for a *Grand orgue* based on 16′ pitch, with three manuals and pedals, suited to the nave of the new church of Sainte-Clotilde in Paris; drawn up by A. Cavaillé-Coll the younger, organ builder, 66 rue de la Rochefoucauld, Paris.

List of Stops
Pédale division
25 notes (2 Octaves) C to C

Foundation Stops

1. *Contre basse*, or *Flûte ouverte*	16′	25 pipes	1,000
2. *Basse*, or *Flûte ouverte*	8′	25 pipes	400
3. *Octave*	4′	25 pipes	300

Reed Stops

4. *Bombarde*	Tin, 16′	25 pipes	1,300
5. *Trompette*	Tin, 8′	25 pipes	500
6. *Clairon*	Tin, 4′	25 pipes	300
		150 pipes	3,800

Positif division (Manual II)

1. *Montre*	8′	54 pipes	500
2. *Prestant*	4′	54 pipes	400
3. *Bourdon*	8′	54 pipes	450
4. *Flûte douce*	4′	54 pipes	350
5. *Salicional*	8′	54 pipes	500

Mutation and Reed Stops

6. *Quinte*	3′	54 pipes	250
7. *Doublette*	2′	54 pipes	200
8. *Plein jeu*	V Ranks	270 pipes	750
9. *Trompette*	8′	54 pipes	550
10. *Cromorne*	8′	54 pipes	400
		756 pipes	4,350

[Ste.-Clotilde continues on p. 117].

Grand orgue Division
54 Notes (4½ Octaves), C to F

Foundation Stops

1. *Montre*	16′	54 pipes	600
2. *Montre*	8′	54 pipes	500
3. *Prestant*	4′	54 pipes	400
4. *Viola di Gamba*	8′	54 pipes	500
5. *Viole d'amour*	4′	54 pipes	350
6. *Bourdon*	16′	54 pipes	700
7. *Bourdon*	8′	54 pipes	450
8. *Flûte harmonique*	8′	54 pipes	650

Mutation and Reed Stops

9. *Octave*	4′	54 pipes	350
10. *Quinte*	3′	54 pipes	250
11. *Doublette*	2′	54 pipes	200
12. *Fourniture*	IV Ranks	216 pipes	600
13. *Cymbale*	III Ranks	162 pipes	450
14. *Bombarde*	16′	54 pipes	1,500
15. *Trompette*	8′	54 pipes	550
16. *Clairon*	4′	54 pipes	400
		1,134 pipes	8,450

Récit Expressif Division
54 Notes (4½ Octaves), C to F

Foundation Stops

1. *Flûte harmonique*	8′	54 pipes	650
2. *Flûte octaviante*	4′	54 pipes	500
3. *Flûte douce*	8′	54 pipes	450
4. *Viole d'amour*	8′	54 pipes	550

Mutation and Reed Stops

5. *Octavin*	2′	54 pipes	400
6. *Trompette harmonique*	8′	54 pipes	650
7. *Basson / Hautbois*	8′	54 pipes	600
8. *Voix humaine*	8′	54 pipes	400
		432 pipes	4,200

[Bayonne continues on p. 118].

Grand orgue division
54 notes (4½ Octaves) C to F

Foundation Stops

1. *Montre*	16′	54	pipes	600
2. *Montre*	8′	54	pipes	500
3. *Prestant*	4′	54	pipes	400
4. *Viola di gamba*	8′	54	pipes	500
5. *Viole d'amour*	4′	54	pipes	350
6. *Bourdon*	16′	54	pipes	700
7. *Bourdon*	8′	54	pipes	450
8. *Flûte harmonique*	8′	54	pipes	650

Mutation and Reed Stops

9. *Octave*	4′	54	pipes	350
10. *Quinte*	3′	54	pipes	250
11. *Doublette*	2′	54	pipes	200
12. *Fourniture*	IV Ranks	216	pipes	600
13. *Cymbale*	III Ranks	162	pipes	450
14. *Bombarde*	16′	54	pipes	1,500
15. *Trompette*	8′	54	pipes	550
16. *Clairon*	4′	54	pipes	400
		1,134	pipes	8,450

Récit expressif division
54 notes (4½ Octaves) C to F

Foundation Stops

1. *Flûte harmonique*	8′	54	pipes	650
2. *Flûte octaviante*	4′	54	pipes	500
3. *Flûte douce*	8′	54	pipes	450
4. *Viole d'amour*	8′	54	pipes	550

Mutation and Reed Stops

5. *Octavin*	2′	54	pipes	400
6. *Trompette harmonique*	8′	54	pipes	650
7. *Basson / Hautbois*	8′	54	pipes	600
8. *Voix humaine*	8′	54	pipes	400
		432	pipes	4,200

[Ste.-Clotilde continues on p. 119].

Summary of Stops and Pipes at the Various Pitches

Division	16′	8′	4′	3′	2′	Pleins-jeux	Stops	Pipes	Price
Pédale	2	2	2				6	150	3,800
Positif		5	2	1	1	1-V	10	756	4,350
Grand orgue	3	5	4	1	1	2-VII	16	1,134	8,450
Récit expressif		6	1		1		8	432	4,200
Totals	5	18	9	2	3	3-XII	40	2,472	20,800

Case-Pipes

The case-pipes, which are to decorate the case and serve as the bass notes of the *Montre* stops in the *Grand orgue* and *Positif* divisions, shall be made of tin, polished and burnished. The tower pipes shall have raised mouths, and the pipes in the flats bay-leaf mouths.

The price of these pipes is not included in the price of the stops; it shall be determined, according to the design adopted for the case, at the rates of 6 f. 50 per kilogram for pipes over 3 meters tall, and 7 f. 50 for pipes under 3 meters.

The average price for a set of such case-pipes is   6,000

Multiple-Pressure Bellows

The bellows for this organ shall have feeders and a multiple pressure reservoir of dimensions suited to the number and compass of the stops.

The new multiple-pressure wind system is an important factor contributing to the power of the organ and the steadiness of pitch. Since wind supplied to the bass is separate from that supplied to the treble, the accompaniment cannot rob wind or shake the melody line, as happens in conventional organs.

The different wind-pressures obtained with this system allow the bass range of the reed stops to speak at the usual pressure, while the treble, being winded at higher pressure, speaks more vigorously and is not overpowered by the bass, as is usually the case when the same pressure is used for all stops. In this manner, the melody retains all its tonal purity and keeps its proper relationship to the bass, without the use of compound flue stops such as the *Cornet,* which blends poorly with the reeds and often makes them sound thin and shrill. This wind system is also a great help in voicing the harmonic stops, also of our invention.

Building this wind system, together with wind-trunks, flexible connections, and operating mechanism, shall cost   4,000

[Bayonne continues on p. 120].

Divisions	Pitch of Stops						Stops	Pipes	Prices
	16′	8′	4′	3′	2′	Pleins-jeux			
Pédale	2	2	2				6	150	3,800
Positif		5	2	1	1	1-V	10	756	4,350
Grand orgue	3	5	4	1	1	2-VII	16	1,134	8,450
Récit expressif		6	1		1		8	432	4,200
						Total price of stops			20,800

Case-Pipes

See description in Specification no. 357, book 13/3 [Bayonne, above]
Usual price of these pipes   6,000

Multiple-pressure Bellows

See above [Bayonne]   Price   4,000

Windchests

Windchest specification as follows:
1. One large chest with two pallet-boxes for the Pédale   1,200
2. One chest with two pallet-boxes, for the 10 Positif stops   1,250
3. One large chest in two sections, with two pallet-boxes, for the 16
   Grand orgue stops   3,200
4. One chest with two pallet-boxes, for the eight Récit expressif stops 1,200
                                                                         6,850

Swellbox

See no. 357, Book 13/3 [Bayonne]   500

Action

See no. 357 [Bayonne]   4,410

Keyboards

See no. 357 [Bayonne]   500

Composition pedals

See no. 357, up to the ninth pedal.
9. The ninth pedal shall add the mutation and reed stops in the Positif
   to the foundation stops.
10. Finally, the tenth pedal shall operate the swell shades on the Récit
    division.

Pneumatic Lever

This organ shall be equipped with a patented device consisting of 54 pneumatic levers, to overcome the natural stiffness of the key action and make the keyboards as easy to play as that of a conventional piano.

[Ste.-Clotilde continues on p. 121].

[Bayonne continued].

Windchests

The windchests specified below shall be built of select oak, and designed so as to permit convenient access for tuning as well as maintenance of the action.

1° One large chest with two pallet-boxes, for the Six *Pédale* stops   1,200
2° One chest with a single pallet-box, for the ten *Positif* stops   1,250
3° One large chest, in two sections and with two pallet-boxes, for the 16
   Grand orgue stops   3,200
4° One chest with two pallet-boxes for the eight *Récit expressif* stops   1,200

Swellbox

A large swellbox with double walls shall be built to enclose the *Récit* stops. The box shall be fitted with shutters and a mechanism enabling the organist to control by means of a pedal the volume of sound throughout all possible degrees, and play with expression.

Building this box and its fittings shall cost   500

Action

The entire system for this organ, including the rollers that relay the key motion to the pallets and the drawstop motion [to the sliders], as well as the various squares and levers, shall be sturdily made and fitted with care and accuracy.

The action and its accessories shall cost   4,410

Keyboards

The three manuals shall be made of select oak, [the naturals] covered with first-quality ivory, and the sharps with ebony; the frames shall be veneered in rosewood.

This work shall cost   500

Composition Pedals

This organ shall be fitted with several mechanical appliances of our invention, operated by nine pedals within the organist's reach and affording him many novel resources.

1° The first pedal shall operate a mechanism coupling the *Positif* to the
   Grand orgue.
2° The second pedal shall couple the *Récit* to the *Grand orgue.*
3° The third pedal shall couple the bass range of the manual divisions —
   the bass of every stop in the organ — to the *Pédale.*
4° The fourth pedal shall operate a sub-octave coupler acting on the
   Grand orgue manual as well as on all the others.
5° The fifth pedal shall control a tremulant acting on the *Récit* stops.
6° The *Pédale* reeds selected in advance by the organist may be added to
   the foundation stops by means of the sixth pedal.
7° The *Grand orgue* reeds may likewise be added to the foundations by
   means of the seventh pedal.

[Bayonne continues on p. 122].

[Ste.-Clotilde continued].

Installation and Voicing

All the parts constituting the organ specified in the present estimate shall be installed and adjusted by us in the church of Sainte-Clotilde.

All the stops shall be voiced and regulated, and they shall be tuned singly and in the various combinations.

This work shall cost   2,500

Cost of the organ, less case 50,960

Organ-case

The case to contain the instrument described in the present specification shall be built according to plans and specifications by Mr. Ballu, architect of the building.

This case, built of select oak and with carved decoration, also of oak, would entail the following expense, which we estimate according to the sketch furnished by the architect:

1. Framework and joinery, both for the case and the overhanging gallery for the organist, including the hardware for steadying of the case and for access doors: 20,000
2. Decorative carvings for said case and gallery according to said sketch, including hardware and other items required for installation:

Approx. 10,000

For the organ case and gallery	30,000
For the organ itself	50,960
Grand total	90,960

Paris, January 21, 1853

[End of Ste.-Clotilde].

[Bayonne continued].

8° The *Récit* reeds may likewise be added to the foundations by means of the eighth pedal.

9° The ninth pedal shall operate the swell box on the *Récit* division.

Designing and building these various appliances shall cost   2,400

Pneumatic Lever

There shall be built and fitted to this organ a patented device consisting of 54 pneumatic levers for lessening the inherent stiffness of the manual action, making the keys as easy to play as those of a conventional piano.

Building this device and all its accessories shall cost   3,000

Installation and Voicing

All parts composing the organ specified herein shall be installed and fitted by us in the Cathedral church of Bayonne.

All stops shall be voiced, regulated, and tuned.

This work shall cost   2,500

Total   50,960

N. B. Packing and shipping costs, not included in the present estimate, shall be the purchaser's responsibility: they shall be receipted upon presentation of bills and invoices.

Pipe-metal from the old organ shall be credited according to the market price and composition of the metal.

[End of Bayonne].

Lettres IV, #2974
Prefect, Department of Seine
Your Excellency,   April 20, 1855

I herewith submit for your kind consideration remarks concerning the construction of the organ in the new church of Ste.-Clotilde. Following the recommendation of Mr. Ballu, the architect of the church, you determined to assign to me the great task of building the organ, by your order dated 22 June last. Since that time, according to Your Excellency's instructions, I have placed myself at the architect's disposal, giving him all papers he might require in order to draw up plans for the case which is to house the instrument.

Nevertheless, Your Excellency, despite our desire to begin work on the organ, so that it might be finished in time for the dedication of the church, we have not yet been able to start.

The architect's weighty responsibilities have no doubt prevented him from giving us the final plans for the case, plans which we must have in order to design our instrument and make it fit the case designed by him.

You are surely aware, Your Excellency, that building a pipe organ is a sizable undertaking, requiring great craftsmanship, precision, and care, not only in designing the mechanical parts with reference to the shape of the case and the peculiar arrangement of the gallery, but in making the various parts that constitute this huge instrument, and particularly in voicing the stops, which task must be left to a single craftsman. We estimate that not less than 18 months will be necessary for us to build and install the organ for Ste.-Clotilde, assuming that the case — to be built under the architect's supervision — is finished in time for us to set up and regulate our instrument: namely, eight months before the date set for the testing of the organ.

We are confident, Your Excellency, that you are no less anxious than we are to see the completion of this organ, which is to adorn the monument your administration has bestowed upon the city of Paris, and we trust you will see to it that the architect provides a speedy solution to the problem of the case that we need for designing and installing our own work.

Allow me, Your Excellency, to take this opportunity to present for your approval a copy of the specification for the organ you ordered 22 June last, and our estimate for the instrument alone at a price of 50,960 francs.

Concerning the decorative part or case, estimated in the same document at about 30,000 francs, we assume the architect designing the work will have it built by his usual contractor.

In closing, we request Your Excellency to return us a copy of the specification and estimate we are submitting for your approval, so that in due course we may have them filed for use in applying for payment. Respectfully yours,

Lettres V, #3468

My dear Mr. Ballu,   June 27, 1857

I have received in due course your memorandum for 272.30, and the other day one for 72.21, totaling 344.51, for scaffolding you caused to be erected at our request at St.-Merry.

As the Council leaves this expense to me, and thus we shall have to pay your bills, kindly inform me in all good conscience of the exact figure to which we may reduce the total of your two memoranda. I shall promptly remit a 90-day note.

I take this opportunity to urge you to expedite the case for Ste.-Clotilde, so that we may not be hampered in installing our instrument. Yours truly,

Lettres V, #3526

Mr. Ballu, architect for the Church of Ste.-Clotilde   September 29, 1857
"Sir,

We enclose a statement of work completed thus far on the organ for the church of Ste.-Clotilde, totaling as of this date thirty-four thousand francs   34,000

Kindly examine this statement for accuracy, and have a payment made to us to cover part of our advances. Respectfully yours,

Etats des Orgues, #207
Ste.-Clotilde (Organ for)
29 September (1857)
Statement of Work Completed on the
Organ for the church of Ste.-Clotilde
in Paris, by A. C.-C. & Co.

All stops listed below have been made according to good practice and as specified, to wit:

1. *Pédale* division, C to D, 27 notes

		(Pipes)	(Price)
1. *Contre basse* or *Flûte ouverte*	16'	27	1,000
2. *Basse basse* or *Flûte ouverte*	8'	27	400
3. *Octave*	4'	27	300
Mutations and Reeds			
4. *Bombarde*	16'		
5. *Trompette*	8'		
6. *Clairon*	4'		

These 3 stops are being made, and thus are not included in the charges.
N. B. These stops were specified at 25 notes and have been increased to 27, thus adding 2 pipes to each stop.

1,700 francs

Positif division, C to F, 54 notes

1. *Montre*	8′		500
2. *Flûte harmonique*	8′		400
3. *Gambe*	8′		450
4. *Prestant*	4′		350
5. *Bourdon*	8′		500

Mutations and Reeds

6. *Quinte*	3′		250
7. *Doublette*	2′		700
8. *Plein-jeu*	V Ranks		750
9. *Trompette*	8′		
10. *Cromorne*	8′		

N. B. The last 2 stops are being made, and are therefore unfinished.

Grand orgue division, C to F, 54 notes.

1. *Montre*	16′	54	600
2. *Montre*	8′	54	500
3. *Prestant*	4′	54	400
4. *Viole de Gambe*	8′	54	500
5. *Viole d'amour*	4′	54	350
6. *Bourdon*	16′	54	700
7. *Bourdon*	8′	54	450
8. *Flûte harmonique*	8′	54	650

Mutations and Reeds

9. *Octave*	4′	54	350
10. *Quinte*	3′	54	250
11. *Doublette*	2′	54	200
12. *Fourniture*	IV Ranks	216	600
13. *Cymbale*	III Ranks	162	450
14. *Bombarde*	16′		
15. *Trompette*	8′		
16. *Clairon*	4′		
			6,000

N. B.   Since the last three stops are not finished, we do not include them in the total.

Récit expressif division, C to F, 54 notes

1. *Flûte harmonique*	8′	54	650
2. *Flûte octaviante*	4′	54	500
3. *Flûte douce*	8′	54	450
4. *Viole d'amour*	8′	54	550

Mutations and Reeds

5. *Octavin*	2′	54	400
6. *Trompette harmonique*	8′		
7. *Basson / Hautbois*			
8. *Voix humaine*	8′		

N. B. The last 3 stops are not finished.

Case-Pipes

All the case-pipes have been made and installed in their respective locations. These pipes are made, according to the specification, of fine tin polished and burnished. Each and every pipe has a raised mouth.

The average value of these pipes is estimated in the specification at

6,000 francs

Mechanical Part
Multi-Pressure Wind System

The bellows have been made and installed in accordance with the specification: they comprise feeders and reservoirs and supply wind at various pressures. There are two large horizontal reservoirs, each with iron stabilizers and two pairs of feeders, operated by pedals.

Complete with wind trunks, flexible conduits and operating mechanism, this wind system is estimated in the specification at   4,000 francs

Windchests

The windchests, as specified below, are made of select oak and designed so as to afford easy access whether for tuning or repairs to the action, to wit:

1. One large chest in two sections, with double pallet-boxes, for the 6 *Pédale* stops, priced in the specification at   1,200
2. One large chest in three sections, with double pallet-boxes, for the 10 *Positif* stops, priced in the specification at   1,250
3. One large chest in two sections, with double pallet-boxes, for the 16 *Grand orgue* stops, priced in the specification at   3,200
4. One chest with double pallet-boxes, for the 8 *Récit expressif* stops, priced in the specification at   1,200

6,850

Swell Box

The swell box is built according to the specification, with double walls and mechanically-operated shutters for controlling the volume of the *Récit* stops. This box and its accessories are priced in the specification at   500

Action

The action is now being built in our workshops.

Keyboards

The keyboards are also being built.

Composition Pedals

This part of the keyboard action is also being built.

Pneumatic Levers

The pneumatic-lever machine has been built in accordance with the specification.

Aside from the customary machine, in order to overcome difficulties arising from location, we have been obliged to build a special mechanism for the *Grand orgue* chests located at the feet of the case towers.

Construction and installation of the new mechanism are priced in the specification at   3,000

Installation and Voicing

Installation of the organ began as soon as work on the case allowed, and has been continued diligently ever since.

Since this work is not finished, we do not include it in our figures here.

Summary of the Present Status of the Work

1.	*Pédale*	1,700	
2.	*Positif*	3,600	
3.	*Grand orgue*	6,000	
4.	*Récit*	2,550	13,650
5.	Case-pipes		6,000
	Total for pipes		19,650
6.	Multi-pressure bellows	4,000	
7.	Windchests	6,850	
8.	Swell box	500	
9.	Pneumatic levers	3,000	
		14,350	
	Total for work to date		34,000
	Less ⅕ for performance bond		6,800
			27,200

Lettres V, #3560

Mr. Ballu, architect for the church of Ste.-Clotilde   December 5, 1857
Sir,

Of the statement we submitted to you on 29 September last for 34,000 francs, you have been good enough to forward to us a first payment of 7,000.

Since then, we have worked continuously, both in our shops and at the church, and the value of the work done to date has significantly increased the extent of our commitment. We shall submit a revised statement as of 1 January next, but in the meantime we should be obliged if you would issue us another payment before the end of the year. Yours,

Lettres V, #3580
Mr. Ballu, architect for the church of Ste.-Clotilde   December 17, 1857
Sir,

Enclosed please find a statement of work completed on the organ in Ste.-Clotilde, amounting to date to 17,998. We have indicated in the statement the work completed during the last quarter of this year, amounting to 13,998, to which figure we have added the total from the preceding statement, submitted by us at the end of last September, amounting to 34,000, bringing the grand total to the figure given above, of 17,998.

We request you, Sir, to issue us another payment so that we may meet our year-end commitments. You have sent us a money order of 17,000, so the balance amounts to 30,998. We should be most obliged, Sir, if you would authorize payment of whatever sum you deem suitable on this balance. Yours truly,

Etat des Orgues, #210
Ste.-Clotilde Organ
Statement of Work Completed
on the Organ for the Church
of Ste.-Clotilde in Paris
as of December 15, 1857.

Since the preceding statement of work completed, submitted at the end of last September, itemizes all the work completed at that time, we shall mention here only that completed during the last quarter of the present year.

Mutations and Reeds

Pédale division

1. *Bombarde*	Tin, 16′	27 notes	1,300	
2. *Trompette*	Tin, 8′	27 notes	500	
3. *Clairon*	Tin, 4′	27 notes	300	2,100

Positif division

1. *Trompette*	Tin, 8′	54 notes	550	
2. *Cromorne*	Tin, 8′	54 notes	400	950

Mutations and Reeds

Grand orgue division

1. *Bombarde*	16′	54 notes	1,500	
2. *Trompette*	8′	54 notes	550	
3. *Clairon*	4′	54 notes	400	2,450

Mutations and Reeds

Récit expressif division

1. *Trompette harmonique*	Tin,	8'	54 notes	650	
2. *Basson / Hautbois*	Tin,	8'	54 notes	600	
3. *Voix humaine*	Tin,	8'	54 notes	400	1,650

Action

The action of the organ, including the roller-boards for connecting the keys with the pallets, the iron rollers for the drawstop action, and the various squares and levers, has been built in accordance with the specification, but is not yet installed. This action is priced in the specification at 4,410 francs, less ⅕ for installation and regulation, or   3,528

Keyboards

The three manuals and the pedal keyboard have been built in accordance with the specification, but are not yet installed. This work is priced at 500 francs in the specification, and is counted here at ⅘, or   400

Composition Pedals

The composition pedals and their action have been built in accordance with the specification, but are not yet installed. This work is priced in the specification at 2,400 francs, of which ⅘ are   1,920

Installation and Voicing

The installation is now in progress. This work, priced at 2,500 francs in the specification, is counted only as far as it is completed, at   1,000

Total	13,998
Total of the previous statement	34,000
Grand total to date	47,998

Paris, December 15, 1857.

Lettres V, #3763

Mr. Ballu, architect for the church of Ste.-Clotilde   July 12, 1858

Sir:

Enclosed please find our statement of work completed on the organ in Ste.-Clotilde as of July 1 of this year, amounting to   49,960

For this work you have issued payments as follows:

1. October 14, 1857, for	17,000	
2. December 30, 1857, for	11,000	
Total	28,000	
	Balance due	21,960

We should be obliged, Sir, if you could issue us a third payment in an amount you deem appropriate. Yours sincerely,

Etats des Orgues, #224
July 12, 1858
Statement of Work Completed
on the Organ in Ste.-Clotilde
in Paris

I. The stops listed below have been made in accordance with the specification, to wit:

Pédale division, C to D, 27 notes.

1. *Contre basse* or *Flûte ouverte*	16′	27	pipes	1,000
2. *Basse* or *Flûte ouverte*	8′	27	pipes	400
3. *Octave* or *Flûte ouverte*	4′	27	pipes	300

Mutations and Reeds

4. *Bombarde*	16′	27	pipes	1,300
5. *Trompette*	8′	27	pipes	500
6. *Clairon*	4′	27	pipes	300
		162	pipes	3,800

Positif division, C to F, 54 notes

1. *Montre*	8′	54	pipes	500
2. *Prestant*	4′	54	pipes	400
3. *Bourdon*	8′	54	pipes	450
4. *Flûte douce*	4′	54	pipes	350
5. *Salcional* [sic]	8′	54	pipes	500

Mutations and Reeds

6. *Quinte*	3′	54	pipes	250
7. *Doublette*	2′	54	pipes	200
8. *Plein-jeu*	V Ranks	270	pipes	750
9. *Trompette*	8′	54	pipes	550
10. *Cromorne*	8′	54	pipes	400
		756	pipes	4,350

Grand orgue division, C to F, 54 notes
Foundations

1. *Montre*	16′	54	pipes	600
2. *Montre*	8′	54	pipes	500
3. *Prestant*	4′	54	pipes	400
4. *Viole de Gambe*	8′	54	pipes	500
5. *Viole d'amour*	4′	54	pipes	350
6. *Bourdon*	16′	54	pipes	700
7. *Bourdon*	8′	54	pipes	450
8. *Flûte harmonique*	8′	54	pipes	650

Mutations and Reeds

9. *Octave*	4'	54 pipes	350
10. *Quinte*	3'	54 pipes	250
11. *Doublette*	2'	54 pipes	200
12. *Fourniture*	IV Ranks	216 pipes	600
13. *Cymbale*	III Ranks	162 pipes	450
14. *Bombarde*	16'	54 pipes	1,500
15. *Trompette*	8'	54 pipes	550
16. *Clairon*	4'	54 pipes	400
		1,134 pipes	8,450

Récit expressif division, C to F, 54 notes

1. *Flûte harmonique*	8'	54 pipes	650
2. *Flûte octaviante*	4'	54 pipes	500
3. *Flûte douce*	8'	54 pipes	450
4. *Viole d'amour*	8'	54 pipes	550

Mutations and Reeds

5. *Octavin*	2'	54 pipes	400
6. *Trompette harmonique*	8'	54 pipes	650
7. *Basson / Hautbois*	8'	54 pipes	600
8. *Voix humaine*	8'	54 pipes	400
		432 pipes	4,200

Summary of Stops, Pipes, and Pitches

Division	16'	8'	4'	3'	2'	Pleins-jeux	Stops	Pipes	Price
Pédale	2	2	2	0	0	0	6	162	3,800
Positif	0	6	2	1	1	1/5	10	756	4,350
Grand orgue	3	5	4	1	1	2/7	16	1,134	8,450
Récit	0	6	1	0	1	0	8	432	4,200
Totals	5	18	9	2	3	3/12	40	2,484	20,800

Case-Pipes

The case-pipes have been made and are installed in their respective locations. These pipes are made, in accordance with the contract, of fine tin, polished and burnished. Each and every one has a raised mouth.

The average price of these pipes is estimated in the contract at   6,000

Mechanical Part
Multi-Pressure Wind System

The bellows have been made and installed in accordance with the contract; they comprise feeders, and reservoirs supplying wind at various pressures. The two large horizontal reservoirs each have iron stabilizers and two pairs of feeders, operated by pedals.

Complete with wind trunks, flexible conduits, and operating mechanism, the wind system is priced in the contract at   4,000

Windchests

The windchests listed below have been built of select oak and are designed so as to facilitate tuning and repair, to wit:

1. One large chest in two sections with double pallet-boxes, for the six *Pédale* stops, priced in the contract at   1,200
2. One large chest in three sections with double pallet-boxes, for the ten *Positif* stops, priced in the contract at   1,250
3. One large chest in two sections with double pallet-boxes, for the 16 *Grand orgue* stops, priced in the contract at   3,200
4. One chest with double pallet-boxes, for the 8 *Récit expressif* stops, priced in the contract at   1,200

(37,650)

Swell Box

The swell box has been built in accordance with the contract, with double walls and mechanically-operated shutters for controlling the volume of the *Récit* stops.

With its accessories, this box is priced in the contract at   500

Action

The entire action for the organ, including roller-boards connecting the keys to the pallets, iron rollers for the drawstops, and various levers and squares, has been built in accordance with the contract.

The action is priced in the contract at   4,410

Keyboards

The three manual keyboards and the pedal keyboard have also been built in accordance with the contract.

These parts are priced in the contract at   500

Composition Pedals

The composition pedals and their action have been built in accordance with the contract.

These parts are priced in the contract at   2,400

Pneumatic Levers

The pneumatic lever action has been built in accordance with the contract.

Aside from the customary machine, as a result of difficulties arising from the location, we have been obliged to build a special machine for the *Grand orgue* chests placed at the feet of the case towers.

Building and installing this new machine are priced in the contract at   3,000

(Brought forward   48,460)

Installation and Voicing

Installation of the organ is now under way. This work is priced in the contract at 2,500 francs, and we count it here for the portion completed at   1,500

Total for work done to date   49,960

Done and Submitted at Paris, July 1, 1858.
Certified true and accurate.

Lettres V, #3846

To Mr. Ballu,
Architect of Sainte-Clotilde Paris   October 18, 1858
Sir:

We wish to remind you of our request for part payment sent you on 12 July last. We must recover part of our advances, and we should be most obliged if you could make a payment of 10,000 francs by the end of this month.

Respectfully yours,

Lettres VI, #4159

Fr. Hamelin
Priest of Sainte-Clotilde   July 7, 1859
Dear Father Hamelin,

I write to remind you of the request I mentioned to you the other day concerning funds you might invest in our firm.

Since we are now engaged in sizable projects that tie up our capital and require extra funds, I should be most obliged if you would credit to our account the sum of 20,000 francs you mentioned to us.

We shall serve you interest on this sum at 6% *per annum,* quarterly or half-yearly, as you prefer. We shall repay on demand part or all of the amount, with three month's advance notice.

As for security, our firm has at the present time a capital of 200,000 francs. in addition to tools and equipment worth 50,000 francs.

In addition, since we deal only with government agencies and thus need not fear the slightest loss, you may be sure that your money would not be in jeopardy.

I should be obliged if you would grant me an appointment to discuss this matter in detail. Meanwhile, I remain

Yours most respectfully,

Lettres VI, #4226
To Mr. Ballu
Architect of Sainte-Clotilde Paris   August 29, 1859
Sir:

Enclosed please find the final statement for work on the pipe organ you engaged us to build for the church of Sainte-Clotilde.

Kindly examine this statement as to its accuracy.

Our prices are based on the estimate we submitted to you on January 21, 1853, quoting the organ at   50,960
and the case at   30,000

Total: 80,000 [sic]

Building this organ, under circumstances that proved most unusual, involved much more labor and expense than we anticipated. You have had occasion to judge for yourself how the extreme height of the gallery required special planning in order to produce an organ that not only was pleasing to the eye but possessed all the characteristics expected of a church organ.

Despite these difficulties, we believe we have succeeded in our task, and we can assure you that the Sainte-Clotilde organ as it stands today is one of the best instruments that has come from our workshops, possessing all the improvements of modern organ-building.

Our statement totals   74,610

This figure, which far exceeds our estimate, may seem unreasonable to you, but we assure you that the organ in La Madeleine, which did not pose the same problems but is about the same size, cost   75,000

We trust that examining our statement on the site will convince you, better than anything we might add, that we have met our obligations and deserve to be rewarded.

We also request a further payment, as we need the cash.

We have received payments to date totaling   40,000
The balance outstanding is thus   34,610
Awaiting your reply, we remain

Yours most respectfully,

Lettres VI, #4302
To Fr. Hamelin
Priest of Sainte-Clotilde Paris   November 8, 1859
Dear Father Hamelin,

Since work on the Sainte-Clotilde organ has been completed since last August, we should like to have the instrument dedicated. We believe early December would be an appropriate season, and we request you to select a date to your convenience for the dedication.

Mr. Ballu, the architect, agrees that as was done for the organ in La Madeleine, the recital should be held about 8 p. m., when the Church is not in use. Furthermore, an evening hour would permit us to expect the distinguished personalities we intend to invite to this function.

We hope you will see fit to endorse our plans and grant us an appointment in the near future so that we may make arrangements.

                                        Yours faithfully,

Lettres VI, #4309
To Mr. Ballu
Architect of Sainte-Clotilde Paris   November 11, 1859
Sir:

I have arranged with the Priest of Saint-Clotilde to set the date of the organ dedication on Monday 5 December next.

Since the ceremony requires that the scaffolding be removed from the organ at least one week beforehand, so that we may make careful adjustments to the instrument, we request that you order the cornices to be mounted on the case without delay and that the scaffolding be taken down by November 25 at the latest.

Confident of your cooperation and with thanks in advance, we remain

                                        Yours truly,

Lettres VI, #4313
Marquis d'Andiqué, Chairman
Council of Sainte-Clotilde
Hunting Lodge near Montfort-sur-Men   November 15, 1859
Dear Sir,

As work on the Sainte-Clotilde organ has been finished since August, we have arranged with the architect, Mr. Ballu, to hold the dedication at the beginning of December. The Priest has been informed of our plans, and he agrees that the dedication recital should be held on Monday, December 5, so that the organ may be used for the services of perpetual adoration to be held a few days later.

The Priest, no less than ourselves, desires that you honor the recital with your presence; therefore, we write asking whether you can agree to the proposed date.

We hope to secure the services of Mr. Lefébure-Wély, former organist of La Madeleine, and Mr. Franck, organist of Sainte-Clotilde. We should be pleased if this letter met with your acceptance, and we ask that you be good enough to reply.

In the meantime, Sir, we remain

Lettres VI, #4337
Mr. Ballu
Architect of Sainte-Clotilde Paris   December 2, 1859
Sir,

Despite our advice, the work just completed in preparation for installing the cornice on top of the case was done so carelessly that the organ has become unplayable. Sawdust, chips, and even sizable scraps, abundantly scattered inside the instrument, have smothered the pipes or spoiled their tone, so that we cannot now put things to rights in time for the dedication scheduled for the fifth of this month.

We must therefore postpone the recital at least two weeks, till December 19, in order to repair, clean, and tune everything that has been disturbed.

These repairs, made necessary by the fault of the contractor or his employees, for whom he is of course responsible will require more than 500 *francs* expenditure on our part. I presume you will see your way clear to charging this expense to those who caused it.

Kindly transmit our complaint to the suitable parties.[3]

This voluminous documentation shows beyond a doubt that the original organ at Ste.-Clotilde had 40 stops and 10 composition pedals. From the Bayonne proposal until the Ste.-Clotilde installation was virtually accomplished, Cavaillé-Coll had made only three relatively minor modifications. Those were (1) the provision of double pallet boxes and the corresponding composition pedal for the *Positif*, (2) a change in the order of manual keyboards so that the *Grand Orgue* was No. 1, and and (3) the expansion of the pedal compass from 25 to 27 notes.

This information is of great importance, because we have been told continually that César Franck registered his *Six Pièces* (composed 1860-62 and published 1863) specifically for the organ at Ste.-Clotilde. All twentieth-century experts have said the organ had 46 stops, rather than 40. The difference is not only a numerical one, because Franck's registrations would not apply to the stoplist we have just established as the original. Yet the original manuscripts for certain of the *Six Pièces* bear registrations as well in Franck's own hand. Therefore we must choose between two unlikely solutions to the problem: either Franck registered the *Six Pièces* for some other organ, or Cavaillé-Coll was persuaded to make substantial and difficult changes to the organ for Ste.-Clotilde at the last possible moment before completing it.

Let us dispose of the first possibility. There was only one other organ in Paris fulfilling all the registration requirements contained in the *Six Pièces*: Cavaillé-Coll's unfinished 100-stop masterpiece at St.-Sulpice. Since the inauguration at St.-Sulpice took place in 1862, after Franck completed the *Six Pièces,* we may reject the notion that Franck abandoned his own new instrument in favor of St.-Sulpice to register the first major publication of his organ works.

As for the second possibility, we know that Cavaillé-Coll frequently altered the dispositions laid out in contracts. But such alterations were made in the course of executing the work, as was the case for St.-Vincent-de-Paul and a number of other organs. The most striking example of additional work, which was ordinarily never authorized until after the fact, is the instrument just cited at St.-Sulpice. This organ was being "restored" during the time when Cavaillé-Coll was building Franck's instrument at Ste.-Clotilde. The St.-Sulpice organ expanded from the 72 stops in the original contract,[4] to the completed instrument (1862) of 100 stops. Thus, during the evolution of its design *after* the contract was submitted, it became the largest organ that had ever been built.[5] We suspect that the inspiration for the dramatic increase in the size of the organ at St.-Sulpice came from Cavaillé-Coll's trip to Ulm in August, 1856, four months after the contract for St. Sulpice was submitted. At Ulm Cathedral, Cavaillé-Coll inspected the almost complete 100-stop organ built by Walcker, "a builder of merit and genius".[6] He wrote to Walcker that the giant instrument was "the largest and most complete of any that exists in Europe."[7]

Unfortunately, the surviving records of the Church of Ste.-Clotilde, found in two folders preserved in the *Archives de la Ville de Paris,* reveal nothing whatsoever about the organ. The record of repairs and alterations, at least up to the time of Franck's death in 1890, has been lost or destroyed. But it is beyond doubt that Cavaillé-Coll was accustomed to making "additional improvements" above and beyond contractual agreements. Had he not brought St.-Denis very close to completion when Mr. Barker happened on the scene?

The change at Ste.-Clotilde from 40 to 46 stops, and from 10 to 14 composition pedals, occurred before the inaugural recital. This is shown by the following comments, and is supported by Cavaillé-Coll's financial statements:

1. Abbé Lamazou, "The organ in Sainte-Clotilde, dedicated December 19, 1859, contains 46 stops."[8]

2. *La France musicale,* "This instrument (Sainte-Clotilde) was to be as large as possible in relation to the size of the church, namely with 46 stops on three manuals and pedal, having fourteen composition pedals and 2,796 pipes."[9]

3. The third and final piece of conclusive evidence is found in Cavaillé-Coll's final accounting, dated August 29, 1859.[10] It had been more than a year since his past progress report, but three accounts had been submitted before that, at quarterly intervals. In a matter of weeks after July 1, 1858, Cavaillé-Coll could easily have finished the instrument, as there was only 1,000 f. of work still to be done.[11] Why, then, was the inauguration still a year and a half away?

We have observed that for Ste.-Clotilde, Cavaillé-Coll had followed the contract to the letter, rather than introducing "supplementary improvements". The final progress report accounted for all provisions of the contract and no extra expense. Such was not true of St.-Vincent-de-Paul, where the final progress report listed numerous substitutions and additions to the stoplist in the contract. There was, accordingly, a request for an additional sum to cover the cost of "additional improvements". The same was true for Luçon, where special circumstances required an upward adjustment of the contract price. We summarize below the financial data for these three organs, similar in size and almost identical in contract price:

Organ	Contract price	Extra costs	Stops	Extra stops	Total	Total cost	% of increase
St.-Vincent-de-Paul	50,000	12,731.00	40	7	47	62,731.00	25.6
Luçon[12]	50,960	5,124.33	40	0	40	56,084.33	10
Ste.-Clotilde	50,960	23,620.00	40	?	?	74,610.00	40.4

Here are the reasons given by Cavaillé-Coll for the extra costs:

1. St.-Vincent-de-Paul: "additional work", that is, seven extra stops and several substitutions.[13]

2. Luçon: change of destination for the instrument, requiring re-voicing and modifications to the action; setting up the instrument at Luçon.[14]

3. Ste.-Clotilde: extra work and unforeseen expense involved in building and installing the organ in a very difficult situation; extreme height of the gallery, which "required studies to make the appearance of the organ pleasing and suitable".[15]

The price increase for St.-Vincent-de-Paul covered the costs of seven extra stops, representing a 17.5% increase in the size of the instrument, and a 25.6% addition to the bill. At Luçon, the added cost clearly resulted from problems attending a change of destination. The instrument was built for the Cathedral of Carcassonne. It stood in Cavaillé-Coll's workshop for over a year, and eventually it was sold to the Cathedral of Luçon. For each instrument, Cavaillé-Coll itemized the extra costs in his letters requesting reimbursement. But for Ste.-Clotilde he did not offer a satisfactory explanation for the unusual extra charge of over forty per cent. Anyone acquainted with organ building knows he could not have spent almost half again the original figure simply because of the unusual height of the gallery. The appearance of the organ was not Cavaillé-Coll's problem, since Gau, the architect who designed the case, was responsible for that. It appears that Cavaillé-Coll made this sizable expenditure for work that he preferred not to disclose when he requested payment for it. The City of Paris had contracted for the organ,[16] and Cavaillé-Coll must have reasoned that he would be paid more promptly if he concealed the technical details from the bureaucrats.

The changes were broad in scope, involving the addition of new stops and the elimination of others. They required major alterations in chest layouts, the removal of pipes, the making of new pipes, a new stop action, and considerable extra voicing. For an instrument that was almost completed, these changes cost even more; and it would have been very difficult to persuade the officials that such alterations were appropriate. Yet today we can find no explanation for the increase of 40%, unless it covered such major alterations or additions.

Only Franck himself could have pressed for changes at so late a date, and Cavaillé-Coll would not have conspired to accomplish them had it not been for his loyalty towards the organist: after all, he had helped Franck to secure the post at Ste.-Clotilde. Franck assumed his duties as choir director on January 22, 1858, after Cavaillé-Coll had begun work in the church. The musician was able to follow daily progress on the organ, especially after Cavaillé-Coll's best voicer, Gabriel Reinburg, began bringing the instrument to life. It may have been in the growing excitement of that first half-year with the first large instrument he could call his own that César Franck conceived the outlines of his immortal *Six Pièces*.

In the new organ as planned, he would have missed some of his favorite sonorities. There was no *Voix Céleste* on the *Récit*, a stop Franck had particularly enjoyed in his little 18-stop organ at St.-Jean-St.-François; no *Bourdon 16'* on the *Positif*, a stop that Cavaillé-Coll had given the organ at St.-Vincent-de-Paul; nor a *Clairon* on the *Positif* or *Récit*. There must have been discussions on these matters and questions about the feasibility of making changes even then, as the voicing was in progress. Eventually, by the summer of 1858, Cavaillé-Coll agreed to introduce changes, but apparently he decided he had submitted enough progress reports and bills. The rest would be done quietly.

In drawing up the revisions, César Franck gave us his first and only essay in organ design, and this in turn inspired him to compose and publish the revolutionary *Six Pièces*. In the registration, Franck seems to have focused attention on the newly-acquired resources in the organ: this is particularly true of the *Fantaisie in C*, the *Pastorale*, and the *Grand Pièce Symphonique*. By way of appreciation, he dedicated the sublime *Pastorale* to Aristide Cavaillé-Coll, and made ample use in that work of one of the added stops, the *Bourdon 16'* on the *Positif*. In the *Grande Pièce Symphonique* he juxtaposed the new *Voix Celeste* in the *Récit* and the new *Unda*

Maris in the *Positif*, demonstrating a combination of sonorities available at no other organ in Paris until Cavaillé-Coll completed his work at St.-Sulpice.

We list below the additions and subtractions, using the stoplist in the contract as the point of reference.

Ste.-Clotilde
Modifications (before August 1859)

1. Additions to *Pédale*:

> Soubasse (Quintaton) 32′
> Basson 16′

2. Additions to *Positif*:

> Bourdon 16′
> Unda Maris 8′ (or Voix celeste)
> Flûte octaviante 4′
> Clairon 4′

3. Additions to *Récit*:

> Voix Celeste 8′
> Clairon 4′

4. Subtractions from *Grand Orgue*:
   a. Viole d'amour.
   b. Fourniture IV and Cymbale III merged to make a Fourniture VI.

Cavaillé-Coll's records show that the organ was originally intended to have 2,484 pipes, including the 12 added for the extra pedal compass. That is 312 fewer than the total reported in *La France musicale*.   A computation of the extra pipes required for the changes listed above reveals that 324 would have been added, excluding the combination of *Fourniture* IV with *Cymbale* III in a new *Fourniture* VI. A loss of 12 pipes in that readjustment would account for the new total of 2,796.

As for the composition pedals, four must have been added to the original ten, if we are to believe the report in *La France musicale*. We infer the changes by comparing the original with a list given by Charles Tournemire,   who was organist at Ste.-Clotilde from 1898 until his death in 1940:

> Tirasse Positif
> Tirasse Récit
> Octaves graves Positif
> Octaves graves Récit to Positif

Adjustments to the earlier list would have been:

a. Replace coupler, *Récit* to *Grand Orgue*, with *Récit* to *Positif*.

b. The old general *tirasse*, coupling all keyboards to pedal was made *Tirasse Grand Orgue*.

c. The old *Octaves graves* coupler for all keyboards was made *Octaves graves* for the *Grand Orgue* only.

Thus, with its additional improvements, the organ at Ste-Clotilde would have received its final voicing by the end of the summer in 1859: the stoplist was as follows:

Pédale
1. Soubasse 32
2. Contrebasse 16
3. Basse 8
4. Octave 4
   Jeux de combinaison
5. Bombarde 16
6. Basson 16
7. Trompette 8
8. Clairon 4

Positif, 54 notes
1. Bourdon 16
2. Montre 8
3. Gambe 8
4. Flûte harmonique 8
5. Bourdon 8
6. Unda Maris 8 (Voix celeste)
7. Prestant 4
   Jeux de combinaison
8. Flûte octaviante 4
9. Quinte 2⅔
10. Doublette 2
11. Plein jeu
12. Trompette
13. Cromorne (Clarinette)
14. Clairon 4

Grand Orgue, 54 notes
1. Montre 16
2. Bourdon 16
3. Montre 8
4. Viole de gambe 8
5. Flûte harmonique 8
6. Bourdon 8
7. Prestant 4
   Jeux de combinaison
8. Octave 4
9. Quinte 2⅔
10. Doublette 2
11. Fourniture VI
12. Bombarde 16
13. Trompette 8
14. Clairon 4

Récit, 54 notes
1. Flûte harmonique 8
2. Viole de gambe 8
3. Bourdon 8
4. Voix celeste 8
5. Basson Hautbois 8
6. Voix humaine
   Jeux de combinaison
7. Flûte octaviante 4
8. Octavin 2
9. Trompette 8
10. Clairon 4

Pédales de combinaison
1. Tirasse I
2. Tirasse II
3. Tirasse III
4. Anches Pédale
5. Octaves graves I
6. Octaves graves II
7. Octaves graves III/II
8. Anches I
9. Anches II
10. Anches III
11. Accouplement II - I
12. Accouplement III - II
13. Tremolo
14. Expression

It was, of course, César Franck who was to give special significance to the organ at Ste.-Clotilde, one of the two or three most famous instruments in France. Unfortunately, his successors at that console have reverently seen fit to have the instrument "restored", or altered, so that at the present time it is no longer much help in the registration of the most important organ music of the 19th century. During the 1930's, under the direction of Charles Tournemire, last surviving pupil of Franck, the organ was electrified and enlarged. The 75-year-old console, at which the master had improvised for Franz Liszt and a host of others, was removed from the church, eventually finding its way to the living room of Flor Peeters in Belgium. There have been more changes during the tenure of the present organist. Whereas the battle still rages over the treatment of the Couperin organ at St.-Gervais, officially "protected" by the government's Organ Commission, Franck's instrument has perished.

CHAPTER TWELVE

Cavaillé-Coll on Electricity

Cavaillé-Coll was interested from his early years in innovative, even revolutionary changes in the art of organ building as he learned it from his father and grandfather. Once he had established his reputation as a pioneer, however, he was content to work within the new limitations imposed by those innovations. Still, as early as the 1850s he was made aware that experiments with the use of electricity could be pointing to yet a more radical change for the future. Indeed, after Cavaillé-Coll's death in 1899, his name was associated with developments in organ building that he himself would have deplored.

As a consequence of correspondence and comments published by Albert Peschard (1899)[1], J.W. Hinton (1909)[2], and the late Marcel Dupré (1972)[3], widespread credence has been given to the notion that Aristide Cavaillé-Coll (1811-1899) actually favored the new electro-pneumatic action in organs. Evidence cited by these authors is far from convincing and should be re-examined from a broader point of view.

Peschard, the inventor of the earliest form of electro-pneumatic action in the 1860s, was not the first to seek Cavaillé-Coll's support for the use of electricity in organ building; but he was the first to claim that old age and infirmity had prevented Cavaillé-Coll from jumping on the electric bandwagon. Once Cavaillé-Coll was dead, Peschard lost no time in publishing his somewhat limited previous correspondence with the great organ builder. He apparently hoped thereby to gain high level recognition for his early role in an expanding commercial activity that had passed him by.[4]

Hinton, an ardent promoter of the "electric organ" in England, admitted that "no little anxiety was shown by organ builders, both in Europe and in the States, to ascertain the attitude which Cavaillé-Coll would assume in the respect of the new system of electro-pneumatics."[5] In seven pages he managed to accomplish little more than to suggest that a man in his eighties was incapable of making intelligent decisions.[6] He could not otherwise explain the fact that Cavaillé-Coll had suppressed the electro-pneumatic action at St.-Augustin (Paris) just the year before his death.

As for Marcel Dupré, self-proclaimed protector of the old Cavaillé-Coll organ at St.-Sulpice (Paris), one senses no ambivalence toward electric action. He was for it. Thus, in his *Recollections,* we note that he invoked Cavaillé-Coll's posthumous sanction by putting words in his mouth: "Albert Peschard, organist of the Abbaye aux Hommes (Saint-Etienne) in Caen and a physics teacher at that city's lycée, invented the electro-magnet used in organ key-chest actions. He approached Cavaillé-Coll, hoping to collaborate with him, as Barker had. But Cavaillé-Coll declined with these moving words: 'I am old, I am sick, and I am poor. I am unable to even think about undertaking such an extensive project. These things are for the future'. He had, therefore, foreseen the numerous refinements that were to be made in organ construction, thanks to electricity."[7] What Cavaillé-Coll could not have foreseen was that only thirty years after his death the company bearing his name would be building electric 'unit' organs for Parisian theatres, incorporating sostenuto devices on all keyboards. Marcel Dupré, a partisan of such 'improvements', praised the last organ built by this *Société Anonyme de Facture d'Orgues (Cavaillé-Coll)* in 1930: "the electric action is absolutely instantaneous, the attack is precise and gentle, and the adjustable combinations are quick and reliable. In short, the instrument is worthy of the Cavaillé-Coll firm's illustrious reputation."[8]

Aristide Cavaillé-Coll's career was not only one of the longest in organ-building history, but one of the most fascinating. His father, to whom he was apprenticed in the 1820s, and his grandfather before him, passed on in practical experience a priceless heritage of the classical tradition, while Dom Bédos provided the textbook. It is quite clear that Cavaillé-Coll leaned heavily on those traditional techniques throughout his long life. Yet his inquisitiveness led him at an early age into numerous experiments: a revision of the accepted procedures for winding, a design for a harmonium, the application of the free reed principle to pipe organs, the invention of a system for operating manual couplers by foot. These were some of the ideas that occupied his mind before he set out for Paris at the age of twenty-two. The key to his success, in an age when novelty was a prerequisite in artistic endeavor, lay in his eagerness to try new approaches, even daring ones; and from the start he set out to achieve new goals. Nevertheless his reputation rested on the craft learned from his father, a sure guarantee of the quality of all work that left his shop. Such an extraordinary combination of innovative talent, technical conservatism, and political wisdom is seldom found in organ builders. For fifty years Cavaillé-Coll was considered a leader on the international level, and in France the chief of them all.

We all know that there are sharp differences between the classical and romantic organs, and that progress in the romantic movement hinged upon the invention of a successful assist for the manual key action. Cavaillé-Coll, acutely aware of this need, was the first to collaborate with Charles Spackman Barker (1806-1879), the inventor of that all-important pneumatic device, and he continued to use the *machine Barker* as improved from time to time. But its utility was not limited to operating pallets in the wind chests. Unquestionably Barker's invention expanded the organ's previous limitations in terms of size, sonority, and wind supply. The pneumatic motors were put to work moving sliders, operating combination pistons, and even moving swell shades gradually. Without the Barker machine or some comparable innovation, Cavaillé-Coll would not have been able to develop his famous harmonic stops, which provided the basis for a new approach to tonal design. His system of multi-pressure bellows would not have been feasible, nor the use of sub- and super-octave couplers, nor the reverse position console. The simple pneumatic pouches, tripped by the action of the keys, the stop-knobs, or pistons, were operated by the same wind that fed the pipes, and they apparently fulfilled the needs of the medium. To Cavaillé-Coll the inconvenience of maintaining a more complex instrument was a small price to pay for such benefits.

Once established, Cavaillé-Coll did not isolate himself. Rather, he traveled extensively in Germany, Holland, and England; contributed to many industrial exhibitions; wrote papers for the *Académie des Beaux Arts;* and corresponded with the leading organ builders and theoreticians, Walcker, Bätz, Hill, Töpfer, and Dr. Gauntlett. He championed the establishment of international pitch, and tried the inventions of his colleagues, such as Walcker's chest with a separate pallet for each pipe.[9] But he was not one to pick up every new fashion because of its novelty or its stylish attraction. He did not like free reeds although he did manufacture them to sell to other organ builders; he made pipes for export voiced on wind pressures up to 15', while his own organs were winded on less than half that amount; he specified a 61-note manual compass for English customers while supporting a 56-note standard at home; and he proposed a stoplist for Norway that never would have suited a French customer in his time.

Cavaillé-Coll was truly an extraordinary man. Here are the words of Albert Dupré, father of Marcel, and organist at Saint-Ouen, Rouen: "Together with an artist's vision and a technically consummate knowledge, he possessed those precious human qualities that inspire liking, gratitude, and affection, the noblest and finest in our hearts. He was kind and benevolent, indulgent with everyone, and touchingly pleasant and easy with his voicers, those pupils of his with the souls of artists under their modest workmen's smocks. And yet he was always a great man, commanding respect and admiration."[10]

One of Cavaillé-Coll's many correspondents was Dr. Henry John Gauntlett (1806-1876), the radical Englishman who campaigned against the old G compass manuals in English organs. Gauntlett had suggested that all the organs built for the Great Exhibition in 1851 be wired up to a single console, so that they might be played separately or together. It was he who took out the first patent for the application of electricity as a communication between the keys and the pallets (1852), and who foresaw that electricity could be used to activate the pneumatic machines. It is quite likely that in the course of their dialogue Gauntlett told Cavaillé-Coll about his scientific activity. But Cavaillé-Coll did not offer to test any of his ideas.

"I received in due course your letter dated May 7, as well as that dated June 12, containing your idea for replacing conventional organ action with electro-magnets. I apologize for my delay in replying, but my everyday work has kept me from studying the matter you kindly submit for my judgment, and thus from answering your letter in as much detail as I desired.

"Until I can give further explanations, here is what I can say on the subject.

"I have not actually looked into the use of electro-magnets in organ building. We have a different scheme for making the key action light, a pneumatic lever invented by Mr. Barcker [sic] which we have simplified and improved. Using electricity would be possible and would, I believe, result in simplicity, as you intend; but keeping a battery charged in order to play an organ for only a few hours each week seems to me costly enough that this should be taken into consideration.

"The *pneumatic lever* has the advantage of deriving its energy from the very source that produces the sound: compressed air is required to make the pipes speak, and the same compressed air is used to overcome the stiffness of the conventional action.

"I must tell you also, so that you may know where your idea fits in, that several years ago Mr. Froment, one of our best electrical engineers, took me into his shop and showed me a keyboard for playing a set of bells; and that subsequently Mr. Stein, a maker of reed organs here in Paris, took out a patent for using electro-magnets with organ keyboards.

"I shall inquire as to the dates of Mr. Froment's appliance and to Mr. Stein's patent, and I shall send that information to you.

"Now if you think you should protect your idea by taking out a French patent, I am at your service for any and all formalities to be completed in your name.

"Yours truly, *etc.*

"P.S.   Kindly convey my respects to Mr. Mandel when you see him, and to Mr. Haas, the builder of the organ in the cathedral of Berne."[11]

In this letter we see Cavaillé-Coll encouraging another to go ahead with experiments in electricity, admitting that to simplify the organ's action with batteries, wires, and magnets was possible. However, he himself rejected the idea politely but firmly, on the basis of principle. The pneumatic machines were to be preferred because they drew energy from the organ's own source of energy, the wind, which also fed the pipes. Expense, inconvenience, lack of dependability, or the danger of fire were sufficient enough reasons for anyone to avoid electricity in those early days, and Cavaillé-Coll knew that much about it. But here he chose a larger issue. Believing that electricity did not belong in the organ, would he be likely to change his mind when someone found a way to make it work?

Of course electricity gained its adherents. That is proven by the following passage, published the same year, 1855, concerning Stein's work (from *Nouveau manual complet de l'organiste*, 1855).[12]

THE ELECTRO-MAGNETIC ORGAN

"We shall close this little volume with a discussion of a remarkable improvement to the organ, one just recently made. Even while it simplifies the action, it affords every possible advantage for performance: we do not think it possible that any further modifications of such significance can be made to that wonderful instrument.

"Every organist knows that before Barker's invention, the manual action was so stiff that it prevented the artist from playing with all the gentleness and rapidity he might need in order to produce certain effects which cannot be obtained otherwise. Today, thanks to the pneumatic Barker lever, installed mainly in large organs, the keys no longer have the stiffness they once did. Still, the motion is not relayed as rapidly as one might wish, and the action's numerous parts are an ever-present source of trouble.

"The long-desired rapidity has finally been obtained by M. Stein the younger. His path to discovery was in fact already marked, for everyone knows that when rapid mechanical results are desired, one usually turns to electricity. So it was that the old-fashioned telegraph gave way to the electric telegraph, which allows thoughts to be transmitted just as quickly as they occur, and over considerable distances.

"What remained for M. Stein the younger to do, then, was to find a means for applying the advantages of electro-magnetism to the organ, and we may say as of now that he has been successful.

"To replace all the complicated mechanism of the tracker action, all he needed was a metal wire running from the key to an electro-magnet placed beneath the pallet. The stop action and the couplers are just as simple.

"Even the bellows are operated by the same method. All the significant advantages of such a system are now plain to be seen, as is the precision that is thus introduced in all parts of the instrument. Rapidity of opening and closing the pallets, which thus seal the channels tightly, and regularity of wind pressure, such are the qualities dreamed of in organ building, qualities which have thus been achieved.

"We may say that M. Stein the younger has just carried his craft a long stride forward, and that his splendid discovery is destined to bring about a radical revolution in the building of organ actions. It is to be hoped that the electro-magnetic organ will replace the old ones and eliminate from the instrument an endless train of accessory parts. We hope we may be forgiven for not including further details of this interesting invention here, as it is the property of its creator.

"Moreover, M. Stein the younger has built an organ which he proposes to send to the Universal Exposition that is to be held in Paris, so that everyone may see for himself the advantages we have indicated.

"We can but express the desire that the great organ intended for the Crystal Palace at Sydenham may be an electro-magnetic organ, and we sincerely hope that this project may be carried out."

Stein and Son did, indeed, exhibit their organ played by electricity in the Paris Exhibition of 1855. According to Hinton, it 'contained many defects—prominent among which was the fact that the electric current proved insufficient to reliably govern the larger pallets'.[13] Cavaillé-Coll doubtless saw it, but was not impressed enough to change his views.

Cavaillé-Coll's conversations with Froment extended also to the question of the use of electric motors for supplying the wind to organs. On July 13, 1855, he wrote this following letter to a potential customer.[14]

"Mr. Duvivier, Saint-Ouen, near La-Ferté-sous-Jouarre
Sir,

"Enclosed please find the description you requested of the residential organ I built for Madame Viardot.

"Enclosed also a sketch of the floor plan and the location of the organ, and the dimensions of the case. As you can see, the irregular shape of the location made the work difficult and expensive. The figure of 10,000 f. I quote is not at all the net price, but rather our cost, without profit. However, I resume that the same organ built under less unusual circumstances would allow us a small profit.

"Concerning the mechanism for operating the bellows, it would be possible and easy to make: it is an outsized turnspit, and although I don't see its dimensions clearly, I suppose we could have it built for 700 or 800 f. However, I am not at all enthusiastic about this kind of machine, for even if we admit that it can be run for ten minutes, which would be a long time, it would take half that long to wind up the weight required to operate an organ of this size.

"When I built Madame Viardot's instrument, I should have liked to install an electric motor to drive the bellows, but after consulting the distinguished engineer Mr. Froment, I had to abandon the idea.

"The care and expense of maintaining a battery, quite apart from the difficulty and expense of installing the drive mechanism (in the opinion of the builder himself), forced us to discard the plan.

"Thus far, the simplest and most economical has been to operate the bellows by means of a pedal, or to have a boy work them with a handle.

"If you intend to purchase an organ like Madame Viardot's, you can send me the floor plan of the location you have in mind, and I shall give you my opinion.

"In case you wish to assign narrower limits to the cost of this organ, I enclose descriptions of two models of 2-manual organs at 6,000 and 5,000 f. respectively, excluding the case: the latter will be built to our specifications, plain or ornate.

"Hoping this information will be of use to you, *etc.*"

A few years later (1861), Albert Peschard, a teacher and organist in Cane, solicited the aid of Barker to work out his idea of applying electricity to the Barker pneumatic machines, rather than directly to the pallets in the windchest. This was shortly after Barker had embarked on his own organ building business in partnership with Verschneider, the respected voicer formerly with Ducroquet. Peschard's electro-pneumatic system was patented on June 6, 1864, and its first application was accomplished by Barker-Verschneider in a small organ at Salon (Bouches-du-Rhône). The only large instrument built by the partners was the famous electro-pneumatic instrument at St.-Augustin, Paris (1866-1868).

Cavaillé-Coll remained interested, but aloof. Peschard had not failed to seek his support by sending him a copy of the bulletin of the *Société des Beaux-Arts de Caen,* describing his electro-pneumatic system. Though Cavaillé-Coll responded with typical warmth and encouragement, nothing came of the conversations.

Some time later, Barker made a final attempt to penetrate Cavaillé-Coll's reserve, a meeting described by Cavaillé-Coll in a letter to Peschard on February 2, 1866. The relationship between these two early collaborators had been continuously strained since Barker had charged Cavaillé-Coll a double royalty for the second use of his pneumatic machine in 1842.

Cavaillé-Coll told Barker discreetly that he was still not interested: "I told Mr. Barker my position in this matter, namely that if the electricity were to appear useful in my work, I should rather ask him to take charge of it himself, than become involved with it directly."[15]

Had Cavaillé-Coll responded with enthusiasm to Barker's and Peschard's overtures, it is barely possible that electro-pneumatic action might have taken hold in France at this juncture. But two more important deterrents caused a temporary moratorium on developments. Those were the Franco-Prussian War of 1870, and the problems encountered with the organ at St.-Augustin. During the siege of Paris,

Barker's shop was ruined, and at sixty-four years of age he left France, never to return. In England, his electro-pneumatic action, which had been patented there in 1868, was ceded to Brycesson of London. Meanwhile, Cavaillé-Coll, whose projects were largely funded by the Imperial government, was confronted once again with an almost insurmountable financial crisis.[16] Though his imposing new workshop and residence on the Avenue du Maine were intact, the activity had practically ground to a halt. Very few organs were built for about a decade. This was no time for Cavaillé-Coll to embark on uncertain and costly ventures. Furthermore, he may not have changed his mind on the subject of the introduction of external sources of energy to the organ.

As to the second deterrent to continuing development of electric action in France, there were difficulties with and objections concerning the organ at St.-Augustin from the day it was inaugurated. Cavaillé-Coll had doubtless heard of them, and Peschard alluded to certain criticisms with considerable pique: "The inauguration was brilliant, but in that second application, certain incidents occurred later on which had nothing to do with the system itself. It was of course necessary to report those chance breakdowns, and to study them. But what comments, what fictitious reports were put forth and spread abroad, and with such brazen bad faith and treachery (actually, more to be scorned than feared)!"[17]

Reviewing general developments in electric action between 1868 and 1890, Hinton observed: "very powerful magnets, with costly batteries, were used *directly* to do comparatively severe and heavy work in opening the valves, admitting air to the pneumatic bellows or motors, which acted on the soundboard pallets. These large magnets involved strong electric currents, costly to produce, and, as will be seen, difficult to control.

"The main drawback and danger resulting from these strong currents was the possibility of *permanently* magnetizing the electro-magnet, thus creating a cipher; or, if the magnetizing were but transient, at least a failure of 'repetition'".[18]

Other difficulties mentioned by critics of Peschard's system were the danger during staccato playing of splashing mercury from the dipping contacts, the increased demands for wind in a system requiring both exhaust and pressure bellows, and the frequent need to replace batteries. The Committee charged with examining a new organ with electro-pneumatic action built by Merklin at Valenciennes (1891) stated the following about the Barker-Peschard instrument at St.-Augustin: "The instrument remained defective. Barker died without finding a remedy for the faults and the system was forgotten".[19] In 1886, after disputing the difficulties experienced at St.-Augustin, Bonnel, of Lyon, concluded: "that action requires considerable energy, and producing it requires current of the necessary power and steadiness. The system employed at St.-Augustin is destined to remain without descendants: it demands too much electro-magnetic energy, and the result-ing difficulties are enormous".[20]

It was Merklin, of Brussels and Lyon, who moved most aggressively with elec-tro-pneumatic action, having obtained exclusive rights for France to the invention patented (1833) by Schmoele and Mols, of Philadelphia. Though Debierre, of Nantes, had occasionally used electricity during the previous decade, there was no activity in Paris until Merklin broke the stalemate. The instrument was an *orgue de choeur*, installed in the chancel of the Church of Ste.-Clotilde in 1888. César Franck, the renowned organist at the *grand orgue* of Ste.-Clotilde, was a member of the committee charged with approving the project. The *Rapport* began: "An organ of electro-pneumatic design has just been installed in one of the leading churches in Paris. This is a historic event in organ building, because of the resources afford-ed by the system which the builders employed. It would be a mistake to expect Sainte-Clotilde to be a replica of the design essayed about twenty years ago by the late Mr. Barker".[21] Full of the customary praise, the report emphasized the com-mittee's approval of the use of the electric action to solve a difficult architectural problem. The console was situated among the choir pews, at some distance from the pipes, which were placed on either side of the chancel; the wind supply was hid-den behind the alter.

Many years earlier, in 1858, before the *grande orgue* at Ste.-Clotilde was fin-ished, Cavaillé-Coll had leased a small *orgue de choeur* to the church for interim use, a gesture that often resulted in a sale. Now, his old friend, César Franck, had declared himself in favor of an organ built by his chief competitor, and with elec-tric action as well. The following year (1889) Franck was again included among the experts reporting on a Merklin electro-pneumatic instrument for another Parisian church: St.-Jacques-du-Haut-Pas. This organ included a truly controversial feature, namely a single console placed behind the alter, which served not only for playing the *orgue de choeur* a short distance away from it, but also for the *grande orgue* at the other end of church, eighty meters away.

There were many objections. In the 1905 edition of the *Encyclopédie Roret* we note strong words of warning about the use of electricity to make organs playable at such a great distance.[22] Lavignac was quoted thus: "for the organist, an auditory torture such that only a deaf person could withstand it. . . this is the first step lead-ing to schemes that will allow organists to play services from home . . . and hear themselves over the telephone!"

Cavaillé-Coll would probably not have reproached Franck for approving Merklin's solution at Ste.-Clotilde, or even, perhaps for the controversial location of the console at St.-Jacques-du-Haut-Pas. But it must have given him pause when he lost a large contract to Merklin on the basis of this procedure. At Valenciennes, in

1891, Merklin offered to make both organs playable from one console, and won the contract.[23]

These events must have been a source of considerable frustration for Albert Peschard. In 1890, he published *Les premiéres applications de l'électricité*, in which he sought politely to remind the public of his work as a pioneer in the development of electro-pneumatic action, and of the similarities between his system, patented in 1864, and that of the Schmoele and Mols, being used by Merklin. But his patriotic ego was very much aroused in 1892 when the following statement appeared in *L'Aquitane*: "Electric organs originated in America. Invented by Messrs. Schmoele and Mols of Philadelphia, they were greeted with skepticism by French builders. M. Merklin alone saw that they represented the future. Paris had still not accepted the marvelous innovation when the church of Saint-Clotilde adopted it (1888)". Peschard pounced angrily on this statement in a pamphlet published that very month.[24]

Despite the success that Merklin was enjoying with his electric action, there seems to have been no substantial change in Cavaillé-Coll's viewpoint during the last decade of his life. However, there is one remarkable action that was not mentioned by Peschard in his attempts to win Cavaillé-Coll to his own cause. The incident takes us back to the organ at St.-Augustin in Paris, and can be considered Cavaillé-Coll's last statement on electricity in organ building, cancelling out his many diplomatic responses made to those who were eager for his endorsement.

The care of the Barker-Peschard instrument at St.-Augustin had been entrusted to Férat, who was connected with the Barker-Verschneider enterprise until he left Paris in 1889. At that point, Cavaillé-Coll was awarded the contract for maintenance. In a letter to Peschard (1890), Cavaillé-Coll noted that his twenty-six-year-old son, who had been experimenting with electricity, was given responsibility for the instrument at St.-Augustin. This letter, published by Peschard after the death of the great builder, formed the core of Peschard's argument that Cavaillé-Coll was sympathetic to electricity. The text of the letter follows, dated October 4, 1890, as quoted by Peschard:[25]

"I learn with great satisfaction that you are going to publish a work on the application of electricity to organs. As you were one of the first promoters of that new system, it will be easy for you to relate its history. I have not forgotten your efforts to introduce me to your discoveries; but after having done my part in another direction, I have not had the courage to undertake new studies for which I am not prepared.

"At the moment one of my sons, age twenty-six, is working on electricity and has already done some good experimental studies. I have assigned him to the restoration of the organ at St.-Augustin. Still today that organ is the most important that has been made with the electrical system.

"In the preliminary restorative work, we did not change the system, as it still functions very well after twenty-five years.

"Later, it will be a question of serious work on the voicing and the specification, but Mr. Gigout, the erudite organist at St.-Augustin, agrees with us that the electrical system should be saved, along with appropriate improvements."

Shortly afterwards, Cavaillé-Coll's son left the business. But that would not have served to warn Peschard of what would occur, as the letter quoted above gives no hint that Cavaillé-Coll might have been dissatisfied with the operation of the notorious electro-pneumatic action. In 1998, on the eve of his retirement, Cavaillé-Coll chose to discard the electro-pneumatic action altogether, and to replace it with his own conventional pneumatic machines and tracker action.

Cavaillé-Coll's reasons for deciding on this "act of vandalism", as Hinton called it[26], may never be fully known. Was it, as Hinton states, "through utter senile impotency"? Cavaillé-Coll was, after all, eighty-seven years old. Or was it the only way the seasoned builder could see to give that instrument a reliable future? He was sacrificing an old and genial association, but felt the professional obligation to re-emphasize part of the creed that had governed most of his artistic career: "The pneumatic lever has the advantage of deriving its energy from the very source that produces the sound."

APPENDIX A

Views on Diverse Matters

The Cavaillé-Coll letters and contracts preserved in Mme. Lapresté's dossiers cover only a portion of the organ builder's long career. They take us as far as December 1859, when the organ at Ste.-Clotilde was completed and the monumental work at St.-Sulpice was in progress. Thirty years had gone by since Aristide was sent alone to Lérida to work on the cathedral organ. In September 1832, Aristide was discovered in Toulouse by Rossini: thirty years later, he completed his greatest organ, the one for St.-Sulpice. That same year, 1862, also saw the publication of Franck's *Six Pièces*, which like Titelouze's *Hymnes de l'Église* were masterpieces without antecedents. We have seen that in little more than thirty years Cavaillé-Coll contributed substantially to that sudden, almost miraculous flowering of Franck's genius as a composer for the organ, as well as creating the French Romantic organ itself.

We have attempted in our various appendices to give the essential contracts and progress reports for the instruments discussed in the text, leaving to future students an extended analysis of the hundreds of proposals not mentioned in this volume. In selecting the letters, our aim has been to provide the reader with a chronological account in Cavaillé-Coll's own words of the progress of his career, the influence political events had upon it, and the financial structure of his company. Students of Cavaillé-Coll's work will wish to refer to the microfilm prints of the entire Lapresté collection, which are available at the Library of the Department of Music at Duke University, or to the films themselves, which are deposited at the library of the Oberlin College Conservatory of Music.

This volume is intended to be neither a treatise on organ building in the 19th century nor a statistical survey of Cavaillé-Coll's surviving instruments. Should the student wish to find exact data on pipe scales, cut-up, chest measurements, key dip, and so on, he may refer to the surviving instruments themselves, or to articles written about them. As for Cavaillé-Coll's standards with regard to scales, weights of pipe metal, or prices, a wealth of information remains to be examined in the Lapresté dossier.

In the following pages, we have drawn from the letters and contracts to quote Cavaillé-Coll on numerous topics.

I. Placement and Acoustics
Lettres I, #817
To Mr. Lenormand, Government Architect, Paris   June 4, 1842

"Enclosed please find a specification for a choir or accompaniment organ capable of producing all the effects required for sustaining and accompanying the choir, as well as allowing the performance of the various selections necessary in the worship service.

"The location of the organ in the church is one of the chief factors determining the sound of the instrument. We must bring this point to your attention, for it is of capital importance both for savings that may be realized in building the organ, and for the effectiveness and power which may result from a favorable location.

"In our opinion, the best location for an organ is as low as possible and as near the center of the church as possible, away from the walls of the building. In this way, as theory indicates and experience confirms, the sound-waves may spread without obstacle: they acquire the greatest possible volume since they are generated in dense air, and travel upwards into progressively thinner air. The sound emanates from the organ in all directions, thanks to a location away from the walls of the building; and the tone and volume are thereby increased.

"The effectiveness of choir organs is a concrete example of the theoretical remarks just made.

"*Grandes orgues* are usually located over the doors of churches, on galleries of various heights, according to the architectural scheme of the building. They lose considerable power because they are far removed from the choir, high above the floor, and enclosed between the walls of the building: the instrument cannot emit sound except through its facade, and consequently loses power.

"As a result, in order that a *grand orgue* possess a volume commensurate with the size of the church, the size of the instrument must be significantly increased so as to fit inside it a larger number of stops: this inevitably increases the expense, sometimes as much as four times what would be required in order to produce the same effects with a choir organ in a suitable location.

"A further advantage of choir organs is that they can both play the service and accompany the choir.

"The foregoing remarks will enable you, Sir, to decide, with reference to the funds the church council may appropriate for the purchase of the organ, whether to locate it in the choir or over the entrance door. In the latter case, a much larger instrument would be required, costing at least twice the price of the organ we suggest. We shall send the specification on your request.

"Please be assured, Sir, that we shall faithfully execute any work you may assign us.   Yours,

"N.B. — sent him a copy of the Specifications on p. 22 of the file, including the price of 7,000 francs for the organ, packing, and shipping. The price of a plain organ-case was estimated at 1,000 francs. Case dimensions:

Height   3m.50 to 5m.
Width   2m.50 to 3m.
Depth   1m.20 to 1m.50."

Advice for a church with a very long nave and a low ceiling elevation:
Lettres V, # 3345, November 29, 1856.
". . . Placed thus at the entrance to the choir, near the center of the nave, the organ could project its sound in all directions, and even its gentlest, sweetest tones could be heard in all parts of the church."

Lettres V, #3509, September 9, 1857
". . . However, I must emphasize that I sold the Saint-Paterne organ for installation in the choir, where it would have been most effective for accompaniment. Nevertheless, contrary to my wishes, it was installed in a gallery, where I knew it would not produce the desired effect . . . Furthermore, I need not remind you, Father, that Saint-Paterne is not only the least attractive but also the least resonant church in the entire diocese, and therefore provides the worst acoustical setting for judging the worth of an instrument."

II. *Positif-de-dos*; solidity in gallery construction.
Lettres V, #4242, September 16, 1859 (St.-Martin à Roubaix)
". . . Following our last conversation and my recent inspection of the site, I consider that it would be most suitable from an artistic viewpoint to have the *Positif* stand in front of the main case. The instrument would also benefit, from a tonal viewpoint."

Lettres VI, #4349, December 15, 1859 (Langon)
". . . The only shortcut we have taken upon ourselves to make, in order to stay within the limits imposed by the contract price, is doing away with the little *Positif* case shown in our first plan: it had no effect on the tonal quality of the organ."

Lettres VI, #4350, December 15, 1859 (Belleville)
". . . we consider that adding a *Positif* case would contribute nothing to the tonal quality of the organ and would require most of the money that the architect could save in designing the case. Adding an independent *Pédale* would be a more substantial contribution to the effectiveness of the organ."

Lettres II, #1123, July 26, 1845 (Ajaccio)

". . . The organ-case, comprising two cabinets, one for the main part of the instrument, called the *Grand orgue,* and the other for the *Positif,* could be modified in such a way as to house the entire organ in the main case, if this were necessary in order to place the orchestra in the organ-loft and keep the singers from being hidden by the *Positif* case.

"The organ itself would be mounted on a frame separate from the case: we shall build this frame and install it at Ajaccio. Our only instructions for you are to make the gallery floor quite solid, not only so that it may bear the weight of the organ, which is considerable, but to make the floor rigid, so that the action of the organ may not be disturbed as a result of settling in the floor.

"Finally, Sir, if you have the case built at Ajaccio, and if you have changes to make in its dimensions or design, we should be obliged if you would send us a tracing of such changes, so that we may judge whether they interfere with the organ itself. Since this case need support only the pipes mounted in the facade, it may be of as light a construction as you think suitable."

III. Detached console.

Devis II, #119, April 18, 1845 (Notre-Dame-de-Metz)

"The manuals shall be installed in a desk-shaped cabinet standing in front of the case, so that the organist shall face the high altar . . ."

Lettres IV, #2132, January 16, 1852

"Mounting the console on a case forward of the organ and facing the altar is indeed to be preferred."

IV. Musical function of the case.

Lettres V, #3386, February 6, 1857 (St.-Paterne, Orléans)

". . . As for the idea of opening the rear doors in order to increase the volume of sound, I do not favor it at all. Apart from the damage that might occur to the instrument, this small increase in noise would destroy the most valuable resources of the organ, to wit: the expression and blending of the stops."

V. Disposition of Stops

a. The *Plein Jeu,* survival of Dom Bédos *Cymbale* disposition

Lettres I, #801, February 26, 1842 (to Dumas, Toulouse)

"We should point out that our *Plein-jeu* consists of the three highest ranks of the *Cymbale* given in Dom Bédos' book. We have numbered the pipes as shown in the book, so you can plant each pipe in its location by following the chart."

b. Suppression of the *Plein Jeu* in small organs.

Lettres III, #1720, April 16, 1850 (to Maillard, Le Havre)
"... For example, the *Plein Jeu* could be replaced by a *Flûte octaviante.*"

Lettres II, May 19, 1845 (Oratoire)
"However, if the Consistory could increase the expenditure, we would suggest a useful addition, to wit: first, replacing the *Mixture* on manual I with a *Flûte.*"

Lettres IV, #2339, December 9, 1852
"I have omitted a *Plein-jeu* from the specification in the belief that since this organ is intended principally for vocal accompaniment, it would seldom need the high, piercing tones of the *Plein-jeu* which, according to you, would not suit the great resonance of the church."

c. The Progressive Mixtures

From the early years, Cavaillé-Coll departed radically from traditional commitments to what is known today as classical tonal design. While he held firmly to the proven technical standards of the craft, referring often to Dom Bédos, his musical aims would have been quite unacceptable to his distinguished predecessor, François-Henri Cliquot. Nevertheless, in early proposals, Cavaillé-Coll is known to have advised that classical *pleins jeux* be preserved, as he did for the church of St.-Laurent in 1836. But, it was inevitable that the classical mixtures should be transformed or discarded, as they sounded "high and piercing" in the trebles with increased wind pressure. Inevitably they would go the way of the *Flageolets, Tierces, Larigots,* and *Cornets.* Cavaillé-Coll responded to his appetite for fundamental strength in the trebles by developing "progressive mixtures". These mixtures, whose primary purpose was to strengthen the trebles of the harmonic trumpets, had no breaks, but added more and more ranks toward the upper range of the keyboard. Thus the traditional bond between mixtures and the plenum was severed.

Cavaillé-Coll's disposition for the harmonic (progressive) mixtures of the *Grand Orgue* and *Positif* at Notre-Dame-de-Paris (1868) are given below, from his notebook. Note the *Tierce* in the *Cymbale.*

Notre-Dame-de-Paris

Grand Orgue, Fourniture harmonique

	10⅔	8	5⅓	4	2⅔
C				4	2⅔
c			5⅓	4	2⅔
c′		8	5⅓	4	2⅔
c″	10⅔	8	5⅓	4	2⅔

Grand Orgue, Cymbale harmonique

	1	1⅓	1⅗	2⅔	2
C				2⅔	2
c			1⅗	2⅔	2
c′		1⅓	1⅗	2⅖	2
c″	1	1⅓	1⅗	2⅖	2

Positif, Plein jeu harmonique III - VI

	16	8	5⅓	4	2⅔	2
C				4	2⅔	2
c			5⅓	4	2⅔	2
a		8	5⅓	4	2⅔	2
f#′	16	8	5⅓	4	2⅔	2

d. Harmonic pipes

Lettres IV, #2373, January 9, 1853 (to Dr. Gauntlett)

"The compass of the harmonic stops I have built thus far has always been 4½ octaves, C to F. However, the harmonic pipes proper begin only with a C pipe 4 pieds long, thus sounding 2′ C. Thus, the three harmonic stops:

1. *Flûte harmonique* 8′, C to F, 54 notes, is composed of 24 conventional pipes, followed by 30 harmonic pipes.
2. *Flûte octaviante* 4′, C to F, 54 notes, has 12 conventional pipes, followed by 42 harmonic pipes.
3. *Octavin* 2′, C to F, 54 notes, begins with a pipe 4 pieds long speaking at 2′ pitch and has 54 harmonic pipes."

e. Mutations

Lettres VI, #3945, January 20, 1859

"We quite agree with your first comment: the *Quinte*, which recurs naturally in the *Plein-jeu harmonique*, shall be replaced by a 4′ *Dulciana* stop."

Devis III, #232, August 21, 1849 (Notre-Dame-de-Valenciennes)

"The following new stops shall be made and installed in the place of several stops in the present organ which sound poor and are never used.

    1. A *Gambe* 8′ instead of the *Gros Nazard.*

    2. A *Gambe* 4′ instead of the *Grosse Tierce.*

    3. A *Flûte octaviante* instead of the *Flûte* 4′.

    4. An *Octavin harmonique* instead of the *Tierce.*"

Devis IV, #674, December 15, 1854 (Notre-Dame-des-Victoires, Paris)

"The *Nazard* and *Tierce* stops, whose strident tones cause them to be avoided by our best organists and always remain silent, shall be replaced to good advantage by the following foundation stops, which have a more pleasing tone when used singly, and blend better in combinations."

VI. Wind and Pressure

a. See above, p. 18 ff. for basic tenets.
b. For typical arguments for multiple-pressure bellows, see page 93.
c. Wind Pressures for pipes made for export.

Devis I, #298, 1847 (Liverpool)

    Grand Orgue: Trompette, Cor anglais, Clairon: 35 centimeters
    Positif: Cor anglais, Basson: 30 centimeters
    Pédale: Trompette 16′, Basson 16′, Clairon 8′: 35 centimeters

Lettres III, #2011, June 26, 1851, (Dublin)

"As you request, the wind pressure will be 64 mm. of water."
d. Typical views on "improving" old wind systems:

Lettres IV, #2426, March 7, 1853 (Pézénas)

". . . Surely it would also be preferable to replace the old bellows, which supply unsteady wind, with a large reservoir . . . I am aware that everything cannot be anticipated at the outset of such a job, but experience has already more than proven to me that repairs of that kind almost always force me to build everything new."

Devis V, #847, February 11, 1859, Compiègne

"The present bellows shall be releathered so as to make them wind-tight, and the mechanism shall be designed for operation by two pedals, enabling the blower to exert greater power with less fatigue. In addition, various regulators and reservoirs shall be added, so as to store a greater volume of air and adjust the wind-pressure near the chests."

e. Insufficiency
Lettres I, #1014, November 11, 1844
  "Your organ sounds like an orchestra where all the wind instruments are played by consumptives."

VII. Pipes
a. Materials
  The materials to be used for new pipes were often listed in contracts. But Cavaillé-Coll seldom discussed these matters in detail. An early exception is found in the appendix to the proposal for restoring the organ in St. Laurent, Paris, 1836. We quote the entire proposal below:

Specification
for Additions to this Organ, Required to Restore it to its Original Disposition or Replace Defective Parts, and Improve its Mechanism Throughout.
  1. The case-pipes for the *Grand Orgue* adorning the case are extremely thin and oxidized, so that their walls are weak and porous. The pipes cannot vibrate properly, and as a result they cannot produce the volume of sound they should. Moreover, these case-pipes are poorly made: the tin used in them is of poor quality, and it contains a considerable admixture of lead and zinc.
  All these case-pipes should be replaced with new ones made of first-quality, pure tin. The thickness of metals used here and in all pipes can be controlled precisely by means of tools which allow us to measure them exactly and without guesswork. Since we can keep the correct proportions of thickness, length, and diameter, we achieve uniformity of tone throughout the compass of a stop. All these pipes would be hammered, to make the metal denser, and they would be polished and burnished with the greatest care.
  2. The three stops that seem once to have stood in the *Grand orgue* should be restored:

1. A *Quarte de Nazard* or *Flûte* 2′, of pure tin	50 pipes
2. A *Fourniture* of V Ranks, of pure tin	250 pipes
3. A *Cymbale* III Ranks, of pure tin	150 pipes
	450 pipes

  3. The *Grosse Tierce* in the *Grand orgue* should be replaced by a *Tierce* sounding the octave of the former. The *Tierce*, sounding a tenth above the *Prestant*, could be used in various registrations: *Cornet, Tierce*, etc., without the unpleasant effect or harsh tone of the *Grosse Tierce* in the various combinations, it being too close to the fundamental.
  Substituting the *Tierce* for the *Grosse Tierce* could be done without charge, as follows: The *Dessus de Tierce* would be installed in place of the *Grosse Tierce*, and the lowest octave would be supplied from the pipes eliminated. The metal in the remaining pipes would about offset the cost of the substitution.

4. The *Dessus de Tierce* should be replaced with a *Dessus de Flûte* 4′, consisting of 39 new pipes of pure tin. This stop could be used alone for flute solos, and it would combine with various registrations such as foundations, *Cornet, Plein-jeu,* etc., rounding out their tone.

5. On the *Positif* chest, there seem to have been two stops, whose locations and controls still exist.

1. A *Plein-jeu* V Ranks		250 pipes
2. A *Doublette*		50 pipes
	Total	300 pipes

These two stops should be restored, using new pipes of pure tin. Thus the organ would be returned to its original disposition, and it would recover the true character of religious music, which it has lost apparently through malice or ignorance.

6. In this organ, the bass or foundation stops lack energy. The *Pédale* or accompaniment stops are higher than the manual stops instead of being lower: the two *Pédale* flues are labeled *Pédale de Flûte* 16′ and 8′ respectively, but they reveal only 8′ and 4′ pipes.

A *Pédale de Flûte* 16′ could be added without interfering with the stops already installed, and this addition would give the *Pédale* or accompaniment tones as deep as those already available on the manuals. Since these tones would be of considerable volume and power, they would pervade the entire tonal structure, and their beautiful voice would impart the awesome character of religious music.

7. The *Récit* chest could be fitted with a box enclosing all the stops and imitating echo effects: this box could be opened gradually so as to simulate a pleasing crescendo.

8. Since the four manual keyboards have acquired a great deal of play, they require extensive repair: they would be better replaced with new keyboards, the naturals capped with ivory and the sharps with ebony, and the frames of rosewood; all parts made with precision. The new keyboards would be stationary; in other words, they would not slide forward for coupling, as in conventional organs, but instead a simple and original mechanism would enable the organist to play the *Grand orgue* and *Positif* together or separately, without disturbing his performance. Thus he could increase or decrease the volume, depending on the number of stops drawn on the various manuals.

9. The pedalboard is in at least as poor condition as the manual (sic).

This pedal keyboard could also be replaced, and in this case it would be designed in the German style, etc. (see *Devis* I, #2, art. 12, Appendix B).

10. All the trackers connected to the various manuals should be provided with adjusting nuts, to facilitate leveling the keys.

11. Once rebuilt as specified under Repairs, restored according to its original disposition, provided with a *Pédale de Flûte* 16′, and improved mechanically as specified above, this organ would be most admirably suited to the nave into which it speaks. By restoring the *Plein-jeu* of the *Grand orgue* and *Positif*, and by adding a *Pédale de Flûte* 16′, the instrument would have everything needed for religious music: the gentle, supple tones of a good *plein jeu*, and the impressive, deep voices of the *Pédale de Flûte,* a rich source of those sublime effects that uplift the soul and inspire religious feeling.

Itemized Estimate of the Additions Specified Above

1. Case-pipes for the *Grand orgue,* made of pure English tin, hammered, polished, and burnished as described in Article 1, would cost   6,000 fr.

2. The *Quarte de Nazard, Fourniture,* and *Cymbale,* totaling 450 pipes of pure Bangka tin, hammered, would cost   1,000 fr.

3. Changing the *Grosse Tierce* into a *Tierce* an octave higher would occasion no expense (as stated in the same article of the Specification): we would either take the 39 remaining pipes or leave them at the disposal of the council. The substitution would cost   30 fr.

4. The *Dessus de Flûte* 4′ to replace the *Dessus de Tierce* 39 pipes made of pure Bangka tin, hammered, would cost   100 fr.

5. The *Doublette* and the *Plein jeu* for the *Positif,* 300 pipes, would cost   300 fr.

6. The *Pédale de Flûte* 16′ stop, consisting of 20 very large pipes made of select Northern pine, and varnished inside and out to improve tone and durability, together with two chests and actions, would cost   1,200 fr.

7. The four manual keyboards, built as described in the Specification, with coupler mechanism and control pedal so that the organist may couple *Grand orgue* and *Positif* at will, would cost   700 fr.

8. The pedalboard of German design, as described in the Specification, made of fine oak, with the naturals capped in brass and the sharps in copper, smoothed and polished with care, would cost   250 fr.

9. The tracker-ends with adjusting nuts to level the keyboards, as described in the Specification, would cost   150 fr.

Total	10,000 fr.
Repairs	5,000 fr.
Total for both Specifications	15,000 fr.

Note

Let us point out here that if the council decided not to authorize this expenditure and were satisfied with the organ as it is, repaired but not restored, we could follow the first Specification for repairs only, which totals   5,000 fr.

Let us also point out that if it were desired to restore the organ at a later time and return it to its original disposition, as described in the second Specification, we could no longer charge the same, for we would have to dismantle the organ a second time, as for repairs.

Let us now point out that if we were charged with repairing the organ or restoring it as we have specified, we would require the council to supply us the scaffolding necessary for dismantling the instrument and laying down various parts, as well as space for working on the repairs.

The time required for repairing the organ as specified would be four to five months, and if we made the additions at the same time, seven or eight months would be required for completion.

Appendix to the Specification for Restoration, Explaining the
Qualities of Tin Used in Making the Pipes for Various
Ranks, and Concerning the Thickness of Pipe-Metal,
in Relation to Diameter.

The resonators or bodies of all new pipes will be made of pure, first-quality tin, with no alloy whatever.

There are two kinds of tin, both very ductile, but with different degrees of malleability, which property allows us to use both to good advantage in various stops, according to the tone- quality sought.

English tin is extremely stiff and has a brilliant sheen. It is also highly ductile, which enables us to forge it with a trip-hammer to close the pores: thus treated, it is very dense and best suited to making large pipes, whether case-pipes or reeds. Since these pipes are very heavy, especially when the thickness of their walls is proportional to their diameter; if the metal is not stiff and evenly forged, the pipes collapse of their own weight. The mouths are deformed and no longer speak, and repair becomes difficult and extremely costly.

Moreover, if the tin used in case-pipes contained the slightest admixture, the pipes would soon lose their sheen; and depending on the amount of alloy, they could oxidize from contact with the air, as the case-pipes in this organ have done.

Bangka or India tin is extremely mild, flexible, and malleable as well. Once forged so as to close the pores, it is well suited to making small pipes for the *plein-jeu, dessus de flûte,* and other treble stops. The timbre of such pipes is very mellow, and tuning them is easy, as they readily submit to reducing or enlarging at the top, by use of the tuning-cone.

The quality of tone and the uniformity of timbre, volume, and power of the pipes, all depend on the proportion between length and diameter, the quality and density of the metal, and especially the precise control of the thickness of the metal, and its relation to diameter.

Since organ-building has been our family's craft for over a century, tradition as well as experience enables us to determine the best relation between thickness and diameter. We have set it at one-hundredth the diameter, and we have made tools that enable us to measure it precisely, without guesswork. We give all our pipes the same proportion of thickness to diameter, so that a large 32′ pipe 50cm. in diameter has walls 5mm. thick.

A 16′ pipe 30cm. in diameter is 3mm. thick.

An 8′ pipe 15.7cm. in diameter is 1.57mm. thick.

A 4′ pipe 11.5cm. in diameter is 1.15mm. thick, and so forth.

Since the diameters of pipes between 32′ C and 16′ C, and between the latter and 8′ C, decrease by geometric progression, their thickness also decreases in geometric progression: the thirteenth terms are those we have given for the thickness of C in the various octaves.

The foregoing comments appended to our Specification, if compared to the samples of tin we provide, will illustrate the quality of the materials we use, and the care with which we prepare them.

1. All case-pipes shall be made of English tin, forged, polished, and burnished like sample A.

2. All *plein jeu* and *flûte* pipes shall be made of Bangka tin, forged like sample B.

3. If reed stops were to require restoration, they would be made of English tin, hammered like sample C.

4. The thickness of metal in every pipe shall be precisely one-hundredth the diameter of the pipe.

b. Use of zinc.

Lettres I, #89, July 16, 1840

"For our part, we are completeley confident that these zinc pipes would fulfill the required conditions of soundness, resonance and durability at least as well as tin pipes.

Devis V, #841, January 25, 1859 (Cambrai Cathedral)

"On the other hand the reed pipes are made of zinc rather than tin, as is customarily being done in good building."

Lettres VI, #4042, April 15, 1859

"This organ, estimated at 5,000 francs without previous examination, was so poorly built that the chests and action would only be good for kindling, and the pipes, for the most part tin-plated zinc and poor material, wouldn't bring 500 francs worth of decent material."

c. Montre pipes.

Lettres V, #3278, September 11, 1856

". . . the sounds of the *montre* pipes are always the most beautiful in the organ." See also p. 153 above, on case pipes for St.-Laurent, Paris.

d. Hammering.

Devis I, #1, 1833 (Notre-Dame-de-Lorette)

(The metal for) "all the interior pipes shall be rolled to the correct thickness and trip-hammered to achieve greater density, thereby making the tone quality even better."

e. Pitch

Devis IV, #675, December 22, 1854 (St.-Merry, Paris)

The pitch should be raised one half tone, and ". . . to conform to the present pitch of modern instruments, the organ should be tuned to standard pitch, with A at 880 cycles per-second."

f. Free Reeds

For the reasons for Cavaillé-Coll's rejection of free reeds, see *Lettres* IV, #2132, January 16, 1852, in Appendix A.

Lettres II, #1107, June 21, 1845

"As for the stops you want, the *Euphone* and the *Cor Anglais*, I have heard them in the Daublaine organs. They may be good for solos, but never in tune and that is detestable."

VIII. Registration and Technique

a. Registration

Lettres I, #138, October 5, 1840

"The 8' stops are never too numerous in organs. They are the principal pitch upon which all harmony is based, and should therefore predominate."

Lettres IV, #2132, January16, 1852

"The *grand choeur* would not be complete without the *Bombarde, Trompette,* and *Clairon* in the *Grand orgue*, sustained in the bass by a 16' *Bombarde* and an 8' *Trompette*.

"Increasing the number of 8' stops would not add much to the volume of sound, but only to the variety of timbres available."

Lettres IV, #2970, April 14, 1855

"Remember, the bigger the crowd, the more you play loud (no rhyme intended)."

Lettres V, #3151, February 27, 1856

"As for the *Voix humaine* and *Voix celeste* effects, they are imitated by a *Tremulant* which when used with a *Flûte* produces a *Voix celeste;* and with the *Hautbois*, a *Voix humaine*."

Lettres V, #4077, May 10, 1859

"I fear that eliminating all the high-pitched stops will deprive the organ of many colorful effects that can be obtained by combinations with other stops. The *Doublette* together with the *Bourdon* 8 imitates the *galoubet*. The *Octavin* with the *Hautbois* is an almost perfect imitation of the *musette*. Even the *Picolo* (sic) which by itself is insignificant, produces a marvelous bell-like effect in certain registrations."

b. On the *Orage*
Lettres V, #3255, July 29, 1856

"As for the storm effect you request me to add to the organ, it can readily be achieved by playing several bass notes at once, but we shall fit a pedal enabling the organist to produce this effect with one foot." This pedal device was offered in dozens of proposals for organs of all sizes. At St.-Sulpice (1862) it was called *tonnerre* (thunder).

c. On *demi-jeux*
Lettres VI, #4086, May 20, 1859

"We build no divided stops, for our new composition pedals enable the organist to play the bass and treble of each reed and mutation stop separately. This new design furnishes eleven more stops without extra knobs; and the composition pedals have the added advantage of enabling the organist to vary and shade the tones of the stops as cannot be done by conventional means."

d. *Tremblant*

Tremulants operated on the *Voix humaine* alone, as for Dinan (*Devis* II, p. 48), Algiers (*Devis* III, p. 354), or Lannion (*Devis* IV, p. 64); or on the entire *Récit* division as for Ste.- Clotilde, above; or on both the *Récit* and *Positif*, as for Manila (*Devis* III, p. 292), and for La Madeleine, Paris.

e. Articulation, "expression", and technique
Lettres IV, #2170, March 9, 1852

"The *Cromorne,* like the *Voix humaine,* would be more effective in the *Récit* division, where the swell box allows the tone to be softened."

Lettres IV, #2628, December 5, 1853

"I should prefer to place the *Cromorne* under expression, to soften the harsh tone always found in this stop unless heard in a large church."

Lettres V, #3151, February 27, 1856

The *Voix humaine* is effective only in a large organ and very far from the audience, so that the sour, shrill tones are mellowed by the distance."

Lettres IV, #2394, January 28, 1853

"Ladies usually have rather clever fingers, but they are seldom skilled in the use of the feet."

Lettres VI, #3988, February 21, 1859

". . . although the organ is sturdily built, it is unfortunate that is should be entrusted to a young man who, as you say, has not studied the organ as a specialty. Although the keyboard is the same as that of a piano, the playing technique is entirely different. The organ requires a *legato* style, while the piano demands a crisp attack: used on the organ, this technique not only produces a poor effect, but causes frequent disorders in the action. Therefore, Sir, it would be preferable from the standpoint of the organ's durability that no other hands play it than those of the accomplished organist of Saint-Louis-d'Antin, or at very least persons whom he considers able to play it."

VI. Restoration
a. General Policy
Lettres V, #3555, November 27, 1857

". . . we have concluded that no restoration would be truly thorough and lasting unless the entire action were replaced, incorporating all the improvements made in instrument building in our time. Thus, the bellows, chests, and action would be replaced.

Pipework that was designed and built to the best standards would be retained in part. However, all the stops from the old organ that are present in the new disposition would be significantly improved. Furthermore, we propose to replace with new stops a few old ones that sound poor and are rarely used today."

Lettres V, #3090, December 12, 1855

". . . we consider it our duty to propose a thorough job, replacing old stops that are seldom or never used with new ones whose tone is more religious and thus better suited to worship services."

Lettres V, #3120, January 19, 1856

". . . but I can say that a single division of the present organ will be more effective than all the old divisions together."

". . . restoration and improvement required by the organ in your church, to return it to perfect condition, improve on its original design, and bring it up to date with modern techniques.

Lettres IV, #2804, July 15, 1854

"The entire action and the bellows, chests and keyboards from the old organ, which are no longer usable, would be entirely replaced according to modern practices."

b. On eliminating the classical *Récit* and *Echo*
Devis V, #846, February 7, 1859 (Tours Cathedral)
"The last two divisions ought to be done away with, as they are incomplete and bear little relation to the others: they should be replaced with a new *Récit* division having the full compass of the other divisions."

Lettres IV, #3662, March 9, 1858
"If we were talking about a junky little 2 to 2½ octave *Récit*, like those found in old organs, we could easily find room for it . . ."

Despite the prevailing attitudes toward early organs and lack of interest in preserving them, Cavaillé-Coll held François-Henri Cliquot in high regard:

Lettres VI, #4000, March 5, 1859
"As for the little three-stop *Récit*, . . . it is a fine little specimen of the Cliquot's work . . . the *Hautbois* is one of the best-made and most successful that can be found."

VII. Policy and Sales
a. Delivery of stock organs
Lettres V, #3293, September 26, 1856
"The last two instruments are in storage and could be ready one month after the order date. The other models could not be shipped until about three months after ordering.

"Since the last eight-stop model is entirely under expression, it could be temporarily installed without a case."

Lettres V, #3409, February 26, 1857
"As for your inquiry concerning organs in storage, we have a few of four, five, six, and eight stops that are ready for installation."

Lettres V, #3154, February 29, 1856
An organ for export: "This organ will be set up and voiced in our shop, where it can be tried by a musician of your choosing before it is packed."

The earliest list of stock organs is found in *Lettres* I, #50, April 1, 1840, in Appendix A; of second-hand organs, in *Lettres* I, #157, December 18, 1840. See also for lists of stock organs *Lettres* I, #176, March 12, 1841; IV, #2832, September 4, 1854; IV, #2440, April 12, 1853; V, #3077, November 10, 1855.

There were also booklets published advertising stock organs: *Maison A. Cavaillé-Coll, orgues de tous modèles*, Paris, 1889.

c. Delivery of custom-built organs
Lettres V, #3302, October 8, 1856

"The time required for building and installing the organ would be no more than one year from the date of the contract, with a penalty of 25 francs for each day's delay."

d. Sub-contracting

There was a long association with Ménard at Coutances, who made pipes and even small organs for Cavaillé-Coll, and with numerous other manufacturers who supplied parts and pipes. The first pipes Ménard made for Cavaillé-Coll were a *Flûte 8'*, a *Prestant*, a *Doublette*, and a *Trompette*. In 1845, Cavaillé-Coll asked him to make a *Trompette* with C 8' "about 13cm. in diameter". By the 1850's Ménard was supplying small organs, completely voiced.

Cavaillé-Coll bought keyboards   and even casework:

Lettres V, #3289, September 22, 1856
"The quotation you sent us of the price for the case you have built is not acceptable . . ."

But he also made pipes to sell to others. One of his regular customers was Mr. Telford in Dublin. To Mr. Burk in Paris, he listed prices for separate ranks; in 1854, he sent a *Trompette* and an *Hautbois* to Hoogbuys in Bruges, and in 1858, he sold several ranks and a pneumatic machine to Mr. Courcelle in Paris: ". . . these stops shall be entirely finished, voiced, and tuned to standard concert pitch . . .

Voix humaine 8', 56 notes	400
Cor anglais 8', free reed	450
Flûte harmonique 4'	350
Pneumatic machines	1200"

e. Commissions

Although Cavaillé-Coll did not charge consulting fees,   he allowed professional reductions on pipes or complete organs sold for re-sale or export. For unvoiced pipes the discount could amount to 20%,   while representatives buying stock instruments for foreign markets divided the profit with Cavaillé-Coll, each keeping 10%. To a stranger acting as middle man for a church, Cavaillé-Coll replied: "Confidential — You inquire as to professional discount. I am not in the habit of granting such, but I shall make an exception by allowing you a commission of 5% or 300 f. on the price of 6,000 f. quoted to the council of the church on whose behalf you inquire." A similar arrangement was offered to an enterprising entrepreneur in Quebec.

VIII. Family

a. Cavaillé-Coll was married on February 4, 1854, to Adèle Blanc. He announced it to Abbé Caussé, professor of music at the seminary in Montpellier in this way: "As Mr. Lazare has sureley told you, I have married the sister of one of our good friends, Mr. Hippolyte Blanc, an office supervisor at the Religious Affairs Department. She is a fine, beautiful wife. When you come to Paris again, you shall meet her and visit our new home at 96 rue de Vaugirard."

We learn that in a two-day interval in 1859 their two children died of "croup". The father was then 48 years old. Subsequently two more children were born, Cécile and Emmanuel.

b. Although from the start Aristide had taken charge of the direction of the *Société Cavaillé-Coll père et fils,* there was friction with Aristide's father, especially after the dissolution of the partnership on Decembeer 31, 1849. Occasional references to family problems appear in the letters, all of which are included in Appendix A, *Lettres* II, #1237; III, #1591, #1609, #1854; IV, #2243, #2353, #2799, #2917.

IX. Travel; a Workshop in England?

In the fall of 1844, Cavaillé-Coll took a 40 day tour of organ shops in Germany, Switzerland, Holland, and England. His letters to organ builders he met along the way give his own confident appraisals of a number of organs famous in their day: St. Nicolas in Fribourg (Switzerland), the Bavokerk in Haarlem, and the Cathedral of Utrecht.

Cavaillé-Coll praised the workmanship of the Dutch builder, Batz, but saved his most extravagant compliments for Walker of Ludwigsburg. On the contrary, Hill's enormous instrument in Birmingham was "an abomination", and its 32′ front pipes looked like "downspouts".

Frequent trips continued to enrich Cavaillé-Coll's experience and to open opportunities for professional exchange. In 1856 he heard Walcker's new 100-stop organ at the Cathedral of Ulm. The instrument, "unquestionably the greatest organ ever built", is discussed in Cavaillé-Coll's letter to the architect, Dwirner, at Cologne. During the same trip (1856) Cavaillé-Coll made the acquaintance of the famous theoretician, in Weimar, Töpfer, with whom he had been in correspondence.

Cavaillé-Coll's unrestrained praise of Walcker's 100-stop organ at Ulm suggests a relationship between that visit and the eventual size of the organ he himself would soon complete at St.-Sulpice in Paris. It was to be his largest, with exactly 100 stops, but with 6706 pipes to Ulm's 6286.

Cavaillé-Coll's correspondence of course extended to areas he never visited. In 1852, he wrote to Ducci in Florence   to thank him for "the little model of an Italian windchest, as well as the scale for the *Corni dolci* stop and many delicious sausages . . ."

Lettres IV, #2373, January 9, 1853
To Dr. Gauntlett, 70 Upper Norton St., Portland Place, London
    . . . Now, Sir, I must say a word in reply to your inquiry whether business relations with England would be desirable. Indeed I should be most proud to work for your great nation, but a favorable opportunity would have to be found.

    "The great Liverpool organ you spoke of some time ago would have been a good means of taking our place among the manufacturers in your country, but you know what became of that negotiation . . ."

    Cavaillé-Coll probably refers to an extraordinary proposal for Liverpool dated September, 1847:

Liverpool (England)

		Three manuals
Grand orgue from low C to A	58 notes
Positif from low G to A	63 notes
Expressif from low G to A	63 notes
Pédales from low C to A	31 notes

Grand orgue

1. Montre 16′
2. Bourdon 8′   tin
3. Flûte 8′   tin
4. Flûte 8′   tin
5. Flûte 8′   wood
6. Flûte 8′   wood
7. Flûte (stopped 8′)
8. Nazard
9. Prestant
10. Prestant
11. Prestant
12. Grosse Tierce
13. Nazard
14. Doublette
15. Doublette
16. Doublette
17. Doublette
18. Doublette
19. Plein-jeu XV
20. Grand Cornet VII
21. Trompette 8′ with 35 centimeters wind pressure
22. Cor anglais 8′ with 35 centimeters wind pressure
23. Clairon 4′ with 35 centimeters wind pressure

Positif

1. Bourdon 12′
2. Montre 8′ metal
3. Flûte 8′ wood
4. Cromorne 8′ wood
5. Salicional 8′
6. Cromorne tin
7. Cor anglais 8′ with 30 centimeters wind pressure
8. Basson 8′ with 30 centimeters wind pressure
9. Bourdon 4′
10. Flûte (stopped) 2′ wood
11. Prestant 4′
12. Flûte 4′
13. Doublette 2′
14. Doublette 2′
15. Doublette
16. Clairon
17. Cornet de Récit VIII

Expressif

1. Flûte 24′
2. Bourdon 12′
3. Flûte 12′
4. Flûte 12′
5. Flûte 12′
6. Bourdon 4′
7. Prestant
8. Prestant
9. Gros Nazard
10. Grosse Tierce
11. Nazard
12. Doublette
13. Doublette
14. Doublette
15. Doublette
16. Flûte 2′ wood
17. Plein-jeu X
18. Cor anglais 8′
19. Trompette 8′
20. Hautbois
21. Cromorne
22. Clairon 4′

Pédales

1. Flûte 32′ tin 30 *pouces* square
2. Flûte 32′ wood 39 *pouces*
3. Flûte 16′ tin 16 *pouces*
4. Flûte 16′ wood 22 by 24 *pouces*
5. Flûte   tin narrow scale
6. Flûte   wood narrow scale
7. Flûte 8′ tin
8. Flûte 8′ wood
9. Bourdon 4′ wood
10. Bourdon 4′ tin
11. Flûte 4′ tin
12. Flûte 2′
13. Cornet II or III
14. Trompette 16′ with 35 centimeters wind pressure
15. Basson 16′ with 35 centimeters wind pressure
16. Clairon 8′ with 35 centimeters wind pressure
     Price for this organ without case 175,000 fr.

X. Inventions, publications, and honors

a. Inventions:

In 1855, Cavaillé-Coll listed the parts of the organ that he had "invented or improved"

"1. The multiple-pressure bellows, of my invention.

2. The double pallet-boxes and the new system of combination pedals likewise of my invention.

3. The new sliderless chests with an individual pallet for each pipe, invented by Mr. Walcker of Ludwigsburg: introduced in France with the inventor's permission in 1844, these chests were used for the first time in the organ I built for the Royal Chapel at Dreux. This new design is also used in the *Montre* division at Saint-Vincent-de-Paul.

4. The new system of pneumatic levers, invented by Mr. Barker.

Finally, the new harmonic stops also our invention, first used in the organ we exhibited in 1839."

It often seemed that Cavaillé-Coll claimed to be the inventor of harmonic pipes. In truth, he realized that harmonic pipes had been known for centuries. Cf. this statement, found in *Devis* I, #91, January 1, 1843, for St. Jérôme, Toulouse: "Although physicists have long known and studied the harmonics in pipes, these tones had not been used in the organ. It is common knowledge that tones of this type are fuller and stronger than those of pipes speaking only the fundamental." But he may not have known that Praetorius and others described harmonic pipes.

Cavaillé-Coll also invented a circular saw, described in Mallet, *Rapport fait à la Soc., d'encouragement pour l'Industrie Nationale sur la scie circulaire de M. Cavaillé-Coll fils;* and a "Precision Winding System provided with a new system or air and gas pressure regulators . . .", useful for acoustical experiments and gas lighting.

b. Publications and Papers (*Académie des Sciences*)

February 24, 1840: *Etudes expérimentales sur les tuyaux d'orgues.*

February 5, 1859: *De la Détermination du ton normal et du diapason pour l'accord des instruments de musique.*

January 23, 1860: *De la Détermination des dimensions des tuyaux par rapport à leur intonation.*

February 23, 1863: *Note sur une soufflerie de précision munie d'un système de regulateurs de la pression de l'air et des gaz.*

1872: *De l'Orgue et son architecture.*

1875: *Projet d'orgue monumental pour la basilique de St.-Pierre de Rome.* Cavaillé-Coll applied for the title *"facteurs d'orgues du Roi".*

Lettres I, #994, July 30, 1844
To M. Le Comte de Montalivet,
Intendant General
"Your Excellency,

We beg to request your assistance in our application for the title of Organ-Builders to the King . . .

If your Excellency consented to solicit from the King the title of Organ-Builders to the King, that title would be for us the most valuable of rewards."

The title was used on the name-plate for the organ at La Madeleine (see above, p. 69), and on other instruments until the Revolution of 1848.

A list of other honors bestowed upon Cavaillé-Coll was published in *Orgues de tous modéles*, 1889, p. 5.

LIST OF THE PRINCIPAL ORGANS
MADE
BY A. CAVAILLÉ-COLL, INC.

CHURCHES AND CHAPELS IN PARIS

Barnabites (église des Pères). — Gr. orgue.
St-Bernard de la Chapelle. — Gr. orgue.
Carmes (église des). — Grand orgue.
Dames de l'Adoration réparatrice. — G. o.
Dames Bénédictines du T.-S.-Sacrement.
Dames des Sacrés-Cœurs. — Gr. orgue.
Dames Sainte-Marie. — Grand orgue.
Dames Sainte-Clotilde. — Grand orgue.
Dames de Sion. — Grand orgue.
Ecole Fénelon. — Grand orgue.
EGL. EPISCOPALE AMÉRICAINE. — G. o.
Eugène Napoléon (Maison). — Grand org.
Fidèles Compagnes de Jésus. — Org. de ch.
Lazaristes (église des). — Grand orgue.
MADELEINE (la). — *Grand orgue de 32 pieds*.
Madeleine (la). — Orgue de chœur.
NOTRE-DAME. — *Grand orgue de 32 pieds*.
NOTRE-DAME D'AUTEUIL. — Gr. orgue.
Notre-Dame de Bercy. — Grand orgue.
Notre-Dame (Congrég. de). — Gr. orgue.
NOTRE-DAME DES CHAMPS. — Gr. orgue.
Notre-Dame des Champs. — Orgue de ch.
NOTRE-DAME DE LA CROIX. — Gr. orgue.
Notre-Dame de la Croix. — Org. de chœur.
Notre-Dame de la Gare. — Grand orgue.
NOTRE-DAME DE LORETTE. — Gr. org.
Petit Séminaire de Paris. — Grand orgue.
Sainte-Anne (Asile clinique). — Grand orgue.
Saint-Augustin. — Orgue de chœur.
SAINTE-CLOTILDE. — *Gr. or. de 32 pieds*.
ST-DENIS DU ST-SACREMENT. — Gr. o.
St-Denis du St-Sacrement. — Orgue de ch.
SAINT-ÉTIENNE DU MONT. — Grand org.

SAINT-FRANÇOIS-XAVIER. — Gr. orgue
Sainte-Geneviève (Panthéon). — Gr. org.
Saint-Honoré. — Orgue de chœur.
ST-JACQUES DU HAUT-PAS. — G. o. de ch.
ST-JEAN-BAPTISTE DE BELLEVILLE.
  — Grand org.
SAINT-JEAN-SAINT-FRANÇOIS. — G. o
Saint-Jean-Saint-François. — Org. de ch.
SAINT-LOUIS-D'ANTIN. — Grand orgue.
Saint-Marcel. — Grand orgue et org. de ch.
SAINT-MERRY. — Grand orgue.
SAINT-PAUL-SAINT-LOUIS. — Gr. org.
Saint-Paul-Saint-Louis. — Orgue de chœur
Saint-Pierre-Montmartre. — Gr. orgue.
SAINT-ROCH. — Grand orgue.
Saint-Roch. — Orgue de chœur.
SAINT-SULPICE. — *Gr. orgue de 32 pieds*.
Saint-Sulpice. — Grand orgue de chœur.
SAINT-THOMAS-D'AQUIN. — Gr. orgue.
SAINTE-TRINITE. — *Gr. orgue de 32 pieds*
Sainte-Trinité. — Orgue de chœur.
SAINT-VINCENT-DE-PAUL. — *Gr. o. de 32 p.*
Saint-Vincent-de-Paul. — Orgue de chœur
Petit Collège Stanislas. — Grand orgue.
Sorbonne (église de la). — Grand orgue.
Temple des Billettes. — Grand orgue.
Temple de l'Étoile. — Grand orgue.
Temple de Grenelle. — Grand orgue.
Temple israélite. — Grand orgue.
Temple de l'Oratoire. — Grand orgue.
TEMPLE DE PANTHEMONT. — Gr. orgue.
Temple de la Rédemption. — Gr. orgue.
Temple Suédois. — Grand orgue.

MISCELLANEOUS LOCATIONS IN PARIS

M. Edouard André. — Gr. orgue de salon.
Mlle Rosine Bloch. — Orgue de salon.
M. le Cte de Chambrun. — G. or. de chapelle.
Conservat. de musique. — G. o. et o. d'étude.
École normale supér. — O. p. exp. d'acoust.
M. le Baron d'Erlanger. — Gr. org. de salon.
Faculté des Sciences à Paris. — O. harm.
M. Eugène Gigout. — Grand orgue d'étude?
M. Charles Gounod. — Grand orgue de sal.

Institution des Jeunes Aveugles. — G. o.
Inst. des Jeunes Aveugles. — 2 org. d'ét.
Opéra. — Grand orgue.
Opéra-Comique. — Grand orgue.
M. le comte d'Osmont. — Gr. org. de salon.
M. Poirson. — Grand orgue de salon.
M. Taskin. — Orgue de salon.
PALAIS DU TROCADÉRO. — Gr. orgue.
Mme P. Viardot. — Grand orgue de salon.

FRENCH CATHEDRALS AND CHURCHES

AIX. — Cathédrale : grand orgue.
AJACCIO. — Cathéd.: gr. orgue et orgue de ch.
Alby. — Couvent de Notre-Dame: gr. orgue.
Alby. — Église Saint-Salvy: orgue de chœur.
Alger. — Temple protestant.
Allevard. — Eglise paroissiale : grand orgue.
AMIENS. — Cathédrale : grand orgue.
Amiens. — Couv. des Ursulines : gr. orgue.
Andelys (les). — Egl. parois. : org. de chœur.
ANGERS. — Cathed.: *grand orgue de 32 pieds*.
Angers. — Eglise Notre-Dame : org. de ch.
ANGERS. — Eglise Saint-Joseph : gr. orgue.
ANNONAY. — Eglise Notre-Dame : gr. orgue.
Antibes. — Baron de l'Espée : grand orgue.
Arc-les-Gray. — Eglise parois. : gr. orgue.
Arles. — Eglise Ste-Trophime : org. de chœur.
Auch. — Cathédrale : orgue de chœur.
Autun. — Cathédrale : orgue de chœur.
Avignon. — Dames des Sacrés-Cœurs : gr. org.
Avignon. — Temple protestant : org. de ch.
BAGNÈRES-DE-BIGORRE. — Eg. d.Carmes.
Bagnères-de-Luchon. — Egl. parois.: g. org.
BAILLEUL. — Eglise parois. Saint-Amand.
Barbeville. — Chap. du baron Gérard : g. or.
BAYEUX. — Cathédrale : grand orgue.
Bayeux. — Cathédrale : orgue de chœur.
Belle-Isle-en-Mer. — Eg. par. du Pal., g. o.
Bellevue. — Eglise paroissiale : grand orgue.
BELLEY. — Cathédrale : grand orgue.
Bergerac. — Eglise Saint-Jacques : gr. org.
BERGUES. — Eglise paroissiale : grand org.
Bétharam (abbaye). — Eglise Notre-Dame.
BÉZIERS. — Cathédrale Saint-Nazaire : g. o.
Bolbec. — Eglise paroissiale : grand orgue.
Bolbec. — Temple protestant : orgue de ch.

Bordeaux. — Eglise des Carmes : grand org.
Boulogne-sur-Seine. — Eg. paroiss. : gr. o.
Bourges. — Dames des Sacrés-Cœurs : gr. o.
Braine. — Eglise paroissiale : grand orgue.
Brest. — Eglise Saint-Martin : grand orgue.
CAEN. — Eg. St-Etienne : *grand org. 32 pieds*.
CAEN. — Eglise Saint-Pierre : grand orgue.
Caen. — Eglise Saint-Jean : orgue de chœur.
Caen. — Eglise de la Sainte-Trinité : gr. or.
Caen. — Paroisse de Vaucelles : grand orgue.
Cambrai. — Grand séminaire : grand orgue.
CARCASSONNE. — Cathéd. : grand orgue.
Carcassonne. — Cathéd. : orgue de chœur.
CASTELNAUDARY. — Eg. St-Michel : gr. o
Cattenon. — Egl. parois. : grand orgue.
Cette. — Egl. St-Joseph : orgue d'accompagn.
Chalon-sur-Saône. — St-Pierre : org. de ch.
Chalon-Saint-Cosme. — Egl. par.: gr. org.
Chantilly. — Egl. parois. : grand orgue.
Charleville. — Egl. parois.: orgue de chœur.
Charly-sur-Marne. — Egl. parois.: gr. org.
Charmes. — Egl. parois.; grand orgue.
CHATEAU-GONTIER. — St-Jean: gr. org.
Châteauneuf-sur-Cher. — Eg. p.:g. o.d'acc
Château-Renault. — Egl. parois.: gr. orgue
Châteauvillain. — Egl. parois.: gr. orgue.
CHAUMONT. — Egl. St-Jean-Baptiste: g. o.
Chaussin. — Egl. parois. : gr. org.
Clamecy. — Egl. St-Martin : grand orgue.
Clesles. — Egl. parois. : orgue de chœur.
Colombey-les-Belles. — Egl. parois.: g. o.
COMPIÈGNE. — Egl. St-Jacques : gr. orgue.
Coulommiers. — Eglise parois.: gr. orgue.
Couzances-les-Forges. Eg. parois.: gr. org.
Creil. — Eglise paroissiale : grand orgue.

Dammartin-en-Goële. — Egl. par. : gr. org.

Dax. — Berc.-de-St-Vincent-de-Paul : gr. org.

Deauville. — Eglise paroiss. : grand orgue.

Decazeville. — Egl. paroissiale : gr. orgue.

Dieppe. — Eglise Saint-Jacques : org. de ch.

DIGNE. — Cathédrale : grand orgue.

Digne. —. Cathédrale : orgue de chœur.

Dinan. — Saint-Sauveur : grand orgue.

DORAT (le). — Eglise collégiale : gr. orgue.

Doulaincourt. — Egl. parois. : grand orgue.

DREUX. — Chapelle du château : gr. orgue.

DREUX. — Eglise paroissiale : grand orgue.

Dunkerque. — Eglise St-Martin : gr. orgue.

Dunkerque. — Chap. des Orphelines : gr. org.

Dunkerque. — Patronage : orgue de chœur.

Ecouen. — Maison de la Lég. d'honn. : gr. org.

ELBEUF. — Egl. de l'Immac.-Concep. : gr. org.

ELBEUF. — Egl. St-Etienne : org. de chœur.

ELBEUF. — Eglise Saint-Jean : grand orgue.

Enghien-les-Bains. — Egl. parois. : gr. org.

ÉPERNAY. — Eglise paroissiale : gr. orgue.

Épernay. — Eglise paroissiale : grand orgue.

Esne (Meuse). — Egl. parois. : orgue de ch.

FÉCAMP. — Egl. Ste-Trin. : gr. o. et org. de ch.

Ferté-sous-Jouarre. — Egl. parois. : g. org.

La-Ferté-St-Aubin.—C. de M. Leroux : o. de s.

Fontainebleau. — Saint-Louis : grand orgue.

Fontenailles. — Egl. paroissiale org. de ch.

Fontenay-le-Vicomte, — Egl. par. : gr. org.

Fréjus. — Cathédrale : grand orgue.

Gaillac. — Egl. St-Michel grand orgue.

GERBEVILLER. Ch. du mᵈ de Lambertye g. or.

Gerbeviller. — Egl. parois. : gr. org. de ch.

Gignac. — Eglise paroissiale : grand orgue.

Givet. — Eglise Notre-Dame : grand orgue.

Gordes. — Eglise parois. : gr. org. de ch.

Grenade. — Eglise paroissiale : grand orgue.

Grenoble. — Cathédrale : grand orgue.

Guéménée-Panfao. — Egl. par. : org. de ch.

LE HAVRE. — Saint-Michel : grand orgue.

Le Havre — Saint-Joseph : orgue de chœur.

Havre (le). — Temple protestant : org. de ch.

Hendaye. — Egl. paroissiale : grand orgue.

Héricourt. — Egl. paroissiale : grand orgue.

Isle-Adam. (l') — Egl. parois. : orgue de ch.

Issy-sur-Seine. — Eglise parois. : gr. org.

Langon. — Eglise paroissiale : grand orgue.

Lannion. — Couvent Ste-Anne : grand orgue.

LAVAL. — Cath. : gr. orgue et orgue de ch.

LAVAUR. — Cath. Saint-Alain : grand orgue.

Lion-d'Angers. — Eglise paroiss. : gr. orgue.

LISIEUX. — Cath. : *grand orgue de 32 pieds.*

Lille. — N.-Dame de la Treille : gr. org. de ch.

Les Loges. Maison de la Lég. d'hon : gr. or.

Long. — Eglise paroissiale : grand orgue.

Longjumeau. Egl. paroissiale : grand org.

Longueville. — Egl. paroissiale : gr. orgue.

Lorient. — Eglise St-Louis : grand orgue.

Loudéac. — Eglise paroissiale : orgue de ch.

LOURDES. — Basilique de Notre-D. : gr. org.

Lourdes. — Basilique de Notre-D. : org. de ch.

LUÇON. — Cathédrale : grand orgue.

Lunel. — Église : grand orgue.

LYON. — Eglise St-François : grand orgue.

LYON. — Maison du S.-Cœur de la Ferrandière

LYON. — RR. PP. Jésuites : grand orgue.

Lyon. — Couvent des Carmes : grand orgue.

Lyon. — Eglise d'Ainay : orgue de chœur.

Lyon, — Couvent du S.-C. des Anglais : gr. or.

Lyon. — Eglise Sainte-Croix : grand orgue.

Lyon. — Couvent des Ursulines : grand orgue.

Mâcon. — Eglise Saint-Vincent : orgue de ch.

Mâcon. — Eglise Saint-Pierre : orgue de ch.

Malakoff (Seine). — Egl. parois. : gr. org.

Mans (le). — N.-D. de la Couture : org. de ch.

Marmande. — Eglise paroissiale : gr. orgue.

MARSEILLE. — Egl. Saint-Charles : g. org.

MARSEILLE. — Eg. St-Joseph : g. o. et o. de ch.

Mayenne. — Petit Séminaire : org. d'accomp.

Mazamet. — Eglise St-Sauveur : grand orgue.

Mesnil-sur-Oger. — orgue de chœur.

METZ. — Cathédrale : orgue de chœur.

Metz. — Chapelle du Séminaire : orgue. de ch.

MOISSAC. — Egl. St-Pierre : grand orgue.

Molay. — Chap. du cte de Chabrol : org. de ch.

Mongré. — RR. PP. Jésuites : grand orgue.

Montargis. — Eglise paroissiale : grand org.

Montélimar. — Couvent des Carmes : g. org.

Montfort-en-Chalosse. — Orgue d'accomp.

Montpellier. — Chap du gr. sémin. : or. de ch.

Moreuil. — Chap. N.-D. de Lorette : gr. org.

Motte-aux-Bois. — Egl. paroissiale : gr. org.

Moulins. — Maison du Sacré-Cœur : org. de ch.

Moutiers. — Cathédrale : grand orgue.

MULHOUSE. — Egl. catholique : grand orgue.

NANCY. — Cathédrale : *gr. org. de 32 pieds.*

NANCY. — Saint-Léon : grand orgue.

Nancy. — Temple israélite : orgue de chœur.

Nantes. — Eglise Saint-Clément : orgue de ch.

Narbonne. — Eglise St-Sébastien : grand org.

Neuilly. — Eglise paroissiale : orgue de ch.

Nevers. — Cathédrale : orgue de chœur.

Nevers. — Saint-Étienne : grand orgue.

Nîmes. — Cathédrale : orgue de chœur.

NIMES. — Eglise St-Paul : grand orgue.

Nîmes. — Eglise Sainte-Perpétue : gr. orgue.

Nuits-sous-Beaune. — Egl. parois. : gr. or.
OLORON. — Cathédr. Ste-Marie : gr. orgue.
ORLÉANS. — Cathédrale : *gr. org. de 32 pieds.*
Orléans. — Cathédrale : orgue de chœur.
Orléans. — Eglise St-Paterne : grand orgue.
Orléans. — Eg. N.-D. de Recouvrance : gr. or.
Orthez. — Eglise Saint-Pierre : grand orgue.
Paray-le-Monial. — Basilique : org. de ch.
PAU. — D. de l'Ador. réparatrice : gr. orgue.
PERPIGNAN. — Cath. . *gr. org. de 32 pieds.*
Perpignan. — Cathédrale : orgue de chœur.
Perpignan. — D. du Sacré-Cœur : gr. orgue.
PÉZENAS. — Eglise St-Jean : grand orgue.
Pézenas. — Egl. Ste-Ursule : grand orgue.
Pierrefitte. — Eglise paroissiale : org. de ch.
Pithiviers. — Eglise paroissiale : grand. or.
POLIGNY. — Eg. par. : gr. org. et org. de ch.
Pontivy. — Eglise paroissiale : grand orgue.
PONTOISE. — Egl. St-Maclou : grand orgue.
Pontoise. — Egl. St-Maclou : orgue de ch.
Port-Louis. — Eglise paroissiale : gr. orgue.
Preuilly. — Chap. du château : grand. orgue.
Puy-en-Velay. — Eglise parois. : org. de ch.
QUIMPER. — Cathédrale : grand orgue.
Rabastens. — Egl. N.-D. du Bourg : gr. org.
Reims. — Saint-Maurice : gr. org. d'accomp.
RENNES. — Cathédrale : grand orgue.
Rennes. — Eglise des Carmes : org. de chœur.
Rennes. — Hospice St-Yves : grand orgue.
Rieumes. — Eglise paroiss. : grand orgue.
Roche-Derrien (la). — Egl. par. . gr. orgue.
Roche-sur-Yon. — Egl. par. : grand orgue.
Rochelle (la). — Temple protest. : org. de ch.
Romorantin. — Egl. paroiss. : grand orgue.
Roubaix. — Egl. des Récollets : grand orgue.
ROUEN. — Eglise de Bon-Secours : gr. org.
ROUEN. — Eglise St-Godard : grand orgue.
Rouen. — Egl. Saint-Godard : org. de chœur.
Rouen. — Eglise St-Gervais : grand orgue.
ROUEN. — Eglise Saint-Ouen : grand orgue.
RUEIL. — Eglise paroissiale : grand orgue.
Rumigny. — Eglise parois. : grand orgue.
St-Amand-Montrond. — Egl. par. : gr. org.
Ste-ANNE-D'AURAY.—Eg. du Pèlerin : g. o.
SAINT-BRIEUC. —Cathédrale : gr. orgue.
SAINT-BRIEUC. — St-Michel : gr. orgue.
Saint-Cloud. — Egl. paroissiale : gr. orgue.
SAINT-DENIS. — Basil. : *gr. org. de 32 pieds.*
Saint-Denis. — Orgue de chœur.
St-Denis. — M. de la Légion d'honneur.

SAINT-DIZIER. — Egl. N.-D. : grand orgue.
St-Dizier. — Couvent de l'Assomption : gr. or.
St-Etienne. — Egl. de Valbenoîte : gr. org.
St-Gaudens. — Eglise paroiss. : grand orgue.
St-Georges-sur-Loire.—Eg. par. : org. de ch.
St-Germain-les-Corbeil. — Egl. par. : g. or.
St-Germain-en-Laye. — Egl. par. : gr. org
Saint-Germain-en-Laye. — Eg. p. : or. de c.
St-Girons. — Eglise paroissiale : gr. orgue
St-Leu-Taverny. — Egl. par. : grand orgue.
St-Malo. — Eglise paroiss. : orgue de chœur.
St-Martin-au-Laërt. — Egl. par. : gr. orgue
ST-OMER. — Cat. : gr. org. à *quatre claviers*
St-Omer.—Dames de Sion : grand orgue.
St-Palais. — Eglise paroissiale : grand orgue.
ST-PIERRE-LES-CALAIS. — Gr. orgue.
St-Pourçain. — Eglise parois. : grand orgue.
St-Quentin. — Hôtel-Dieu : grand orgue.
St-Servan. — Couvent Sainte-Anne. : gr. or.
ST-SERVAN. —Eglise paroiss. : grand orgue.
St-Servan. — Egl. paroiss. : orgue de chœur.
St-Sever. — Couvent des Ursulines : gr. or.
Sceaux. — Eglise paroissiale : grand orgue.
SÉEZ. — Cathédrale : grand orgue.
Séez. — Cathédrale : orgue de chœur.
SEGRÉ. — Eglise paroissiale : grand orgue.
Sèvres. — Eglise paroiss. : orgue de chœur.
TARARE. — Sainte-Madeleine : grand orgue.
TOULOUSE. — Cat. : gr. org. et org. de ch.
Toulouse. — Eglise St-Jérôme : grand orgue.
TOULOUSE. — Eglise de Jésus : gr. orgue.
TOULOUSE. — Saint-Sernin : *gr. org. de 32 p.*
Tournus. — Eglise paroiss. : grand orgue.
Tours. — Temple protestant : org. d'accomp.
Trouville-s.-Mer. — E. N.-D. des Vic. g. or.
Tunis. — Cathédrale provisoire : grand orgue
Ussel. — Eglise paroissiale : grand orgue.
Vanves. — Eglise paroiss. : orgue de chœur.
Vaucluse. — Asile clinique : grand orgue.
Verneuil. — Eglise Sainte-Madeleine : gr. or.
VERSAILLES. — Cathédrale : grand orgue.
Versailles. — Cathédrale : orgue de chœur.
VERSAILLES.—Chapelle du Château : gr. or.
Versailles. — Sainte-Elisabeth.
Versailles. — Temple israélite : gr. orgue.
Vichy. — Eglise Saint-Louis : grand orgue.
Vidalon-l.-Annon. MM. Canson et Mongolfier.
Villeblevin. — Eglise paroissiale : gr. orgue.
Vire. — Egl. de l'Hôp. St-Louis : grand orgue.
Vitry-le-Français. — Hôtel-Dieu : gr. orgue.

APPENDIX B

Selected Letters in English Concerning Cavaillé-Coll's Travels

November 11, 1844.

Monsieur Régnier

Upon my return here on the last day of October, I was told that we had received a letter from you. My dear father misplaced that letter, and I have just now found it. Having read it, I see, as from the letter I received at Vogt's in Fribourg, that I owe you some advice about your organ.

I cannot promise how good my advice will be, since I do not have the time to consider it at length. I have a huge amount of work that accumulated during my forty days absence. But so that you will not have to wait another forty days, I shall rely upon your letter and my memory of the brief inspection that we made together, to tell you what I think.

1. The wind system has the defects not only of providing unsteady wind to the organ, as a result of the system's design, but also of having a pressure that is too weak and wind trunks that are incapable of doing their job, due both to the size of the trunks and the distribution of wind carried to the various parts of this vast instrument. The shaking and weakness which abound in the wind supply of the organ are as much the result of the inadequate size and their arrangement as of the faulty design of the bellows.

2. The wind chests have too many stops for them to sound together properly with the same pallets. The reeds, the *plein jeu* and all *nazards* and *tierces* should be supplied with a separate pallet box, different from that of the foundation registers. This is my opinion and my fundamental principle. I contend that no organ is really a good one without such a

scheme, whether it be in Nancy or Fribourg, Haarlem or Frankfurt. In each case, the wind is weak because large and small pipes are winded by the same pallets.

3. The 32′ *Bombarde* has never been good and is now completely unsatisfactory. What a pity. I heard a very good one in the organ under construction by Monsieur Walker in the cathedral at Stuttgart. The metal walls of the *Bombarde* are much too thin for the sound emitted by the reed to reverberate properly. The columns of air in these enormous pipes are no better contained than if the pipes were made of paper. The result is that you hear only the sound of the reed as if it were speaking freely in the air. Since the pipe walls are too thin, they are now coming apart, and their sound is thereby completely lost.

4. The *Récit* and the *Echo* with their half stops should be omitted from so large an instrument to make room, as you say, for a new division which would have the compass of the organ's other manuels and which, equipped with a swell box, would be an advantageous replacement for both the *Récit* and *Echo*.

5. The number and compass of the keyboards should remain as they are. The keyboard omitted due to the disappearance of the present *Echo* could be advantageously adapted for playing reeds in the *grand orgue*, adding a new division, namely, the *Bombarde*. I will not go into detail here regarding how good or how bad each stop is, for I cannot remember them that well. As for the disposition, some *Quartes* and *Tierces* should surely be omitted; but all this does

not get us to the heart of the matter, nor to the heart of the organ. My only criticism deals with the lungs, for here is where the trouble lies. You would do well to replace all your stops and adopt the German system of *Gambes*, but the organ would sound no better. As things are now, your organ sounds like an orchestra where all the wind instruments are played by consumptives.

Before ending my letter, I should tell you a little about my trip. To begin, I confess I did not find a *Voix Humaine* anywhere except in the fingers and knowledge of your friend Vogt. I assure you that there is no more a *Voix Humaine* in the Fribourg organ than in all the organs I have had the opportunity to see and hear there. As you say in your letter, I did not find a Vogt; but the *notaire* who is substituting for him enabled me to see and hear the organ. The first impression of the *grand choeur*, which started the demonstration was disconcerting to me. Not that I was disconcerted, but the weakness of the wind in this beautiful organ was so obvious; the *Cornets* and the *Fournitures*, mixed in the with the *great Trompette*, are so far from forming an ensemble that I was reminded of the finest tin-pan band. I was more pleased with the foundations, which are beautiful, the *Gambes*, and with the solo stops in general. The *Récit*, where the famous *Voix Humaine* is located, is very pleasing. This part of the organ speaks into the vestibule, and the sounds are modified in the vaulting, instead of traveling directly to the congregation's ears. What a magical effect the sounds from these stops have! It is impossible to characterize these stops, modified as they are by their location more than by any special construction. Some call them all *Voix Humaines*. It is true that they are less shrill than they are in other organs. I myself call them pretty stops. To sum up my ideas on this organ, whose reputation is due, I believe, as much as to Vogt as to Moser, I will say that it is a new old organ, where the work is conscientiously done; where each stop, considered by itself, has a beautiful timbre (with the exception of the reeds); but where the organ as a whole is not worth a farthing. The lungs are bad; the veins and the arteries are defective.

Moser claims to have created a masterpiece with his wind system. He took care to put it in a box to hide it from profane eyes. I think he did a wise thing; for while the rest of his work is handsome, this part alone is, in my opinion, wretched. I still have a great deal to say regarding this organ and the great praises sung throughout the world by its many visitors, but I must stop here. You wish me to tell briefly of the other organs, and I must not cause you to pay twice, three, or four times the normal postage. Before going to Fribourg, I saw the organs in the *Temple Neuf* and the Cathedral at Strasbourg; you are familiar with them. The organ in the *Temple Neuf* is very good; he only problem is that it is a bit old and consumptive.

I went to Ruffach to visit the workshop of Callinet, who was away. I tracked him down in a mountain village called Lutter, near St.-Denis, which consists of four to five houses and two churches. There he was installing an organ with two manuals and independent pedal, which impressed me very much, given the size of the village church.. The work seemed good enough to me: nothing new, no outstanding quality. I judge from my inspection of his work and his workshop that Monsieur Callinet is a good builder who should make money.

Next I went to Basel where I saw the Rhine and the House of Three Kings. That was all very beautiful, but I needed organs. I went to Bern to look for them since I knew one was being constructed there. I expected to find the builder at the church, so I went there right away. After I crossed his palm with silver, the caretaker opened the doors for me. While he pointed out the paintings, I turned my whole attention to the organ. I've made a mistake, I said to myself. This is an old organ. Since I did not hear a single hammer, I asked if repairs were being made on this organ. The answer was yes. Having asked if the workers were at lunch, I was told that they were working in town. Finally, in order not to waste my admission fee, I visited the tombs and then approached the partition that the Protestants built to divide te church in two, since it was too large for them. The caretaker opened the door leading to the choir. There I found superb 32' pipes.

laid out like giants' coffins. Seeing them gave me a good impression of the man who made them. Let's get the tomb of Dagobert over with quickly, since my concern is the organ. I told my guide to take me to the builder. He responded in German and my heart sank. Fortunately, my guide was somewhat ambidextrous, and I was able to make known my name and profession. I was then received with open arms, and without further ado, he showed me all his work. All I could say was *gout [gut] and cheun [schön]* (correct my spelling if you can), for all his work seemed to have been done with the utmost care. It was only ten in the morning then, yet we did not part until eleven that evening. After inspecting his work, we had to chat for a while. My interpreter translated badly, but we improvised a kind of telegraphic language. With pencil in hand, arm and finger gestures, and with the aid of the eyes, we spent a most interesting artistic day.

I am beginning to see that if I took you through every sketch we made, my task would be long and tedious for you to follow. Therefore I will conclude with just a word about the builder himself. His name is Haas, and he is thirty-three years old — tall and handsome like an Alsatian. He is a student of Mr. Walker, the famous builder at Ludwigsburg, of whom I shall have occasion to speak at the proper time. He is a fine young man, married to a girl from Basel who speaks a little French but who does not know the language of organ-builders. All the work seemed to have been done to the greatest perfection; and if this bird's song is as fine as its feathers, then the Fribourg organ won't be worth a row of pins any more. I spoke for a long time with Mr. Haas about the lungs of his organ. I gave him my ideas on this subject, and he thought they were good; although this part of the organ was already partially installed, I suspect he will make significant changes and thereby cure the organ of the disease that plagued all the organs I saw during my long trip.

I must really go to bed now. It is midnight. Goodnight.

November 15, 1844.
Monsieur Carl Gottlieb Weigle, Organ-builder, Stuttgart

Dear Monsieur and colleague,

Upon receipt of your letter, I went immediately to a friend who could explain its contents to me, for you know with only a dictionary were we able to exchange a few words during my stay at Stuttgart.

You are proposing to send your brother to work in our shop in Paris to improve his knowledge of the profession. I told my father and brother of your request, and they join me in accepting your proposal with pleasure. Please advise us of his arrival date in Paris so that we can have a position ready for him in our workshop. Rest assured that we will pay him a fair wage and see that his time is spent in the best way possible. So, the matter is settled.

Now I must tell you about the rest of my trip. I was well received in Frankfurt by the organist, Monsieur Petsch. Monsieur Kocher's letter of intoduction was most helpful. Please thank him for me. The organ in St. Paul's is good, but the church itself is not. There is such lack of clarity in the sound of the instrument that the overall effect of the organ is seriously hampered. As always, I found your work well executed; but the layout seemed to me to be somewhat congested, which must seriously hinder maintenance. I think Monsieur Walker must have found himself limited by the space allowed him by the architect. Architects, at least in France, are the enemies of organ-builders. When they can imprison us, they will not hesitate to do so in order to preserve architectural lines.

In Holland, I saw some very beautiful organs with respect to the extraordinary proportions of the *façade* or the *montre*, or *Prospect*, as you call it in German.

In Rotterdam, there are 32' pipes, (32 *futs*) in number. The entire organ is at least seventy feet high from the gallery floor to the top, without touching the vault. To climb into the interior, there is a large staircase composed of six flights, just as in a large house. A Dutchman told me that it is possible to walk around inside smoking a three-foot pipe, without touching anything. This gigantic organ was begun by Messrs. Meere and Zoon in 1790 and finished in 1823 —

thirty-eight years in the making. You would think it would have been good, but alas, that is not the case. Already Messrs. Batz & Co. of Utrecht are making major repairs.

In Haarlem, I went to see Monsieur Schumacker, the organist. Monsieur Kocher was wrong to correct my spelling of his name – I called him Schuman. He really is a "Schumacker", who makes shoes only for money. He did not want to show me the organ, even though I had already paid three florins to the bellow-boys to let me hear it for about fifteen minutes. Perhaps he too was waiting for a tip. If I had known the truth about him beforehand, I would have brought along a coach whip to deliver the payment that so base an artist deserves.

Well. enough of Monsieur "Schuman" or "Schumacker". The organ at Haarlem also has vast architectural proportions: a very beautiful facade of 32' pipes. Sound echoes well throughout the church; and although the organ is old, it produces beautiful tones.

After leaving Haarlem, I went to Utrecht to meet the organ-builder, Monsieur Batz. He received me very warmly and showed me his workshop, where everything was in good order, as well as the organ he built in the cathedral. Regarding this installation, the work has been soundly and carefully done, and the organ's tone is good. The organist who plays it is a charming young man with much talent. The work of Monsieur Batz is not characterized by genius, as is that of Monsieur Walker. Rather, it is based on traditional plans and conscientiously done. In London, I first saw Monsieur Hill, Organ-Builder to the Queen, who welcomed me warmly thanks to the letter of introduction from *Chevalier* Neukomm. With him, I visited the most important organs in this city, which are neither large nor beautiful. I also went to Birmingham to see the famous 32' organ installed by Monsieur Hill in resent years. It is a large instrument, but the workmanship is horrendous. They tried to build a 32' wooden pipes, three feet square, made with frames and panels. These enormous pipes, occupying a great deal of space, sound worse than your old pipes in your organ at Stuttgart. To be perfectly accurate, they hardly sound at all.

In this organ, as in all those I saw in England, all the metal pipes are of lead, including those in the façade. The tin we import from England is unknown to English builders and is not found in the organ of Birmingham. The pipes in the façade or *Prospect* are of zinc, just like rainspouts and gilded, with quite visible soldered seams. Even so, these zinc pipes produce a rather nice tone. What I found to be the most outstanding feature of this organ is a trumpet, voiced on high pressure, which dominates because of its intensity. All the stops together yield a beautiful result. I am quite sure this results from a conversation I had sometime ago with *Chevalier* Neukomm on this subject. He passed along my ideas to Monsieur Hill, who used them to good advantage.

I urge you, whenever you have the opportunity to try to increase the wind pressure on the reeds. You will see that the intensity and quality of the sound from the *Trompettes* can be significantly improved.

I just realized my letter is getting a bit long. I don't want to close, however, without expressing the great pleasure I got from visiting your workshop and Monsieur Walker's. I can still hear you superb 32' *Bombarde*. I can still see the thousands of valves opening and closing in the new chests (*vind lade*). And how I admire the light touch of your keyboards! In my letter to *Chevalier* Neukomm thanking him for the letters of introduction he gave me for my artistic journey, I did not forget to mention you and to classify Monsieur Walker, with his genius and painstaking work, as the best builder among all those I visited.

Please give my regards, Monsieur *Confrère*, to your uncle and his wife, and my sincere compliments to Mr. Kocher. I still expect you for the dedication of our organ at La Madeleine, as you promised.

January 28, 1845.
Monsieur Callinet, Sr. in Ruffach

My dear Monsieur and Colleague, I owe you a letter of thanks for the enjoyable day I spent with you in Luther's capital city. I have often spoken at home of that delightful day. I have not forgotten that beautiful royal highway where the carriage, always below ground level and thus safe from overturning, was first a boat then a cart as we arrived by land and by sea at the base of the cathedral which overlooks the great city of Luther and contains an organ by Herr Callinet. I must admit that I was worried for a moment that I wouldn't see you. From the looks of that village, who in the world would imagine that an organ could have been built there? Certainly, no one who grew up in southern France: organs are scarcer in our part of the country. Then another dilemma arose: what to do for dinner? With my appetite whetted by the mountain air and my stomach absolutely empty, would I have to go all the way back to St.-Denis? Such were the questions I was asking myself as I approached that great city. As I stood at the very door of the church, my throat already parched with thirst, my heart nearly stopped when I asked for Monsieur Callinet and no one answered. I recovered somewhat when I saw the organ. When my guide asked the villagers for Herr Callinet and I finally heard, "Ja, Ja, Herr Callinet," I recovered completely. I recall vividly all the circumstances of that delightful day, the most pleasant one I spent during my trip. Nor have I forgotten how you eased my hunger with the excellent lunch you ordered – a meal which I thought I would miss. Neither Tokay nor champagne could have made me lose that memory. So I thank you now, though a bit late, for the time you gave to me and for that day so well spent. I thank your wife for being such a fine hostess. Finally, I thank Monsieur Vidor for making possible my visit to his fine workshop and for the trouble he took to see me to the train. You were kind enough to write us last December 15, and among other things you asked me for a brief description of my trip. I will tell you about it very succinctly, for it was so rapid that I cannot go into detail without risking inaccuracies. After leaving you at Luther, I went to Bern as I said I would, where I found Monsieur Haas instead of Walker, whom I had been told to expect. Yet, I must admit that I was very satisfied with his work. Everything I saw was made conscientiously, with care and precision. It remained to be seen whether the "song fit the bird".

That is a matter which I could not judge because nothing had been set up yet, and as a result, I didn't hear a single note from the instrument.

At Fribourg, I found that Wagl was absent, and consequently so was the *Vox humana* of the organ. Nevertheless, I heard the organ played by his substitute. I found all the individual stops charming, but the ensemble wasn't worth a farthing. The problem is that the lungs are bad. This famous organ needs a lot of nursing if it is to deserve the reputation it has generally been given. I inspected the interior of the instrument and found all the work well done and properly arranged. I believe that with a good wind supply, this instrument could gain a great deal. Unfortunately Mooser was mistaken: what he believed to be the best and wanted to hide (the wind supply), is the worst part of the organ. At Zürich I saw Haas' organ in the *Temple neuf* in which, as you know, the components are good, but the plan is bad; and the lungs are as defective as those of the Fribourg organ.

The organ in the Cathedral, which ought to be dismantled, succeeded in hurting my ears. Here the components, the arrangement of the organ, the construction of the pipes, everything corresponds to the tone of the instrument. In other words, everything was horribly managed. Packing-crates are better made than the wooden pipes. Gutters are better soldered than the tin pipes. I say tin, but perhaps I give the builder too much credit, because ordinary zinc is much purer than his metal. Finally the tone of the pipes is like that of a tin-pan band back home. But I've said quite enough about this bad organ; let me save space for something better.

At Winterthur, I saw the organ begun by Mooser and finished by Haas. Here, either because of the organ or the organist, who is excellent, I was very pleased when I heard this instrument. It does, however, have some bad reed stops, but fortunately there are not many of them. On the other hand, the foundation stops, the strings, and the flutes are well-made and effective.

Then I arrived in Stuttgart. At the cathedral I found a 32' nave organ, which Monsieur Walker of Ludwigsburg had almost finished. I heard the organ Sunday, the day I arrived, and I left that evening for Ludwigsburg without having inspected the instrument which I could see anyway on my way back. I found Monsieur Walker very comfortably settled in his workshop, and he showed me all the details of his work. While there, I saw a 16' nave organ, well made and with a good sound, completely set up in a suitable location. Monsieur Walker is, in my opinion, a builder of merit and genius. Upon my return to Stuttgart, I heard a 32' *Bombarde* with a fine sound, the only reed stop finished so far. If the rest is comparable, this instrument will leave little to be desired. His foundation stops are beautiful as well as the strings and the flutes. Everything is well done.

I visited the organ with Monsieur Walker's nephew, Carl Weigle, who is a very skilled worker. He has sent us his brother, Ernst Weigle, who is not very skilled, so that he can learn French and learn more about his craft. He claims to have worked for you. I would like to know what you think of him, what his position was, and what work he did. Up to now I have thought of him as an apprentice, because he is quite unskilled. Please tell us something about him.

I rushed onward by train and steamboat and eventually arrived at Frankfurt. I saw Walker's organ in the new Protestant church. I'm not as pleased with it as I am with the instruments I have already told you about. It is not a "platitude", as you say of the Zürich organ, but rather a "depression". The church is curved in the form of an ellipse. The organ is set against the wall and follows the same curve; and since it is sizable, it is cramped in its case. Resonance in the church creates a great confusion of sounds, so that nothing very powerful or distinct can be heard. I think the architect did a great disservice to the builder in both the shape of the case and the design of the church.

I won't tell you about Mainz, Cologne, Nijmegen, but will simply say that I left for Rotterdam. I inquired about the organ. I was told it was being repaired and that the best organ builder in Holland, Mr. Bätz of Utrecht was in charge of the work. I was brought into the church, and they told me that the front pipes were 32 feet. I didn't believe it at first, although the façade seemed quite beautiful to me. I measured the width of the church, that is of the nave, by pacing it off. My twenty-three paces, according to the length of my pace, came to 46 feet. It was then that I began to get an idea of the size of the organ. Nonetheless, I was not quite convinced of the height of the pipes until I had climbed 5 or 6 levels inside the organ, and could put my arms around the top of the largest pipe, which was 10" in diameter. Looking down it like a chimney-sweep, I had admitted that my eye had fooled me and that the case pipes were indeed 32 feet. This is the largest I've ever seen. You can walk around inside the organ, a Dutchman told me, smoking a three-foot pipe without touching anything. It's true. The work was not finished. The foundations were excellent, but the sound of the organ is not proportional to the gigantic size of the instrument.

In Haarlem, I had a letter of recommendation to the organist, Monsieur Schumann, who, as it turns out, would make a better *Schumacker* (shoemaker). After I had coaxed him quite a bit he told me to give the blowers three florins, and I could hear the organ. He would not let me see the instrument, telling me on one hand that he didn't have the keys, yet on the other hand that it was he who tuned the organ. So I asked him if he could teach me his method of tuning an organ without ever going inside. This would be the best way to protect these instruments against fire, wouldn't it? Finally I heard the organ, and that convinced me. This organ produces a good sound; it is better supplied with reeds than German organs. It is a large 32' instrument, pleasing in appearance and sound, although a bit old. It is unquestionably the largest instrument built to date.

Let's not leave Holland yet. I went up to Utrecht, and there met a fellow builder Monsieur Bätz, for whom I had no letter of recommendation. Nevertheless, I was very well received by him; it was the nicest welcome, next to Herr Callinet's in Luther, that I had on my trip. I spent a profitable day with this good man, to whom I am late in writing, by the way, in spite of the promise I made to him, as I did to you, to write as soon as I arrived in Paris. But that's the fashion. Good children always get served last. You have a very fine fir, but Monsieur Bätz has a very fine oak. What magnificent wood! After visiting his shop, we went to the church to see a 16' organ, built by him not long ago. It is well built and laid out for easy maintenance, speaks well, and has well-voiced reeds and foundations. Nothing new in the way of inventions, but it's like an old organ, well built and quite fine.

Next I crossed the sea from Rotterdam to London. I vomited on the trip over, and I almost vomited when I saw the organs there. Where I thought I would find perfection, I found the sloppiest work. With the Royal Organbuilder, Monsieur Hill, I visited the principle organs in that wretched city. I must first tell you that even the largest organ didn't have the 12' front pipes; and if some had 16' pipes inside, that's certainly the upper limit. Pipes of lead as black as coal filled the inside of the organ. The façade also consisted of lead pipes, and the mouths had been pounded flat with the fist. Raised mouths are unknown in this country of factories.

Their organs produced nevertheless a rather decent sound. The foundations are strongly voiced. There are also the swell boxes, which ensure power for the instrument.

I have no more space here to tell you about the organ in Birmingham, which I also visited, covering ninety leagues in the same day on a devil of a train that hurled us along at the speed of lightning. (It's getting dark now and I can't see clearly.) The organ in Birmingham was constructed on the same scale as those in London. The front pipes, however, are 32' made of gilded zinc. The action is as stiff as those made for carillons. Unsuccessful experiments have been made, such as 32' wooden pipes, three feet square made with framed and panels, and sounding like wet drums. It is hardly a masterpiece. Here I am at the end of both my paper and my trip. Please excuse my scribbling – time is short. I am too lazy to recopy my letter. Please give my kind regards to your wife and daughter. Remember me to Monsieur Vidor, and the doctor, with whom I had the plea-sure of dining in your home, and please accept from all of my family our best wishes.

January 29, 1845.
Monsieur Bätz, Organ-builder at Utrecht

My dear Monsieur Bätz, since last October 31, date of my arrival in Paris, I have thought of writing you; but to do that, I had to find a moment of peace – a moment I am still waiting for, because of the mountain of work I found upon my return home. Nevertheless, I am going to fulfill my promise today and describe for you the remainder of my trip.

I have already given you my opinion of the organs that I was able to see during my brief stay in Utrecht, which you made so very pleasant for me. Your associate, Monsieur Witte, has probably told you that I spent a few moments with him at the organ in Rotterdam. I found it very interesting to see that organ again. Once again, I beheld the gigantic proportions of that colossal instrument. It is truly the most monumental organ case I have ever seen. I don't believe a larger organ exists anywhere in Europe. Nevertheless, the interior arrangement does not do justice to the beautiful proportions of the façade. With all the space afforded by the interior of that big box, the various parts of the instrument could be better arranged. It is too bad that the work was not better planned in the beginning. Still, the extensive repairs you are making will give it many qualities that it didn't have originally. Monsieur Witte, who familiarized me with the changes made to the original construction and those you were about to add, gave me a most favorable impression of all the improvements.

I still remember with pleasure your organ and organist in Utrecht. All flattery aside, it is the best work I saw during my trip. Your organ had the most logical arrangement and the most painstaking and conscientious workmanship. It has the most charming tone, is the best suited to its location and, according to my taste, was played the best by the organist.

I left for London and arrived in that great city amidst fog and smoke. I went straight to the Organ-builder to Her Majesty, Monsieur Hill, for whom I had a letter of recommendation from *Chevalier* Neukomm. I went with my colleague to see the principle organs of the city. First, I must mention that the largest organ in London doesn't reach the top of your organ in Utrecht or, for that matter, even the "belt" of the great organs of Holland. This is not their major shortcoming. The inside of these instruments is as black as coal. The inside pipes were generally of lead, only slightly alloyed. Those in the facade were also of lead but gilded. The mouths were beaten flat with the fist; raised mouths, normally found on front pipes, are completely unheard of in this country. The wooden pipes are of fir and are built like packing-crates. The action and all the rest of the instrument are in similar style. I assure you I did not expect to find organs of such poor quality in England. I was as pleased with the detailed craftsmanship in Germany and Holland as I was displeased with the negligence one finds in English organs. Monsieur Hill's workshop is certainly not of the same caliber as Monsieur Bätz' in Utrecht.

I went to Birmingham to see the famous 32' organ built by Monsieur Hill. The organ is located in a large concert hall and the front pipes are indeed 32'; but good Lord, what pipes! They are made of zinc; and with all their seams, they look like downspouts. Again the mouths have been beaten flat with the fist, and gilded to boot, which made the poor workmanship stand out even more. The sound is nonetheless, good. These pipes speak well; but on the other hand, there are 32' wooden flutes in the organ, three feet square, and their speech is relatively poor, or, more accurately, nonexistent. The pipes were put together with panels and frames, in such a way that the faulty construction robbed the pipes of all the power that could have been obtained from pipes of such extraordinary size, if they had been correctly made. In all, this work is of no better quality than the organs in London of which I have already spoken. The keys have a stiff touch. The action is rather badly built and poorly installed. The overall effect of the organ is more than sufficient, considering the size of the hall, but I believe that it would lose ninety-nine percent of its power and tone, if it

were placed in the church in Rotterdam.

Well, my dear Monsieur Bätz, that was how my artistic journey ended. You can see that the last was hardly the best. In Germany and Holland, there are really artistic craftsmen building organs; in England, they are simply organ-builders.

So now I must thank you for your hospitality and all the beautiful instruments that you showed me. I must also ask you to thank your excellent organist for his delightful concert on your organ. Please thank Monsieur Witte for the kindness he showed me, and tell him how much I regret not having been able to talk with him at greater length. I would like very much to see you again, all of you together or as many as possible, either in Paris, where I would be delighted to welcome you with the same hospitality you showed me, or in Holland. In any event, I shall not fail to reciprocate. The organ we are building for la Madeleine will be installed in July. I will be happy to tell you when the dedication ceremony will take place. You must try to come see us on that occasion. You won't see a gigantic organ, like yours in Holland, but I hope you will see some innovations that will be to your liking.

I would have to use the margins, for want of space, and to retrace my steps, as in my trip, to describe everything from beginning to end. When you see Monsieur Schumann, call him Shoemaker for me. I certainly wouldn't call him an artist.

My father and brother, who know you by reputation, have asked me to send you their kind regards. Please remember me to Monsieur Schmidt, Royal Organist in the Hague, and to his friend or brother-in-law, the flutist, whose name I don't recall.

Here we are back at the point of departure. So my dear Monsieur Bätz, thank you again for your warm hospitality. Please accept my sincere expression of lasting friendship. Your devoted servant.

September 11, 1856.
Mr. Dwirner, Architect of the Cologne Cathedral
Sir:
Upon my return to Paris I told Mr. Hittorff about the warm welcome you gave me upon

his recommendation. I thank you, and should like to comment on your plan for an organ for your magnificent cathedral.

After leaving Cologne, we made a brief excursion through the north of Germany in order to see the most outstanding organs in that area. In Berlin, we saw the works of Mr. Buckholtz, one of the best organbuilders. Those include the new organs in the churches of Saint Peter and Saint Nicholas, as well as the one he restored in the parish church, etc.

These moderately-sized instruments are very compatible with the churches in which they are installed. Modern cases with 16' pipes and gothic styling are not really exceptional, insofar as architecture is concerned. One generally finds more harmonious proportions in cases dating from the seventeenth and eighteenth centuries.

We also visited the organ of Weimar. The learned author, Mr. Töpfer, who has written a treatise on organ-building, lives there. There is little noteworthy about the case, which is old, and even less about the instrument, which is of modern construction. It follows the principles of the learned organist of Weimar. Next we went to Frankfurt, where we found an organ under construction by the celebrated builder of the organ in Saint Paul's at Frankfurt, Mr. Walker [*sic*], of Ludwigsburg, whom we know. He urged us to inspect the organ which he is about to complete in the Cathedral of Ulm.

So we went to Ulm to see this great instrument, of which you yourself had spoken. It is unquestionably the largest organ which has ever been built, and it is this organ in particular that I should like to discuss with you.

Upon entering that huge church, one is immediately struck by the modest dimensions of the woodwork on the case. The two large side towers each house 5 big pipes 2 feet in diameter; together with them are tiny cases containing very small pipes that clash with the big ones, like dwarfs standing beside giants. The crowns of these large towers are also disappointingly small. The wooden parts, which should serve as frames and support for the pipes, seem like ivy clinging to the pipes themselves. Although all this work seems well done when viewed up close,

the effect is completely lost when the case is seen from the floor of the church. The case is, for the most part, too small. Heavier beams should be used to frame such large pipes; an organ really ought to give the appearance of a musical instrument, since it is said to be the king of instruments. Above all, there must be a reasonable progression in size between the large and small pipes. Besides, low tones should not be simply juxtaposed with the high tones; they should be separated by the tones of the middle register. If a gradual progression is observed between the small and large pipes, then there will be a homogenous succession of sounds in the display. We must not forget that the sounds from the display pipes are always the finest in the organ.

We also noticed that the vault of the porch is a bit low and could have been raised a few feet without difficulty.

There is another observation which seemed to agree with your opinion: placed as it is behind the great vault at the end of the nave, the organ seems imprisoned by the large pillars, which hide a major portion of the case.

In our opinion, it would have been better to place the instrument in front of the two pillars, where the old organ was. This location seems all the better because the site is naturally defined by the two bays of the blank wall in front of the arches of the nave.

We believe this example should be reason enough for discarding the idea of similar placement for the organ in the Cathedral of Cologne. Considering the vast size of the church, if this location were chosen, it would be absolutely necessary to move at least the façade of the organ in front of the pillars, in order to allow the sound to travel as freely as possible. Another fault which we believe to be very serious, and which will surely shorten the life of the instrument, if the hole which was left inside the organ for access to the bell tower and for construction materials. Besides the accidents which might occur while the work is in progress, this hole would necessarily cause dust and debris to collect in the organ, soon spoiling the sound of the pipes.

Therefore, Sir, we believe that if the

north-transept location that you favor were accepted, this would be the best location for an organ worthy of the Cathedral of Cologne.

As soon as we have received the tracings that you offered, we shall hasten to submit our ideas on the disposition of the instrument and the size of the case in relation to the size of your immense Cathedral.

In the meantime, please accept our thanks for your warm hospitality. With kindest regards, *etc*.

APPENDIX C

Several Contracts in English

Devis I, #1, 4 October 1833
Church of Notre-Dame-de-Lorette, in Paris
Specification for a 16′ Organ, for the New Church
of Notre-Dame-de-Lorette.

Pédale
Compass: 25 notes, A to F, 2 Octaves.
1. *Flûte ouverte* 16′, from C   25 pipes
2. *Flûte ouverte* 8′, from C
3. *Flûte ouverte* 4′, from C
4. *Trompette* with ravalement,
    F to F   25 pipes
5. *Trompette* with ravalement   25 pipes
6. *Clairon* with ravalement   25 pipes

Grand orgue
Compass: 54 notes, C to F, 4½ Octaves.
1. *Grand Cornet* VII Ranks,
    from F   37[8] pipes
2. *Montre* 16′: bass pipes of wood,
    up to the largest that can be
    placed in the façade.
3. *Montre* 8′
4. *Solicional* [sic] or *Seconde*
    Montre 8′
5. *Bourdon* 16′, from second C
6. *Bourdon* 8′
7. *Prestant*
8. *Flûte* 4′
9. *Dessus de Flûte conique,* from
    third C
10. *Nazard*
11. *Quarte*
12. *Grosse Fourniture* IV Ranks
13. *Petite Fourniture* IV Ranks
14. *Cymbale* IV Ranks
15. *Bombarde:* lowest octave in unison
    with the *Trompette*
16. *Trompette*
17. *Doublette*
18. *Clairon*
19. *Voix humaine*

Positif
Same Compass as *Grand orgue*
1. *Cornet* V Ranks
2. *Bourdon* 8′
3. *Flûte* 8′
4. *Prestant* 4′
5. *Flûte* 4′
6. *Nazard*
7. *Tierce*
8. *Doublette*
9. *Plein jeu* V Ranks
10. *Trompette*
11. *Clairon*
12. *Basson*

Third Manual (*Récit*)
Compass 37 notes, F to F, 3 Octaves.
1. *Bourdon* 8′
2. *Flûte* 4′
3. *Cornet* III Ranks
4. *Flûte octaviante*
5. *Flûte traversière*
6. *Flageolet*
7. *Cor anglais*
8. *Trompette de Récit*

Jeux expressifs: same manual
9. *Voix humaine*
10. *Hautbois*

Windchest Arrangement

Two windchests shall be built for the *Pédale* and located inside either end of the organ case, slightly above the gallery floor. Each chest shall have twice as many channels as there are notes in the pedalboard: each pedal shall operate two pallets, one for the flue stops, and the other for the reeds. As a consequence of this arrangement,

1) the pedal action can be relayed to the pallets by rollers alone, mounted against the inside of the organ case and lying parallel to the gallery floor.

2) The large *Pédale* pipes have their mouths placed as low as possible, so the sound is projected into the nave with but one deflection. We may point out that since the gallery where this organ is to be installed has only the arch for admitting sound into the nave, the organ must be designed in such a way that the largest pipes have their mouths as far below the arch as possible. Thus instead of placing the *Pédale* chests about 3 meters above the floor, as in conventional organs, we find it preferable to locate them as we have stated.

Grand orgue Windchests, and *Positif* Windchest

These two chests shall form a single unit, mounted at the same height as the *Pédale* chests, and built in the same manner, to wit: the channels for the *Grand orgue* stops shall alternate with those for the *Positif*. This chest shall be divided into four sections, all mounted at the same height, and spaced far enough apart to afford easy access for repairs and tuning, as well as for various other purposes, as the need may arise.

Récit Windchest (Manual 3)

Compass: 3 Octaves, F to F: 37 notes.

This chest shall be located above the *Grand orgue* chests so as to hinder maintenance of the pipework as little as possible where the *Grand orgue* is concerned, and so as to permit the best possible projection of the sound from the *Récit* stops into the nave.

The majority of the *Récit* stops shall be enclosed in a box so as to imitate echo effects, and the box may be opened gradually, by means of a pedal, thus imitating a pleasant *crescendo*.

Beneath this chest a reservoir shall be fitted: it may receive wind from the bellows when desired, and by means of a pedal placed above the pedalboard, the organist may vary the pressure in the reservoir. Thus he can increase or decrease the volume of the *jeux expressifs* placed on this chest, swelling the sound from *pianissimo* to *fortissimo,* and rendering every shading known to music.

Detailed Description of Keyboards.

The pedalboard shall be built in German style: the naturals shall be levers on which the entire foot may rest; and the sharps shall be arranged in such a way as to be playable with the toe. This design allows playing *legato* scales, both diatonic and chromatic, with a single foot, which is impossible with conventional pedalboards. Moreover, since the pedals are exposed and space is left between them, dirt or sand cannot lodge between the pedals and cause them to stick, as sometimes happens with conventional pedalboards.

The three manual keyboards shall be similar in construction to those of the finest pianos. Like the pedalboard, the manuals shall be located at the rear of the organ: the organist can see the priest and the altar through the action and between the case-pipes.

All the rollers relaying the key action to the pallets shall be made from iron bar stock of dimensions suited to the function; the pivots shall be turned, and the bearings shall be made of brass, perfectly fitted and carefully polished throughout their length.

The rollers shall be placed inside the rear of the case, as required by the location of the manuals, and the roller-arms shall face the organist. Thus, by removing some panels in the rear of the organ, it will be possible to see the entire action, and so to correct with the greatest of ease any disorder that may occur.

All the vertical rollers relaying the drawstop action shall also be made from iron of the necessary dimensions, and the pivots shall be turned so as to fit precisely into brass bearings. All levers shall also be made from iron of suitable size, such as those used in the drawstop action, etc.

All traces shall be made of choice pine, clear and straight-grained, and they shall be fitted at either end as suits their function. For example, in the drawstop action, the traces and drawstops shall be slotted and provided with two plaques of hard wood: these shall be drilled to fit exactly the pins linking the traces to their levers, and furthermore the pins shall be threaded at one end so they cannot work loose. All trackers, from the manuals to the rollers and from the latter to the pallets, shall be fitted with brass wires at either end, and one set of wires shall be threaded. The unthreaded wires fit the roller arms, and the others are provided with nuts, to facilitate leveling the keys. All trackers, traces, and other wooden rods, etc., shall be varnished, to avoid warping through exposure to the air.

Wood is preferable to metal for trackers and traces, for metal expands and contracts with changes in temperature, causing variations in the level of the keys if iron or brass wire is used for trackers. Now since straight-grained wood does not vary in length according to the temperature, it is better for making these parts.

All three manuals shall be stationary, and two pedals placed at the end of the pedalboard shall permit coupling two or all three together without interrupting the performance. Thus, a final chord may be strengthened two or three degrees in volume, depending on the number of stops drawn on the various manuals.

Two more pedals shall be provided near the pedalboard: one, for opening the *Echo* box; and the other for adding expression to the *Récit* stops.

Bellows.

Bellows shall be provided in sufficient number to supply all the wind the organist can require, even if he draws all the stops. The bellows shall be conveniently located and shall take up as little space as possible at the rear of the gallery.

All valves and pallets in the bellows and the windchests shall be simplicity itself to remove and return to their places: this will permit clearing them of any dirt that may lodge on them.

All metal pipes shall be made of tin, and the thickness of the metal in every pipe shall be precisely controlled with instruments which enable us to measure exactly and without guesswork. Thus the thickness of the metal is pro-

portional to the length and diameter of each pipe, and timbre is uniform throughout the compass.

All case-pipes shall be hardened and polished with the greatest care.

All inside pipes shall be made of metal rolled to the proper thickness, then hammered for greater density, thus affording better tone-quality.

All wooden pipes shall be of the finest workmanship, and they shall be varnished inside and out, to improve their tone and durability.

The majority of the reed pipes shall be built to new scales, to wit: instead of being simply cones, soldered to blocks, they shall resemble the various instruments whose names they bear. For example, the *Trompette* pipes shall have bells at their tops; the *Hautbois*, a narrow inverted bell; and the *Clairon, Basson, Clarinette, Cor anglais,* etc. shall be similar in design to the corresponding instruments. This will imitate their tones as closely as possible, whereas inclusion in the organ [usually] detracts from their character.

The two principal manuals shall have a compass of approximately four and one-half octaves: from C to F in the fifth octave (54 notes). The third manual (*Récit et expressif*) shall have a compass of three octaves: from F in the second octave to F in the fifth (37 notes). I shall point out here that in contrast to old organs, the C# of the bottom octave shall be included, as well as three additional notes in the top octave. I shall also point out that the organ is entirely different from the piano: a compass of five, six, or seven octaves is not required as in the piano, for the organ contains stops at the octave of each other; and by drawing these stops on various manuals, a compass of five, six, seven, or eight octaves may be achieved at will. Therefore, the compass indicated here is not that of the instrument. Moreover, most stops, and especially the reeds, cannot extend upwards beyond F in the fifth octave.

Case.

The case shall not be my responsibility. I shall furnish only the plan for arranging the principal components, and I shall indicate the best arrangement for projecting the sound into the nave with the greatest effectiveness. Then a skillful architect must use these data in designing an elegant case to harmonize with the style of the church.

Summary of the Specification for this Organ.

Chests	Number of Stops	Number of Pipes
Pédale	6	108
Grand orgue	18	1,590
Positif	12	960
Récit	12	440
		3,098

Cost of this Organ   30,000 francs
Completion Time   3 Years.

P. S.   I point out that the price of the instrument could be reduced by decreasing the number of stops.

I also point out that if required, we could undertake to complete the organ in a shorter time. However, since wood is an important material in the principal parts of the organ, such as windchests, for example, there is never any disadvantage in letting them stand for some time once they are completed: then they can be examined and repaired (if any disorder has occurred), before they are installed.

Note Appended to the
Specification Respectfully
Submitted to the Chairman
and Members of the Council,
Notre-Dame-de-Lorette.

According to the organist's request, the pedal compass is not sufficient for him to play the various plain chants that go below C. We undertake to extend the compass down to F, which will give him two octaves instead of one and one-half. I point out, however, that adding this half-octave to the stops listed in my Specification would increase the cost by 7,000 francs. Moreover, since the bass pipes of the *Bombarde* would then be 24 *pieds* tall, they could not be placed in the gallery where the organ is to stand. Now to overcome this obstacle and avoid great additional expense, while still increasing the pedal compass, I respectfully suggest the following:

In place of the *Bombarde,* we could install a wide-scaled *Trompette* with ravalement whose tallest pipe would measure 12 *pieds.*

The *Trompette* listed in the Specification could also have a ravalement, making its lowest pipe 12 *pieds* tall instead of 8, and the *Clairon's* lowest pipe would be 6 *pieds* tall instead of 4. Thus, while doing away with the lowest five pipes of the *Bombarde,* costing 600 francs, we would add 21 new pipes costing 1,100 francs. Therefore, the cost of adding this half-octave would be only the difference between the two, or 500 francs. In this way, the pedal compass could be increased to two octaves from one and one-half, and an expenditure of 500 francs could effect an augmentation that would otherwise cost 7,000 francs. Of course, the lowest reed pipes would be only 12 *pieds* tall instead of 24, as in the *Bombarde* with a ravalement, but I point out that pipes 12 *pieds* tall are low enough in pitch and vigorous enough in tone to accompany and sustain all the reed stops listed in my Specification: 24' pipes found in the ravalement of a *Bombarde* are used only in the largest organs.

The foundation or flue stops of 16', 8', and 4' pitches would be retained as specified: since they are not used playing plain chant, their compass is adequate as planned.

Summary and Composition of
Pédale Stops.

Pedalboard compass: 2 octaves, from F to F.

1. *Flûte* 16', from C	18	pipes
2. *Flûte* 8', from C	18	pipes
3. *Flûte* 4', from C	18	pipes
4. *Trompette,* ravalement beginning at 12' F	25	pipes
5. *Grande Trompette,* from C	25	pipes
6. *Clairon* with ravalement	25	pipes
	Total 129	

Such is the new composition of the *Pédale,* as seems to us most appropriate for augmenting the division specified by us.

11, Quai Voltaire
27 November 1833.
Copy of the Report submitted to the Council of Notre-Dame-de-Lorette by Messrs. Séjan, Benoist, and Miné, organists in Paris, concerning the new organ for said church and the Specification submitted by Messrs. Cavaillé-Coll & Son, organ-builders.

To the Members of the Council, Church of
Notre-Dame-de-Lorette.

Gentlemen:

We have carefully examined the specification drawn up by Messrs. Cavaillé-Coll & Son, and we believe we are justified in stating that it meets your goals fully: the organ will be well built; the materials, superior; and the workmanship, sound.

We have conferred with the younger Mr. Cavaillé, requesting that he explain certain points in his specification that were not entirely clear to us, and we advise that the explanations given by him seemed to us to be conclusive.

We paid particular attention to the mechanism of the organ, which represents considerable difficulty because of the space available. Mr. Cavaillé stated that he was confident he could resolve all problems and build an excellent organ that would be as effective as possible, using methods peculiar to him.

Here are the modifications we consider necessary: Extending the *Grand Cornet* in the *Grand orgue* down to F, requiring seven sets of pipes more than specified. Extending the *Flûte* down to G, requiring five additional pipes. A *Grosse Trompette* in place of the *Bombarde* specified.

Transferring the *Voix humaine* from the *Positif* to the *Grand orgue*.

Adding a *Doublette* to the *Grand orgue*.

Replacing the *Voix humaine* in the *Récit* with the *Cromorne* from the *Positif*. Enclosing all eight *Récit* stops in a *boîte expressive*.

The organist has written to request extending the *Pédale* down to F. We believe it would be sufficient to extend the reed stops only as far as A, since the flue stops have an adequate compass (C) as specified.

We also consider it indispensable to make the *Bourdon* 16' in the *Grand orgue* a full-compass stop. The pipes required for these augmentations are:

3 for the *Bombarde* 16', pure tin.
3 for the *Trompette* 8', pure tin.
3 for the *Clairon*, pure tin.

For the *Bourdon* 16' in the *Grand orgue*:
12 stopped wooded pipes, the largest being 16'.

The organ shall be completed in two years.

Having reached agreement among ourselves, we have made the foregoing report, and we endorse Mr. Cavaillé's Specification, in the belief that his ability will deserve your confidence and ours.

As to the price of the augmentations we request and advise you to have made, if you desire a well-balanced instrument, we suggest the figure of 2,000 francs entered in the Specification, with the comment that these additions involve the low notes, whose pipes are the largest and thus the most expensive.

We believe, Gentlemen, that we have considered this matter with all the care you expect from us, and we hope that our efforts may deserve your confidence.

Yr. humble servants,
Signed   L. Séjan, Benoist, A. Miné
Paris
6 December 1833

Memorandum of modifications and additions proposed by Messrs. Séjan, Miné, and Benoist, organists.

The modifications as indicated by these gentlemen that involve no additional expenses are as follows:

Replacing the *Bombarde* by a *Grosse Trompette*.

Transferring the *Voix humaine* from the *Positif* to the *Grand orgue*.

Enclosing all eight *Récit stops* in a *boîte expressive*: most of these stops are already specified as being under expression.

The additions proposed by those Gentlemen are as follows:

1833	
Notre-Dame-de-Lorette	Totals
7 notes in the *Grand Cornet* VII	49 pipes
5 notes in the *Flûte*	5 pipes
a *Doublette*	54 pipes
a *Cromorne*	54 pipes
the lowest octave of the *Bourdon* 16'	12 pipes
ravalement of the *Bombarde* in the *Pédale*	3 pipes
Carried forward	177 pipes
Ravalement of *Trompette* (*Pédale*)	3 pipes
Ravalement of *Clairon* (*Pédale*)	3 pipes
Total pipes	183 pipes

Price of these additions: Two thousand six hundred twenty francs   2,620 f.

At this point, I respectfully bring to your attention the fact that in order to install these pipes, we must extend the pedalboard, roller-board, and *Pédale* windchests, in order to install these three notes in the lowest octave.

In the *Cornet* for the *Grand orgue,* the addition of 49 pipes requires enlargement of the toeboards and increasing the number of tubes.

The *Grand orgue* requires a new slider and the corresponding drawstop-action for the *Doublette* stop; the addition of a *Cromorne* to the *Positif* also requires a new slider and its mechanism.

These additions to the action are rather expensive, and together with the cost of pipes as listed, they will exceed the sum of 3,000 francs. Nevertheless, we shall complete the alterations for this price, if the Church Council sees fit to authorize them.

27 December 1833.

Devis I, #2, 7 October 1833
Royal Church of Saint-Denis
Specification for a 32′ Organ.

1.   *Pédale*, compass 2 octaves
  1. *Flûte ouverte* 32′
  2. *Flûte* 16′
  3. *Flûte* 16′ *octaviante* (8′ pitch)
  4. *Flûte* 8′
  5. *Flûte* 8′ *octaviante* (4′ pitch)
  6. *Flûte* 4′
  7. *Flûte* 4′ *octaviante* (2′ pitch)
  8. *Gros nazard octaviant* (at the fifth of
     the *Prestant*)
  9. *Bombarde*
  10. *Trompette*
  11. *Cor de chasse*
  12. *Clairon*
  13. *Clairon*, octave higher
  14. *Clairon*, two octaves higher
  15. *Grosse caisse, Cymbales,* and *Chapeau
      chinois*
  16. *Caisse roulante*

2.   *Positif*
  1. *Cornet* V
  2. *Montre* 8′
  3. *Prestant* 4′
  4. *Bourdon* 16′
  5. *Flûte* 8′
  6. *Flûte* 4′
  7. *Nazard*
  8. *Quarte*
  9. *Tierce*
  10. *Larigot*
  11. *Doublette*
  12. *Fourniture* V
  13. *Cymbale* IV
  14. *Trompette*
  15. *Basson*

3.   *Grand orgue*
              Manual II
  1. *Grand cornet* IX
  2. *Montre* 32′, from 24′ F
  3. *Montre* 16′
  4. *Montre* 8′
  5. *Violoncelle* 8′
  6. *Bourdon* 16′
  7. *Bourdon* 8′
  8. *Flûte ouverte* 8′

9. *Gros nazard* 8′ [*sic*]
10. *Prestant* 4′
11. *Flûte* 4′
12. *Nazard*
13. *Quarte*
14. *Tierce*
15. *Doublette*
16. *Grosse fourniture* IV
17. *Grosse cymbale* IV
18. *Fourniture* IV
19. *Cymbale* VI
20. *Trompette à pavillon*

              Bombarde
              Manual III
  1. *Grand cornet* IX
  2. *Flûte* 16′
  3. *Flûte* 8′
  4. *Flûte* 4′
  5. *Prestant*
  6. *Nazard*
  7. *Quarte*
  8. *Tierce*
  9. *Bombarde*
  10. *Trompette*
  11. *Clairon*

Stops Mounted Horizontally Relative to the
    Other Pipes, Outside the Organ-Case
  12. *Trompette*
  13. *Clairon*, with one break
  14. *Clairon*, octave higher, with 2 breaks
  15. *Clairon*, 2 octaves higher, with 3 breaks

(5.)   *Récit*
              Manual IV
  1. *Flûte conique* 8′
  2. *Bourdon* 8′
  3. *Cornet* VI
  4. *Trompette*
  5. *Hautbois*

      Jeux expressifs, Mounted on the
              Récit Chest
  6. *Basson*
  7. *Cor anglais/Hautbois*
  8. *Voix humaine*

9. *Trompette expressive,* mounted outside
10. Set of Bells, played from Manual IV.

6.   *Echo*
                          Manual V
  1. *Bourdon* 16'
  2. *Flûte* 8' (*ouverte*)
  3. *Flûte* 4'
  4. *Cornet* V
  5. *Violon*
  6. *Clarinette*
  7. *Voix humaine* 16' pitch
  8. *Flûte traversière*

7.   Windchest Arrangement
                    Pédale chests

Two *Pédale* chests shall be built, and they shall be installed slightly above the gallery floor, at either end of the organ-case, inside same. Each chest shall have two pallet-boxes, one above and the other below. Each chest shall also have twice as many channels as there are pedals, so that two separate wind-supplies, of different pressures, may be had: the lower pressure is intended for the flues, and the higher pressure for the reeds, as is required by the tone-quality of the various wind instruments to be imitated. Thus each pedal shall open two pallets: one for the reeds, and one for the flues.

This arrangement achieves the following results: 1) the pedal action can be relayed to the pallets by rollers alone, these rollers being mounted inside the panels of the organ-case, and lying parallel to the gallery floor. 2) the huge *Pédale* pipes use space which in all organs is generally left vacant, and thus they do not encumber the valuable space they usually occupy along the sides of the organ at the level of the *Grand orgue* chests, which stand about 3 meters above the gallery floor. Therefore, although many of the 32' pipes and some of the 16' pipes extend above the *Grand orgue* chests, it will nevertheless be seen that the majority fit below them, and that I obtain considerable space beside the chests. I can use this space for the bass pipes of *Grand orgue* stops, whereby these pipes are made easily accessible for maintenance.

8.   *Positif* Windchest

This chest shall be built with all the care and precision required by its function. The pallets will open upwards, as is customary, and the key-action will be relayed in the usual manner, through first-class levers extending beneath the organist's bench. Note, however, that the pivots for these backfalls, rather than being pins let into a dado cut along the beam supporting the levers, will be carefully fitted, individual pivots, each lying perpendicular to the motion of its backfall.

9. *Grand orgue* and *Bombarde* Windchest

These two chests shall form a single unit. It will be built in similar manner to the *Pédale* chests, in that channels for *Grand orgue* and *Bombarde* stops will alternate. Two pallet-boxes will be fitted, one at the front and one at the rear of the organ: each will contain one set of pallets, each controlling the channels corresponding to the two manuals. This chest will be divided into four sections, mounted at the same height, and shown in the order of their division. The divisions will be so made as to allow convenient access to the pipes for tuning, repair, and various other purposes as the case may arise. Note that in this chest, as in the *Pédale* chests, the wind-pressure for the *Grand orgue* will be different from that supplied to the *Bombarde*. The reason is quite simply that by their nature, reed stops, like the corresponding instruments, require greater wind-pressure than flues.

The last four reed stops listed in the *Bombarde* division shall be mounted horizontally with reference to the other ranks and on the front of the case, so that their resonators are directed into the nave.

10.   *Récit* Windchest
                    Manual IV.

This chest shall be installed beneath the *Grand orgue* chests in such a way as to create the least possible obstacle to maintenance of the action, and to permit the best possible path for the sound from the ranks mounted in the *Récit* to reach the nave. Like the *Pédale* and *Grand orgue* wind-chests, this chest will have two pallet-boxes. The *jeux expressifs* will be isolated from the other ranks immediately when the wind-pressure in the corresponding pallet-box is increased or decreased by means of a pedal, which device permits the expression of various shadings, as required by the score.

The two pallets controlled by each key can be operated separately or together, by means of a simple mechanism.

This single manual also controls the Bells, so that the following registrations are possible: *Récit* stops, *Jeux expressifs*, Bells, *Récit* and *Jeux expressifs*, *Récit* and Bells, Bells and *Jeux expressifs*, and all three together.

11.   *Echo* Wind-chest.

The Echo chest shall be installed above the *Grand orgue*, in the center of the organ. All its stops shall be enclosed in a box, so as to imitate as closely as possible the effect that gives this division its name. By means of a pedal, the box may be opened gradually, thus imitating a pleasant *crescendo*.

12.   Construction of the Keyboards.

The pedalboard shall be built in the German style, each natural key in the compass being long enough to accommodate the entire foot, and the sharps arranged for playing with the toes. This design allows playing *legato* scales with the same foot, either chromatically or diatonically, which is impossible with conventional pedalboards. Furthermore, since the sides of the pedals are exposed and there is space between them, dirt or sand cannot cause them to bind.

13. The five manual keyboards shall be made like those of the best pianos.

14. All roller-boards — mechanisms for relaying the key motion to the pallets — shall have dimensions appropriate to their functions, their pivots lathe-turned, their bearings of brass and carefully fitted, and their entire length carefully polished.

15. All vertical rollers shall be made from iron of the appropriate dimensions, their pivots lathe-turned, and their bearings of brass and carefully fitted: each part shall be carefully filed and polished.

16. All levers shall also be made from iron of the appropriate dimensions, and their pivots shall be lathe-turned to fit brass bearings. Such levers shall be used, for example, in the draw-stop-action.

17. All traces shall be made from select, straight-grain pine, and they shall be fitted at either end in a manner appropriate to their function. For example, the drawstops shall be fitted at the yokes with brass plates, drilled to fit the pins linking them to their respective levers: these pins shall be threaded on one side of the yoke, to keep them from falling out while in use.

18. All trackers, from keys to rollers and from rollers to pallets, shall be (round), fitted at each end with a brass wire, one engaging the roller-arm, and the other provided with a nut, to allow leveling the keyboard.

19. All trackers, as well as traces and other wooden rods, shall be varnished, to prevent warping through contact with the air.

20. Wood is preferable to metal for trackers and traces, for metal expands and contracts with changes in temperature: the keyboards go out of adjustment when iron or brass wires are used. Since straight-grained wood does not vary in length with the temperature, it is preferable, as our experience has shown.

21. All five manual keyboards shall be stationary, and three pedals placed beside the pedalboard shall permit coupling two or three manuals together, without interruption in performance. Thus the fourth manual may be coupled to the third, so that by using the *Bombarde* manual, the Bells may be played.

22. Three more pedals shall be arranged beside the ones previously described, controlling the *Grosse Caisse, Cymbale,* and *Chapeau chinois;* the *Caisse roulante;* and the *Echo* box, respectively.

23. The expression pedal shall be placed at the center of the pedalboard, a bit above it.

24. The three overblowing stops placed in the *Pédale* may raise a question as to why I have used such large pipes to produce sounds which might be obtained from pipes half their size. My answer is that they are not the same sounds, and they can be distinguished by their characteristic timbres. The latter are produced by a vibrating column of air with a node at its mid-point, so that although the pitch is the same, the tone is more aggressive and the volume greater. If we take the volume of air as an index of the volume of sound, the ratio with a conventional pipe of the same pitch is $1:2^3$, or $1:8$. Therefore, the sound of overblown pipes is eight times greater than that of conventional pipes at the same pitches; so if I

devote space to these larger pipes, I obtain greater effects from them.

25. The reed pipes mounted horizontally on the front of the organ-case have a similar advantage over inside pipes, for their sound reaches the nave without obstacle, so that a single stop thus mounted outside is more effective than two placed inside: the *Trompette expressive* mounted horizontally and played from the *Récit* manual can make itself clearly heard, and it replaces for solo work the keyed and valve trumpets used in concerts.

26.   Bellows

The bellows shall be cuneiform, as in old organs, and they shall be provided in sufficient number to supply all the wind the organist may require, even when he draws all the stops. The bellows shall be conveniently located in the room behind and above the gallery, at about the level of the *Grand orgue* wind-chests: they shall take up as little space as possible. They shall be arranged in two rows, one above the other, and they shall furnish wind at pressures suited to the tone of the various stops.

27. The wind-trunks leading from the bellows to the chests will extend through the wall, and their length will not exceed two meters; thus, the wind will lose none of its pressure, since the lines are short.

28. I shall point out here that if I use conventional bellows as old builders did, I am not governed by habit or routine: I should use feeders and reservoirs if they afforded any improvement, but I believe that in organs, conventional bellows are an advantage, as I shall attempt to prove.

29. It is common knowledge that flue or mutation stops change pitch as their wind changes pressure: the pitch rises as the wind-pressure increases, and it falls as the pressure decreases. Therefore, in order to ensure stable pitch, the wind pressure must be made uniform. Now let us see which type of bellows is better suited to this purpose.

30. Let us then imagine a bellows composed of three boards: the center one stationary, and the top-board hinged to the former to make a cuneiform reservoir, or rising parallel to the center-board to form a so-called "lantern" reservoir. Either arrangement will suffice for our demonstration. Let us also imagine the bottom-board opening as usual to take in the air which it then forces into the reservoir. Let us now consider this system in operation: I notice that in order to be forced into the reservoir, the wind in the feeder must be compressed more than it is already. This is natural, for if the two pressures were equal, they would balance each other, and the wind in the feeder would not enter the reservoir. Hence I conclude that at each stroke of the feeder, the wind-pressure in the reservoir varies: as we have already observed, this variation in pressure affects the pitch of the pipes, so it represents a fundamental defect in this type of bellows.

Let us now examine cuneiform bellows alone.

31. It is common knowledge that each bellows is mounted in such a way that its top-board is raised by means of a lever, thus filling the bellows with air; then the weight of the board, together with any added weight, produces the necessary wind-pressure. As the top-boards fall and the wind is exhausted, they are raised again, and constant wind-pressure is maintained only by the uniform weight of the boards. Now the construction of these bellows does not ensure uniform wind-pressure, for when the top-board is fully raised, the ribs forming the sides add their weight to that of the board: this extra weight decreases as the top-board descends. However, this defect is easily remedied once observed, by means of a compensating weight which increases as the pressure exerted by the board decreases. Therefore, with cuneiform bellows constructed as I have outlined, the uniform wind-pressure required for stable pitch is sure to be obtained.

32. It may be objected that the compensating weights fitted to cuneiform bellows may also be applied to reservoirs. This is quite true, but such compensation in no way corrects the shortcoming which we have observed in this type of bellows.

Therefore, it seems to me preferable to use conventional bellows, especially when, as in the present instance, we have the room necessary for their installation. In my opinion, feeders and reservoirs should be used only when space does not permit using conventional bellows.

33. All valves and pallets, both in the bellows and the wind-chests, shall be so made that

they can be removed and installed with the greatest of ease: this allows removal of dirt that may lodge on them.

34. All metal pipes shall be made of tin, and the thickness of the metal in each pipe shall be gauged with the utmost care, using instruments which allow us to measure precisely and without guesswork. Thus, the metal in each pipe will have a thickness proportional to the length and diameter of the pipe, giving uniformity of tone throughout the rank.

35. All display pipes shall be hammered, polished, and burnished with the utmost care. All inside pipes shall be made of metal whose gauge has been determined by rolling and whose density has been increased by hammering: this results in superior tone quality.

36. All wooden pipes shall be thoroughly seasoned and in addition varnished inside and out, to improve both their tone and their durability.

37. The largest display pipes and any others of considerable weight shall have an iron hoop soldered around the top and an iron bar mounted across the diameter: from the middle of this bar, and thus from the center of the pipe, an iron rod shall extend upwards through a wooden beam secured to the case-work: a nut threaded on this rod will allow hanging the pipe or at least steadying it in its original position. It often happens, when this precaution is neglected, that these enormous pipes collapse into their feet through their sheer weight, thus deforming the mouths and preventing speech. Repairing these pipes is difficult and expensive.

38. Most of the reed pipes shall be built to new scales: instead of having plain conical resonators soldered to the blocks, as is customary, they will resemble the various instruments for which they are named. The *Trompette*, for example, shall be fitted with bells at their tops; the *Hautbois*, with a narrow, spindle-shaped top; and the *Clairons, Bassons, Clarinettes, Cors anglais*, etc. will be designed so as to resemble those instruments. This is done to imitate the various sounds as closely as possible, since ordinarily the true character of these instruments is altered through subordination to the tonal scheme of the organ.

39. The compass of the three principal keyboards shall be about 4½ octaves, from C to

the F in the fifth octave above (54 keys). The *Récit* and *Echo* manuals shall have a compass of 3 octaves, from F of the second octave to F of the fifth (37 keys). Note that in contrast to old organs, low C# will be included here, and the upward compass is extended by three notes. Note also that the organ keyboard is entirely different from that of the piano. It is not necessary that the organ keyboard have a compass of 5 to 7 octaves, for the stops differ among each other by as much as 4 octaves. Thus, by drawing certain stops on the various manuals, we may obtain a compass of from 5 to 10 octaves, at will. Therefore, the manual compass which I specify is more than adequate: most stops, particularly the reeds, do not speak higher than F in the fifth octave.

40. The bass pipes in the *Montre 32'*, *Montre 16'*, and the *Flûte 16'* of the *Bombarde* up to and including 8' C, shall be winded from a separate chest: by means of a pedal or a drawstop, these pipes shall be playable either from the pedalboard or their respective manual keyboards.

The results of this arrangement are 1) that in *bravura* pieces where the tempo is fast, these bass pipes may be silenced: they do not speak promptly enough, and they merely waste wind; and 2) that by adding these bass notes to the *Pédale*, the latter will reinforce their tone, while for broad passages, the manuals will include 16' and 32' stops throughout their compass.

41.   Organ-Case

I shall not assume responsibility for the case-work, for if I did, I should perhaps design a less elegant case in my efforts to secure the most effective design from the viewpoints of acoustics and sound projection. Therefore I shall give only the arrangement of the various divisions and their chief components, showing the best scheme for projecting the sound into the nave, where it is to be heard: a skillful architect must then design a case which ensures these tonal qualities and harmonizes with the style of the Church.

42.   Summary of the Present Specification:

Divisions	Number of Stops	Number of Pipes
Pédale	16	350
Positif	15	1,284

Grand orgue ..	20	1,962
Bombarde	15	1,026
Récit	10	555
Echo	8	444
	85 [84]	5,621

Price of the Organ   80,000 francs.
Time required for Completion 3 years.

P. S. Note that the cost of this organ could be reduced by 12,000 francs if the *Montre* 32′ were eliminated; a greater saving could be effected by omitting various other stops.

Note also that if my proposal is selected, I shall require spacious quarters for a work-shop during the construction. Further, if required, the time for completion could be reduced. However, since wood is the chief material used in building essential parts of the organ (windchests, for example), there is never any disadvantage in letting these parts stand for a time after completion, since any defects may be corrected before the parts are installed.

Devis I, #5, 10 January 1834
Royal Church at Saint-Denis
Proposal for a 32′ Organ, Designed in Accordance with the
Requirements laid Down by the Academy of Fine Arts.

This organ shall have six keyboards: five manual and one pedal.

The five manual keyboards shall have a compass of approximately four and one-half octaves, from C to the fifth F above: 54 keys, from the lowest note (C) of the 'cello to the second F above G in the treble clef.

The pedal keyboard will have a compass of two octaves, F to F: from the lowest F in the bass clef to the third F above.

I point out here that although the Requirements specify a pedal compass of three octaves and an overall compass for the organ of five octaves, playing would be greatly facilitated by a pedal keyboard of two octaves only. Given equal dimensions, the pedals can be more widely spaced, so that when the organist uses this keyboard, he need not look at his feet, in order to avoid playing two notes at once, as would inevitably be the case with a three-octave pedal keyboard. It is well to point out also that the 32′ *Flûte* would begin at low C, rather than at the 24′ F, as specified in the Requirements. Similarly, the 16′ *Flûte* would begin a t24′ F instead of 16′ C; the 8′ *Flûte* at 12′ F; and the 4′ *Flûte*, at 6′ F. Thus, the *Pédale* is augmented by 28 of the largest pipes, which would effectively compensate for the treble pipes in the third octave not provided, making the *Pédale* complete throughout its compass.

Bellows

The bellows shall consist of eight rectangular reservoirs of the parallel or lantern type, the dimensions of each being as follows:

> Length: 3 meters
> Width: 1.50 meters
> Height: 1 meter.

Each will have a capacity of four cubic meters, so the eight reservoirs will have a combined capacity of 36 cubic meters (1,050 cubic *pieds*). The plate accompanying the present specification shows one of these reservoirs, fitted with a mechanism of our design which maintains the top-board parallel with the bottom and is free of friction: there is also a compen-

sating weight to regulate the pressure of the top-board, insuring uniform wind-pressure.

Beneath each [pair (? erased)] of reservoirs is fitted a feeder operated by a lever, which feeder supplies its capacity of wind to each of two reservoirs in alternation. The intake and exhaust valves will be arranged in such a way that when the intake valves (for example) open, the exhaust valves close, and *vice versa*. As a consequence, each time wind is supplied to the reservoir, the exhaust valve is closed, thus shutting the reservoir off from the wind-chest: thus, the variations in wind-pressure that result from forcing wind into the reservoir cannot affect the speech of the pipes, as is the case with conventional feeders. It will be seen that this system offers all the advantages of bellows, and those of feeders as well: as with conventional feeders, we have a lantern reservoir, which contains twice the wind in a given space as do wedge-type bellows; while as with bellows, we have the priceless advantage of uniform wind-pressure, without the attendant disadvantage of making the organist's performance dependent upon the whim or the inexperience of the blower.

Arrangement of the Windchests
Pédale Chests.

Two windchests shall be built for the *Pédale,* to be installed slightly above the floor of the organ-loft, against either end of the organ case, and inside the same.

Each chest will have twice as many channels as it contains notes, so that each pedal opens two pallets: one for the flue stops, and one for the reeds.

As a consequence of this arrangement: 1) the pedal action may be relayed to the pallets by rollers alone, mounted on the inside of the case and lying parallel to the gallery floor. 2) The huge *Pédale* pipes occupy space which in most organs is left vacant. Thus, they do not obstruct the valuable space that they usually occupy at either end of the case at the level of the *Grand orgue* windchests, which lie approximately three meters above the gallery floor. Although a large number of 32′ pipes and a few 16′ pipes extend above the *Grand orgue* chests, it is nonetheless obvious that the majority of these pipes are contained below chest level, and that much space is thus gained at the ends of the chests. This space may be used to offset the bass pipes of *Grand orgue* stops for ease of maintenance.

Positif Chest(s).

Both *Positif* wind-chests will be built with all the care and precision required by their function, and they will be mounted in the lower part of the organ-case, between the *Pédale* chests and the manuals. The key-action will be achieved by rollers, rather than the backfalls usually employed.

Grand orgue Windchest and *Bombarde* Chest Controlled by the Second and Third Manuals.

These two large chests will form a single unit. It will be built in a manner similar to that used for the *Pédale* chests: it will contain twice as many channels as are required by the compass of the keyboards, so that *Grand orgue* and *Bombarde* channels alternate. Two pallet-boxes will be fitted, one at the front and the other at the back of the organ, each containing the pallets to be controlled by the *Grand orgue* and *Bombarde* manual keys respectively. This windchest will be composed of four sections, all mounted at the same height and separated by spaces adequate to allow access to the pipes for tuning, repairs, and other purposes, as the need may arise.

Récit Windchest, Controlled by the Fourth Manual.

The *Récit* and *Echo* windchest will be mounted above the *Grand orgue* chest at the center of the organ. All these stops will be enclosed in a box, so as to imitate echo effects. A pedal will allow gradual opening of the box, thus simulating a pleasant *crescendo*.

Windchest for the *Jeux expressifs*, Played from the Fifth Manual.

This chest will be mounted at the same level as that for the *Récit* and *Echo*, and attached beneath it will be a reservoir which can be filled with wind as desired: a pedal placed above the pedal keyboard will allow the organist to increase or diminish the wind-pressure, thus increasing and diminishing the volume of the *Jeux expressifs* placed on this chest. In this manner, he can go from *pianissimo* to *fortissimo* either in an instant or gradually, thus rendering every nuance contained in musical art.

Construction of the Keyboards.

The pedalboard shall be built in the German style, each natural key in the compass being long enough to accommodate the entire foot, and the sharps arranged for playing with the toes. This design allows playing *legato* scales with the same foot, either chromatically or diatonically, which is impossible with the customary pedal arrangement. Furthermore, since the sides of the pedals are exposed and there is space between them, dirt or sand cannot cause them to bind, as happens with conventional pedal keyboards.

The five manual keyboards will be made like those of the best pianos, and they will be stationary rather than sliding in and out for coupling, as is customary. Instead, by means of a simple mechanism original with us, the organist can couple the first and second manuals, the second and third, the third and fourth, or the fourth and fifth, as he wishes and without disturbing his performance. He can also couple three together: manual one with two and three, two with three and four, or three with four and five; or four manuals together. Finally, he can couple all five manuals at once. All these combinations can be achieved with only four control pedals. Thus it will be seen how easily the organist can obtain various combinations, and without interrupting his performance, as we have said: he can achieve five different levels of volume, depending on the number of stops drawn in each of the divisions.

Action.

All rollers — parts which relay the key action to the pallets — will be made from iron bar stock of suitable diameters, with the pivots lathe-turned; the bearings, of brass, and perfectly fitted. Such rollers will be used for the key action to the *Grand orgue, Bombarde, Positif, Récit,* and *Jeux expressifs.*

All vertical rollers will also be made from iron of suitable diameters, the pivots turned and fitted to brass bearings.

All levers will also be made from iron of suitable dimensions, levers for the drawstop-action as well as others.

All traces will be made of pine selected for straight grain, and the ends will be reinforced according to the effort applied to them. The drawstops, for example, will be reinforced with brass at the fork, and a hole will be drilled to the precise diameter of the pins linking them to the levers: furthermore, these pins will be threaded so as to engage one side of the fork, making it impossible for them to fall out.

All trackers from keys to pallets will be fitted with brass wires at either end, one connected to the roller-arm and the other threaded to allow leveling the keyboard by means of nuts.

All trackers, traces, and other wooden rods will be varnished to avoid warping through changes in the atmosphere. Wood is preferable to metal for trackers and traces, for metal expands and contracts according to the temperature. The regulation of the manuals is uneven when iron or brass is used for the trackers. Therefore, since straight-grained wood does not change its length with the temperature, it is preferable for use in making these parts, as our experience has shown.

All valves and pallets in the bellows and windchests can be removed and installed with the greatest of ease, allowing the removal of dirt whenever necessary.

All metal pipes will be of pure tin, and the thickness of the metal in every pipe will be determined with the greatest care, using instruments which allow us to measure precisely, with no guesswork. In this manner, the gauge of the metal is made proportional to the length and diameter of each pipe, so that the tone is uniform throughout each rank.

All front pipes will be hammered, polished, and burnished with the greatest care.

All inside pipes will be made of metal whose thickness has been determined by rolling: it has also been forged with a trip-hammer, thus becoming more dense and ensuring an even better tonal quality.

All wooden pipes will be of northern pine, perfectly seasoned, and varnished inside and out, to ensure tone and durability.

The largest front pipes, and all others whose weight is considerable, will have an iron hoop soldered around the top, and a bar will be secured to this hoop across the diameter of the pipe. From the center of this bar, and thus from the center of the hoop and the pipe, an iron hanger will extend upwards through a wooden beam secured to the organ-case. By means of nuts on the hangers, these huge pipes may be suspended, or at least steadied, in the desired position. Usually, when this precaution is neglected, large pipes sag into their feet: as their mouths are deformed, they no longer speak. Repairing these collapsed pipes becomes difficult and very expensive.

Casework.

The organ-case shall not be the builder's responsibility, as it does not belong to his craft. Therefore, he merely supplies the plan for the arrangement of the organ's principal interior components, the best scheme for projecting the sound into the church, and the most favorable acoustic relationship among the various divisions. From this point forward, the architect's skill must devise an elegant case, in harmony with the style of the church, and suited to projecting the sound.

Description of the Stops in Each Division.

Pédale.

1. Flûte 32'
2. Flûte 16' [with compass extended down to] 24', à ravalement
3. Flûte 8' [with compass extended down to] 12', à ravalement
4. Flûte 4' [with compass extended down to] 6' à ravalement
5. Nazard at the fifth of the 8' stops
6. Bombarde 24' [16'] wood
7. Basson 12' [8'] wood
8. Bombarde 12' [8'] tin
9. Première Trompette 8'
10. Seconde Trompette 8'
11. Clairon
12. Clairon octave

Positif: 18 Stops

1. Bourdon 16'
2. Montre 8'

3. *Prestant 4'*
4. *Bourdon 8'*
5. *Flûte 4'*
6. *Nazard*
7. *Doublette 2'*
8. *Tierce*
9. *Cymbale* **IV**
10. *Fourniture* **IV**
11. *Flûte octaviante 8'*
12. *Flûte octaviante 4'*
13. *Flûte 2'*
14. *Trompette 8'*
15. *Cor d'harmonie / Hautbois*
16. *Cromorne 8'*
17. *Clairon 4'*

Grand orgue: 20 Stops
Manual II

1. *Grand Cornet* **III**
2. *Montre 32'* from 24' **F**
3. *Montre 16'*
4. *Montre 8'*
5. *Prestant 4'*
6. *Bourdon 16'*
7. *Bourdon 8'*
8. *Dessue de flûte (traversière)*
9. *Flûte Viole*
10. *Nazard*
11. *Flûte octaviante*
12. *Doublette*
13. *Grosse Fourniture* **III**
14. *Grosse Cymbale* **III**
15. *Fourniture* **III**
16. *Cymbale* **III**
17. *Trompette (à pavillon)* to 16' **C**
18. *Basson / Cor anglais*
19. *Clairon*
20. *Voix humaine*

Bombarde: 12 Stops
Manual III

1. *Grand Cornet* **IX**
2. *Bourdon 16'*
3. *Bourdon 8'*
4. *Flûte 8'*
5. *Prestant 4'*
6. *Flûte 4'*
7. *Quarte 2'*
8. *Bombarde*
9. *Première Trompette de Bombarde*
10. *Seconde Trompette de Bombarde*
11. *Premier Clairon*

12. *Second Clairon*

Récit & Echo
Manual IV

1. *Flûte (harmonique) 8'*
2. *Prestant 4'* (replaced by a *Flûte octaviante harmonique*)
3. **Bourdon 8'**
4. *Flûte octaviante 4'*
5. *Doublette 2'*
6. *Trompette harmonique*
7. *Clairon harmonique*
8. *Voix [humaine] harmonique*

2 Jeux expressifs
Manual V

1. *Cor anglais*
2. *Voix humaine*

Itemized Estimate of Prices for the Present Proposal.

Bellows, consisting of 8 reservoirs with a combined capacity of 1,050 cubic *pieds*, with appliances for guiding the top-boards and regulating the wind-pressure, together with feeder-pistons for each, wind-trunks, supports, handles, etc.:

10,000 francs

Windchests.

Pédale chests, 2 *Positif* chests, 4 **Grand orgue** chests, 4 *Bombarde* chests, *Récit* and *Echo* chests, and the chest for the *Jeux expressifs,* with its variable-pressure reservoir and the *Echo* box:

12,000 francs

Keyboards.

Pedalboards, *Positif, Grand orgue, Bombarde, Récit* and *Echo* keyboards, and the keyboard for the *Jeux expressifs,* 6 in all:

1,500 francs

Action

Roller-boards or relay mechanisms from keyboard to pallets, for *Pédale* chests. Roller-boards for *Grand orgue, Bombarde, Positif, Récit,* and *Expression,* with trackers; and draw-stop action, including vertical rollers, levers, and traces:

12,000 francs

Stops, with the Number of Pipes
Contained in Each

Pédale

12 Stops, containing 286 pipes of large dimensions, the lowest being 32 *pieds* high,
6½ *pieds* in circumference, and having a
volume of 80 cubic *pieds*.

10,000 francs

Positif

18 stops, containing 1,482 pipes, with a
total value of

5,000 francs

Grand orgue

20 stops, containing 1,886 pipes, some huge
pipes being of pure tin, polished and burnished, to be mounted in the case: the tallest of
these is 24 *pieds* high and 4 *pieds* in circum-

ference. Tubes etc.:

24,500 francs

Bombarde

12 Stops, containing 891 pipes, with a total
value of

6,000 francs

Récit & Echo

12 Stops, containing 648 pipes, with a total
value of

2,500 francs

Expression

2 Stops, containing 108 pipes, played from
the fifth manual:

1,500 francs

Total number of pipes in the
organ: 5,301.

Total cost of this 32' Organ 85,000 francs

Devis I, #10, 16 September 1836
Church of Notre-Dame, Pontoise
Specification of Repairs and Additions Needed in this Organ.

1° The bellows must be taken down and each unit reconditioned with the greatest care.

2° All the pipes inside the organ must be removed, cleaned, and carefully repaired. Since these pipes are rather well-made, especially the *Trompette, Clairon,* and *Hautbois,* they may all be retained except for a few pipes which are too badly deteriorated: these must be replaced with new pipes.

3° All the case-pipes in the organ must be replaced. They are extremely [thin] and oxidized, and therefore their speech is faint. This is the chief reason why the bass of the organ is too weak in relation to the treble.

4° All the tubes supplying wind to the bass pipes of the *Bourdon* and the 8′ *Montre* must be replaced with new tubes of larger diameter, so as to strengthen the bass of these stops.

5° All the windchests must be thoroughly examined, and any ciphers or runs must be corrected.

6° The *Grand orgue* chest must be provided with a slider for the *Cornet de Récit,* so that this stop may be played at will from the third manual.

7° The entire mechanism must be examined and repaired with the greatest care; and any defective sliders, vertical rollers, or roller-boards must be replaced.

8° The *Grand orgue* chest contains the toeboards and sliders for a 5-rank *Plein jeu*: the 240 pipes of this stop must be made and installed, so as to obtain the fullest tone possible without altering the original disposition of the organ.

9° The *Grand orgue* chests also contain the toeboards, sliders, and drawstop mechanism for a single rank, of 48 pipes. A *Doublette* should be made so as to fill out the tonal scheme of the *Plein jeu* mentioned above, as well as for use alone or in other registrations.

10° The *Tierce* in the *Positif* should be replaced with a 4′ *Flûte* of pure tin: this stop could be combined with the foundation stops, the *Plein jeu,* or the *Cornets* to reinforce them; or it could be used alone, or with the *Bourdons,* for flute solos, etc.

11° The *Grand orgue* should receive an 8′ *Flûte* of full compass: all the pipes would be open, the lowest octave being of Northern pine, and the rest of pure tin. Since this stop should strengthen the bass of the organ, it should be wide-scaled; then it would combine with the two 8′ *Bourdons* to provide a good *Pédale de flûte.*

12° Carrying out the repairs and additions listed above would make this organ as complete as possible within the limits of its original disposition.

The new case-pipes, made of pure tin and with suitable diameters and gauges, would have a more vigorous tone and much greater volume than the extremely thin, oxidized pipes now in place.

Replacing the tubes with larger ones would permit greater volume to be obtained from the bass pipes in the *Bourdon* and the *Montre,* and adding a *Plein jeu* and a *Doublette* to the foundation stops would achieve the true character of religious music.

The 4′ *Flûte* added to the *Positif* would produce a pleasing effect in flute solos and in various combinations with other stops. The 8′ *Flûte* added to the *Grand orgue* would allow flute solos of a more solemn nature. Finally, adding these two stops to the foundations would restore the impressive character of the bass register, as well as correcting the weakness in tone and volume that now characterizes this organ, especially in the bass.

Completion of the work specified above, using all the care required by our craft and all the improved methods developed during our long experience in building organs, would cost three thousand five hundred francs.

3,500 francs

Please note that should the Council deem this figure too high and desire to reduce the expense, 500 francs could be saved by eliminating the two stops described in articles 8 and 9. However, if it were decided to add these stops after the organ was repaired, we could not do so without a greater expense, as we would have to return a second time. Therefore, we could not undertake the installation of these two stops without increasing the price beyond the present figure.

If the present specification is approved by the Council, we undertake to complete the work by 15 March 1837 at the latest, and we consent to any and all expert examination of the work done.

Payment shall be made in installments, as follows: the first, equal to two-thirds of the total, will be made by the Council when the work has been installed and approved by specialists; and the remaining third owed by the Council will be paid in installments to suit the convenience of the Council, after the work has been finished.

Drawn up in duplicate at Paris, 16 September 1836.

signed A. Cavaillé-Coll & Son.

Devis I, #91, 1 January 1843
Organ for the Church of St.-Jérôme at Toulouse
Specification for an Organ with 8' Case-pipes and a 16' *Pédale*.

This organ shall have 2 manuals and a pedalboard.

Manual 1 shall have a compass of 4½ octaves, C to F.

Manual 2 shall have a compass of 3 octaves, F to F.

The pedals shall have a compass of 1½ octaves, C to F.

Stoplist
Manual 1
Foundations

1. *Montre* 8', tin	54	pipes
2. *Violoncelle* 8', tin	54	pipes
3. *Bourdon* 8', tin	54	pipes
4. *Flûte harmonique* 8', tin	30	pipes
5. *Prestant* 4' tin	54	pipes
6. *Quinte*, tin	54	pipes
7. *Doublette*, tin	54	pipes
8. *Plein-jeu*, III ranks, tin	162	pipes
9. *Trompette* 8', tin	54	pipes
10. *Clairon* 4', tin	54	pipes
total	624	pipes

Manual 2.

1. *Flûte traversière*	37	pipes
2. *Flûte octaviante*	37	pipes
3. *Octavin*	37	pipes
4. *Clarinette*	37	pipes
5. *Cor anglais / Hautbois*	37	pipes
6. *Voix humaine*	37	pipes
total	222	pipes

Pédale

1. *Flûte ouverte* 16'	18	pipes
2. *Bombarde* 16'	18	pipes
	36	pipes

Summary of Stops and Pipes, According to Pitch:

	Stops	16'	8'				Pipes
Manual 1	10	0	5	2	2	1	624
Manual 2	6	0	4	1	0	1	222
Pédale	2	2	0	0	0	0	36
	18	2	9	3	2	2	882

Multi-pressure Bellows

The wind supply for this organ shall consist of a two-tiered reservoir supplied by two feeders, whose alternating action shall provide steady and constant wind.

This new multi-pressure bellows system has a great influence on the organ's volume and the steadiness of pitch. Since the wind for the bass range is separate from that supplied to the treble, the accompaniment cannot disturb or weaken the melody line, as happens in conventional organs.

The different wind-pressures obtained with this system also allow winding the bass range of reed stops at the usual pressure, while the treble receives a higher pressure. Thus, the treble speaks more energetically and is not overwhelmed by the bass, as usually happens when the same pressure is used throughout. As a result, the melody retains all its tonal purity and balances with the bass without the use of compound flue stops such as *Cornets* and *Fournitures*. Since the latter blend poorly with reeds, the effect of the reed stops becomes thin and shrill.

This wind-system is also very helpful in voicing the harmonic stops — also our invention — which will be discussed later.

Windchests

The windchests shall be built of choice Holland oak, and they shall be designed in such a way that tuning as well as mechanical repairs and maintenance are easy to carry out.

The *Récit* chest shall be enclosed in a *boîte expressive* which the organist can open at will by means of a pedal, thereby achieving every possible nuance of sound and playing with expression.

Mechanism.

All the rollers, relaying the key action to the pallets, shall be made of iron: the pivots shall be turned, and fitted with precision.

All vertical rollers for the drawstop action, as well as the levers, squares, etc., shall be made of iron and not of wood, as is customarily done.

Keyboards.

The two manual keyboards shall be capped

with first-quality ivory. The sharps shall be capped with ebony, and the frames shall be veneered with rosewood.

The German-style pedalboard shall be made of oak.

The keyboards shall be mounted in a desk-shaped cabinet standing in front of the organ case, so that the organist faces the altar.

Composition Pedals.

Both manuals can be coupled at will by means of a mechanism controlled by a pedal.

The foundations and reeds on Manual 1, in whatever combinations the organist has chosen by drawing stops, shall be available separately or together on the same manual. Pedals shall be provided to achieve the following combinations:

The first puts the bass reeds on or off, as desired, so that the treble reeds may be played against an accompaniment of foundation stops.

The second has the opposite function, cancelling the treble reeds only.

The third puts all the reeds on or off, instantly, and throughout the entire compass of the stops.

We must point out that the various combinations available by means of these pedals can be produced as promptly as a note on a manual keyboard, with the result that while playing a single piece, the organist can use six different levels of volume. Hitherto, such variety was possible only on large organs with four or five manuals.

The bass range of the manuals can be coupled at will to the pedals, by means of an original device also controlled by a pedal. This mechanism enriches the *Pédale* with the bass range of every stop in the organ, as well as allowing the organist to expand his performance on the manuals by including intervals often beyond the reach of the hands.

This organ shall also possess a mechanism for coupling the octaves in the manuals, allowing the organist to play twice as many notes as on ordinary keyboards, and in effect doubling the number and power of the stops in the organ.

Case.

The case shall be built as follows: framework of hardwood, and panels of Northern pine. It shall be without carving, but otherwise its style shall resemble that of the building. The case shall be painted and varnished to imitate aged wood, and the handsome case-pipes shall be made of pure polished tin.

The principal dimensions shall be:
5.3 meters high
4.4 meters wide
1.5 meters deep.

Harmonic Stops.

Although physicists have long known and studied the harmonics in pipes, these tones had not yet been used in the organ. It is common knowledge that tones of this type are fuller and stronger than those of pipes speaking only the fundamental. The air-column in harmonic pipes is divided into two, three, four, or more portions, accordingly as it speaks the first, second, third, or higher harmonic. This air-column modifies the tone, giving it better quality and greater power, without making it strident.

The wind instruments in the orchestra can give us an idea of the superiority of harmonic tone over fundamental tone. In the French horn, for example, since the various pitches are produced by a single instrument, the steps are achieved through harmonics of the fundamental. We observe that the tone becomes fuller, purer, and more beautiful, the higher the pitch and thus the greater number of portions are vibrating within the air-column. The sound of the transverse flute compared to that of the recorder may also convince us that an instrument containing a greater volume of air than a similar, but smaller instrument, will always be superior. Indeed, if the same pitch be sounded on both instruments, all other things being equal, it will be seen that the transverse flute has a volume and a purity never to be equaled by the recorder.

The experiments we have carried out concerning the production of harmonic tones in organ pipes — a field in which science had as yet no concrete data — have enabled us to create several original stops whose superiority was recognized by the Jury at the Exposition of 1839. The organ we submitted for examination was the first ever to contain these new stops.

The broader use we have made of harmonic stops since that time, at St.-Denis and St.-Roch in Paris, has proven the superiority of these new stops over conventional ones.

Four stops listed in the present Specification, namely: *Flûte harmonique, Flûte traversière, Flûte octaviante,* and *Octavin,* shall be built according to this original design. They will give the organ a variety of novel effects, hitherto unknown in conventional instruments.

The price of the organ, excluding packing and shipping, which are left to the Council, but installed by us in the Church of St.-Jerome at Toulouse, shall be   18,000 fr.

If the Council desires to take charge of the case, having it built locally, we shall reduce the price by   2,000 fr.

Thus, the price would be   16,000 fr.

Devis I, #139, 20 March 1844
Cathedral of Nantes (Organ in)

Contents
1. Inventory, and Report on the Deterioration of this Instrument
2. Detailed Estimate of Repairs, Additions, and Improvements Suitable in this Organ.

Inventory, and Report on the Deterioration of this Instrument.

Report.

This organ is one of the largest and most important instruments still extant in France. It appears to date back to the last years of the seventeenth century. The large case-pipes and several stops inside the organ are at least that old: their metal is rather substantial, but the pipes are spoiled by rust spots and oxidation on the outer surfaces.

A thorough rebuilding was carried out by the justly famous builder, Clicot [*sic*], as shown by an inscription on one case-pipe. This able builder added several new stops: the manual *Bombarde* and the *Trompette* in the *Positif* are excellent stops, and they reveal the style of this craftsman. All the reed stops [were] repaired, and their compass was extended at the same time, and they are in general of good quality. The irregularities observed in their tone are the results of neglect, or rather of incompetent maintenance. The low notes are especially remarkable for the fullness and purity of their tone, together with a promptness of speech rarely found elsewhere.

Other minor repairs seem to have been made since Clicot's, but they are surely the work of (less) skilled craftsmen. Although this work had as its purpose mere cleaning of the organ, (some) pipes (have suffered) damage that has detracted considerably from the quality of the instrument. The flue stops, already too few in relation to the reeds, are in general weak, poorly voiced, and disparate in tone quality. The *Pleins-jeux* have had the cutup increased or (have been) voiced in such a way that their tone has been made strident, and it overpowers the full organ in a manner both shocking and unpleasant.

The *Cornet* stops are in a better state of preservation. Their tone is in general good, but although their function in each manual division is to reinforce the reeds, they further emphasize the weakness of the flue stops.

The mutation stops, such as *Gros Nazard, Grosse Tierce, Nazard, Quarte,* and *Petite Tierce,* are in our opinion too numerous in relation to the foundation stops, and give the flue chorus a tone quality similar to that of street-organs. Moreover, several mutations are not used by organists today, and could be replaced to good advantage by foundation and octave stops, thus giving the flue chorus the volume and power it now lacks.

The flue stops in the *Pédale* are also very weak in relation to the reeds in this division. The fundamental bass, which the former stops are intended to provide, lacks power and depth. This division could be noticeably improved by replacing the existing stops with new 16' and 8' stops of full compass.

The case of the organ is quite undistinguished both in its design and its ornamentation.

The construction of the case is careless and flimsy. A large number of iron stays, rather poorly made, have been added between the main case and the wall behind it, to hold the case upright. To strengthen the case, and thus to preserve it, uprights should be added that extend from the gallery floor and are joined to the framework of this large case. The main case has five towers and four flats in the façade. The central tower, containing the three largest pipes in the façade, is triangular in shape.

The *Positif* case has three towers — one triangular — and two flats.

Aside from being nothing spectacular from the standpoint of design, the façade has been coated with a yellow wash that spoils the dignified, austere appearance of this monumental instrument.

Present Condition of the Stops

Positif
(Manual 1)
1. *Cornet* V ranks, 30 notes, C to F 150 pipes
   Good scaling and quality.

2. *Montre* 8'   54 pipes
Speech faint in general. Bass pipes well made but oxidized and dented: could be repaired, better replaced.
3. *Prestant* 4'   54 pipes
Uneven. Keep.
4. *Bourdon* 8'   54 pipes
4 lowest pipes of wood; rest of rather good metal.
5. *Cromorne*   54 pipes
Uneven; hard to reach, it would be better in the location of the *Clairon*. Replace latter by a *Dessus de Flûte* or a *Flûte harmonique* of 30 notes.
6. *Nazard* wide scale   54 pipes
Keep.
7. *Doublette*   54 pipes
Average: Keep.
8. *Tierce*   54 pipes
Useless: Replace with another stop.
9. *Dessus de Flûte* same scale   30 pipes
Average: speech weak.
10. *Plein jeu* VII ranks   378 pipes
All pipes defective: cutup too high, so too shrill. Remove, to space out the other stops.
11. *Hautbois*   37 pipes
Good quality; rather light in the bass.
12. *Trompette* good scale   54 pipes
Well made, good tone. Basses mitered (Clicot).
13. *Clairon* medium scale   54 pipes
Old. Remove to make room for *Cromorne*.
                            total 1,081 pipes

Remarks

The *Positif* chest is not tight. With all sliders closed, many pipes speak when keys are depressed with both hands. However, there do not seem to be any runs. The ranks are very crowded, especially the reeds, and there is no balance between the reeds and the few weak foundation stops.

Considerable weakness of wind, even using the smallest stops.

The channels and pallets are too small to wind all the stops, from the bass up to the third F. From there up, all stops speak properly.

Grand orgue and *Bombarde*
(Manuals 2 and 3)

Stops in order of position on the chest.

1. *Cornet* V ranks: 150 pipes
30 notes, C to F
2. *Cornet* V ranks: 149 pipes
29 notes, C to F
both *Cornets* the mounted on the same toeboard. They are well scaled and of good quality.
3. *Montre* 16' old pipes   54 pipes
the large pipes are oxidized. They appear well made, but their tone is weak and poor.
4. *Montre* 8' old pipes   54 pipes
all pipes offset to the case. Well made, but tone weak or poor.
5. *Bourdon* 16' wide scale   54 pipes
Very faint. Bass pipes offset in front of the *Montre* crowd the other stops (change the voicing).
6. *Flûte* 8' (treble)   37 pipes
Average, uneven.
7. *Prestant* 4' old pipes   54 pipes
Replace.
8. *Bourdon* 8' with chimneys   54 pipes
Weak in the bass.
9. *Gros Nazard* with chimneys   54 pipes
Useless: Replace with a *Gambe* 8'.
10. *Grosse Tierce* open,
Medium scale   54 pipes
Useless: Replace with a 30-note *Flûte harmonique*.
11. *Nazard* very wide scale   54 pipes
Shrill in the treble: Replace with a *Flûte octaviante*.
12. *Quarte de Nazard*
medium scale   54 pipes
Replace with a *Dessus de Flûte harmonique* of 30 notes.
13. *Tierce* wide scale   54 pipes
Useless: Replace with an *Octavin*.
14. *Doublette* medium scale   54 pipes
Average: Keep.
15. *Fourniture* VI ranks   324 pipes
16. *Cymbale* VI ranks   324 pipes
All pipes cut up too high: sound shrill, overpowers all the foundations.
17. *Voix humaine*   54 pipes
Eliminate, or transfer to *Positif*: only the bass is tolerable.

Manual 3

18. *Bombarde* 16'   54 pipes
Very well made, excellent tone: Clicot.
19. *Trompette* same scale   54 pipes

Old pipes: average.
20. *Clairon*   54 pipes
Old pipes: average.
21. *Première Trompette*   54 pipes
Good, repaired by Clicot.
22. *Clairon* medium scale   54 pipes
Average.
23. *Seconde Trompette* narrow scale 54 pipes
Old pipes, average.

                        total   1,952 pipes

Manual 4

1. *Flûte* 8'   37 pipes:
2. *Bourdon* 8'   37 pipes:
Keep for new *Récit* division.
3. *Cornet* IV ranks   148 pipes
Wide scale, good tone.
4. *Trompette* 8'   37 pipes
Average, uneven.
5. *Hautbois*
Keep.

Manual 5: *Echo*

1. *Flûte* 8'   37 pipes:
2. *Cornet* V ranks   165 pipes:
3. *Trompette*   37 pipes:
This chest would be supplanted by a large *Récit* under expression.

                                 276 pipes

Pédale
(32 notes, F to C)

1. *Bourdon* 16'   25 pipes
Speech very faint.
2. *Flûte* 8'   25 pipes
Speech faint. 10 pipes in the 2 side towers of the case. Good tone.
3. *Bombarde* 16' with ravalement   32 pipes
4. *Trompette* 12' with ravalement   32 pipes
Uneven; average.
5. *Clairon* 6' with ravalement   32 pipes
Uneven, but keep.

                                 146 pipes

Aside from being extremely weak, the flue stops lack depth here, as everywhere else in the organ: the reeds do not balance the foundation stops.

The *Bourdon* 16' should be replaced by a *Flûte* ouverte 16' with ravalement to 24' F. The *Flûte* 8' should be extended down to 12' F.

The two side towers contain *Pédale* pipes, the bass of the *Flûte* 8'.

Summary of the Stops and Pipes According to Pitch.

Foundations and Mutations

Pitch:	16'	8'	4'	Nazard (Quinte)	2'	Grosse & Petite Tierce	Pleins jeux & Cornets	Stops	Pipes
Manual 1 (*Positif*)		3	1	1	1	1	2	9	882
Manual 2 (*Grand orgue*)	2	3	1	2	2	2	3	15	1,424
Manual 3 (*Bombarde*)							1	1	150
Manual 4 (*Récit*)		2					1	3	222
Manual 5 (*Echo*)		1					1	2	202
Pédale	1	1						2	50
Totals	3	10	2	3	3	3	8	32	2,930

Reeds

	16'	8'	4'					Stops	Pipes
Manual 1 (*Positif*)		3	1					4	199
Manual 2 (*Grand orgue*)		3	1					4	216
Manual 3 (*Bombarde*)	1	1	1					3	162
Manual 4 (*Récit*)		2						2	74
Manual 5 (*Echo*)		1	1					2	74
Pédale	1	1	1					3	96
[Reed] Totals	2	11	5					18	821
Flues	3	10	2	3	3	3	8	32	2,930
	5	21	7	3	3	3	8	50	3,751

Mechanism

The wind-supply, consisting of ten large cuneiform bellows measuring 2.4 meters by 1.3 meters, is in poor condition. A further disadvantage is that the bellows furnish quite unsteady wind: this defect, inherent in the old design, together with the present deterioration of the bellows, must lead to discarding the old system in favor of one containing either a single or multi-pressure reservoir.

The *Grand orgue* windchest is well built and rather well preserved. The channels and pallets are inadequate to supply all the ranks properly, but a second pallet-box can be added so as to wind the reeds and the *pleins-jeux* independently from the foundation stops.

The *Positif* chest is in poorer condition. It loses much wind between the sliders and the toeboards [erasure] the ranks are crowded and rather poorly arranged. A few stops should be eliminated, in order to space the essential stops better, and to facilitate maintenance and tuning.

The *Pédale* chests may be retained if fitted with a second pallet-box, so as to wind the flues separately from the reeds [erasure].

The *Récit* and *Echo* chests, although rather well preserved, should be eliminated because of their limited compass, and replaced by a *Récit expressif* having the full compass of the chief manuals. Several stops from these two divisions could be used in the new one.

The entire mechanism of the organ is in poor condition. The roller-boards, vertical rollers, and other relay mechanisms, would need to be rebuilt, moreover, because of the double pallet-boxes required to wind the various divisions, as well as for the inclusion of new mechanical accessories to be described in the Specification.

The manuals and pedalboard are in poor condition and work badly: they should be replaced by new keyboards.

Specification
of Repairs Urgently Needed, and of Additions and Improvements Suitable to this Organ.

1) Multi-Pressure Bellows. As stated in the preceding Report, the present bellows are too worn and too defective in design to merit repair. It shall be replaced with a new wind-supply having horizontal reservoirs, whose dimensions are commensurate with the number and requirements of this large organ. This wind-supply (shall be) built according to our new system with different pressures, based on an original principle of our invention. The bellows are made to furnish different wind-pressures, the purpose being to wind the various stops according to their character and power, and to wind the bass and treble ranges separately, correcting the weakness usually observed in the treble, by means of higher wind-pressure. The new system usually has the further advantage of avoiding the insufficient and unsteady wind always encountered in large organs.

This wind-supply will be fed by two double feeders worked by two blowers operating two pairs of pedals, and would furnish steady and abundant wind to all ranks.

Building this wind-system, together with the framework, mechanism, and wind trunks to convey the wind to the various divisions shall cost   6,000 fr.

Windchests.

2) The *Positif* chests shall be removed and thoroughly reconditioned: the toeboards, sliders, and table shall be dressed true, in order to correct wind leaks. The pallets shall be refaced with new leather, as well as the bungboards. The toeboard nails shall be replaced with woodscrews, to allow better adjustment of the sliders. Toeboards and rackboards for the *Cromorne, Tierce,* and *Plein jeu* shall be replaced with new ones, to receive three new stops.

This work shall cost   325 fr.

3) The *Grand orgue* chests shall also be rebuilt: a second pallet-box and pallets shall be fitted, so that the reeds and *pleins jeux* may be winded separately from the foundation stops. The channels shall be divided at mid-length so that each pallet need supply only half the number of stops it new does. This will eliminate the insufficiency of wind when all the stops are played together. The pallet-boxes shall also be divided so as to permit separate wind-supplies for bass and treble. Finally, the toeboards for the *Gros Nazard, Grosse Tierce, Nazard,* and *Petite Tierce* shall be eliminated,

and new toeboards shall be fitted for four new stops.

This work shall cost   1,150 fr.

4) The *Pédale* chests shall be entirely rebuilt, in the same manner as above: a second pallet-box shall be fitted so that the foundations may be winded separately from the reeds. New toeboards shall be fitted to receive the new foundation stops, as well as toeboards for offset pipes.

This work shall cost   500 fr.

5) A new *Récit* chest shall be built, with a compass of 4½ octaves and space for 8 stops. The chest, of choice Holland oak, with the *boîte expressive*, shall cost   1,100 fr.

6) The entire mechanism of the organ shall be replaced with a new one:. rollerboards for the *Grand orgue, Positif, Pédale*, and the new *Récit*; vertical rollers for the drawstop action; levers, squares, tracker-wires, and traces.

3,750 fr.

7) Four new manuals shall be built with a compass of 4½ octaves, and a new pedalboard of German design; these shall replace the present keyboards. The manuals shall be capped with first-quality ivory and the sharps with ebony, and the frames shall be veneered with rosewood. The pedalboard shall be made of oak.

These keyboards shall be fitted with sets of levers to which the action shall be attached, so that the manuals and pedals may easily be removed to remedy sticking keys, without disturbing the action.

This work shall cost   1,000 fr.

8) The main keyboard shall be fitted with a patented device which lessens the resistance of the keys and makes them as easy to play as those of a piano. Based on the principle of the steam engine, this device has as its motive force the air compressed by the bellows. Instead of pulling directly on the large pallets, the key serves as a kind of trigger, controlling the motion of the device, which in turn opens and closes the pallets.

For each key there is a small bellows, to which is attached the tracker connected to a pallet in the chest. These bellows are designed in such a way that when a key is depressed, the corresponding bellows fills with wind: the elasticity of the wind causes it to fill the bellows promptly, and this opens the pallet.

When the key is released, the small bellows empties immediately, and the pallet closes.

Building and fitting this device shall cost   3,000 fr.

9)   Composition Pedals

Various pedal-operated mechanisms shall be built, producing the following combinations:

Pedal 1 shall open and close the *boîte expressive* in order to achieve every possible nuance of volume from the *Récit* stops.

Pedal 2 shall couple the treble of the reeds to the *Récit*.

Pedal 3 shall couple the bass of the reeds to the foundation stops.

Pedal 4 shall couple the *Récit* manual to the *Grand orgue*.

Pedal 5 shall couple the *Bombarde* manual to the *Grand orgue*.

Pedal 6 shall couple the *Positif* manual to the *Grand orgue*.

Note that since all the coupling is done with the *Grand orgue* manual, where the device described above shall be fitted, the touch of the keys will not be increased even when all the manuals are coupled.

Pedal 7 shall couple the octaves, thereby doubling the number and power of the effects obtainable from the stops.

Pedal 8 shall control a mechanism that couples to the *Pédale* foundations any combination of reeds previously selected, and cancels them at will.

Pedal 9, finally, shall couple to the *Pédale* the bass range of all the stops. Without increasing the number of stops, this mechanism will considerably augment the power of the *Pédale* division, and will give the foundation tone of the organ the impressive character now lacking.

This work shall cost   2,250 fr.

10)   Repairing the Stops Now
   in the Organ, and Adding New Stops.

Positif.

All the pipes in the *Positif* ranks shall be repaired according to good practice. The flues shall be rounded and revoiced. The reeds shall also be repaired: shallots, tongues, and tuning-wires shall be cleaned, and all speaking parts reconditioned or replaced where defective.

This work shall cost   500 fr.

New stops shall be made and installed in the *Positif*, as follows:

1. *Gambe* 4', 54 notes   400 fr.
2. *Flûte harmonique* 8', 37 notes   300 fr.
3. *Flageolet* 2', 54 notes   300 fr.
                                   [1,000 fr.]

11) The existing stops in the *Grand orgue* shall likewise repaired and revoiced; particularly, the wooden bass pipes for the *Bourdons* 16' and 8' shall be modified at the mouth, so as to make them more powerful.

This work shall cost   750 fr.

New stops shall be added to the *Grand orgue* as follows:

1. *Gambe* 8', 54 notes   630 fr.
2. *Flûte harmonique* 8', 54 notes   650 fr.
3. *Flûte octaviante* 4', 54 notes   400 fr.
4. *Octavin* 2', 54 notes   300 fr.
                                     1,980 fr.

12) The reed stops and the *Cornet* in the *Bombarde* shall also be carefully repaired and revoiced.

This work shall cost   600 fr.

13) New stops shall be made for the new *Récit* division, as follows:

1. *Flûte douce* 8', 54 pipes   450 fr.
2. *Flûte harmonique* 8', 54 pipes   650 fr.
3. *Flûte octaviante*, 54 pipes   400 fr.
4. *Octavin*, 54 pipes   300 fr.
5. *Trompette harmonique* 8',
     54 pipes   555 fr.
6. *Clairon* 4', from the
     old organ, 54 pipes   100 fr.
7. *Cor anglais*, 37 pipes   350 fr.
8. *Voix humaine*, from the
     old organ, 54 pipes   150 fr.
                                   [2,955 fr.]

14) The *Pédale* reeds shall be taken down, straightened, and thoroughly gone over.

This work shall cost   600 fr.

The flue stops eliminated shall be replaced by the following new stops:

1. *Flûte ouverte* 16', with
     short octave   15,000 fr.
2. *Flûte ouverte* 8', with
     short octave   640 fr.
3. *Flûte ouverte* 4', with
     short octave   320 fr.
                                   [2,460 fr.]

15) All case-pipes, both in the main case and the *Positif*, shall be replaced with new pipes, of pure tin, polished and burnished.

This work, after credit for the metal from the old case-pipes, shall cost   4,500 fr.
                        Grand total   34,420 fr.

Note: The approximate value of 4,500 fr. for the new case-pipes may be established more accurately in a different way, to wit: the new pipes would cost 6 fr. per kilogram. The metal from the old pipes would be credited according to the price of tin and the analysis of the metal.

Summary

1) *Positif*:

Repair all stops. Repair or replace the case-pipes. Place the *Cromorne* in the location of the *Clairon*, which is removed. Eliminate the *Tierce* and the *Plein-jeu*. Replace them with a *Flûte harmonique* of 30 [or ?] 37 notes, a *Flûte octaviante*, and an *Octavin*.

2) *Grand orgue*:

Repair or replace the *Montres* 16' and 8'. Eliminate the *Gros Nazard*, *Grosse Tierce*, *Nazard*, and *Tierce*: replace them with:

    Gambe 8'
    Flûte harmonique 8'
    Flûte octaviante 4'
    Octavin 2'

Eliminate the defective *Plein-jeu* pipes in the *Grand orgue*, and replace them with pipes from the *Positif*. Transfer the *Voix humaine* to the *Récit*, and rebuild the trebles, which are poor. Repair all other stops.

3) *Bombarde*:

Repair the reeds in this division.

4) *Récit*:

Eliminate the present division, retaining the *Flûte* and the *Bourdon*, extending their compass, and similarly for the *Trompette* and *Hautbois*. Propose new stops throughout the *Récit*.

5) *Echo*:

Eliminate the present division, retaining the *Flûte*, *Trompette*, and *Clairon* for replacements in defective ranks elsewhere.

6) *Pédale*:

Eliminate the *Bourdon* 8' and the *Flûte*: they are not powerful or strong enough. Replace them with: *Flûte* 16' with ravalement to 24' F, *Flûte* 8' to 12' F, and *Flûte* 4' to 6' F.

Repair the reed stops.

7) Bellows:

Replace the existing bellows with a multi-pressure system.

8-10) Windchests:

(8) Repair the *Grand orgue* chests and fit a second set of pallet-boxes so as to wind the *Pleins jeux* and *reeds* separately.

(9) Repair the *Positif* chests and change the stops as indicated.

(10) Repair the *Pédale* chests and fit second pallet-boxes, making the necessary changes to install the new flue stops.

Notes and citations

INTRODUCTION

1. Lettres IV, 2341, November 12, 1852.
2. Lettres II, 1488, September 9, 1848.
3. Lettres III, 1550, October 13, 1849.
4. Lettres VI, 4111, June 8, 1859.

CHAPTER ONE

1. Sir James Jeans, *Science and Music* (Cambridge, 1937), pp. 142-3.
2. Curt Sachs, The History of Musical Instruments (New York, 1940), p. 407.
3. Hamel at the Cathedral of Beauvais, 1827; Daublaine-Callinet at St.-Eustache, Paris, 1844. Hamel's free reeds at the Cathedral of Beauvais were named: Conoclyte, Termopèle, and Dermogloste.
4. Rev. Mus., VI, 14, October 30, 1829, p. 109 ff.
5. Pierre-Marie Hamel, *Nouveau Manuel Complet ou Traité Théorique et Pratique de l'Art de Construire les Orgues* (Paris, 1849), III, p. 432.
6. In addition, Abbey is credited with the first *orgue d'accompagnement* in Paris, installed in 1829 for the accompaniment of chant in the church of St.-Etienne-du-Mont.

CHAPTER TWO

1. Letters of Felix Mendelssohn-Bartholdy, trans. Lady Wallace (Boston, n.d.), p. 335, from letter of Paris, January 21, 1832.
2. We have noted Erard's use of pedals to control the stop action.
3. *Revue Musicale*, published by Mr. Fétis, VII, 46, Paris, Saturday, December 14, 1833, pp. 369-70.
4. *Revue et Gazette musicale de Paris*, V, 43, October 28, 1838, p. 430.

CHAPTER THREE

1. See Lettres I, #30, June 14, 1838.
2. Contracts I, 19, December 2, 1839.
3. Lettres I, #63, p. 28, May 14, 1840.
4. Lettres I, #121, p. 45, August 31, 1840.
5. C. and E. Cavaillé-Coll, *Aristide Cavaillé-Coll* (Paris, 1929), p. 42.
6. Lettres I, #301, p. 99.
7. See above p. .... ff.
8. In 1845, Cavaillé-Coll proposed for St.-Eustache (Paris) an immense organ with four sets of Barker machines, for *Pédale, Grand Orgue, Bombarde*, and *Récit*. See Dev. 3, #147, p. 49, August 17, 1845, and below, p. 44.
9. Lettres II, #1090, p. 43, May 3, 1845.
10. *Manuels-Roret, Nouveau manuel complet de l'organiste*, 1905, p. 107.
11. C. M. Philbert, *L'Orgue du Palais de l'Industrie d'Amsterdam* (Amsterdam, 1876), p. 34 ff.

CHAPTER FOUR

1. Cavaillé-Coll had put forward a remarkably convincing argument to the authorities at St.-Roch, favoring the Barker machine even before the results at St.-Denis were known. See Letters I, 109, August 13, 1840.
2. Lettres I, #832, July 28, 1842.
3. Lettres II, #1083, April 3, 1845.
4. *Manuel du Factuer d'Orgues*, I, xxvi, as quoted by Ply, *La Facture moderne* (1878), p. 51.
5. Rev. Mus. VII, #29, August 17, 1833.
6. Rev. Mus., VII, #34, September 21, 1833, pp. 265-66.
7. See Hamel, *Manuel du Facteur d'Orgues*, 1849, p. 413 ff; and Ply, p. 53 ff.
8. Abbé H.-J. Ply, *La Facture moderne étudiée à l'orgue de St.-Eustache* (1878), p. 43.
9. *Nouveau Manuel Complet de l'Organiste*, Paris, 1905, p. 118.
10. *Revue et Gazette Musicale de Paris*, XI, #27, July 7, 1844, pp. 230-32.
11. *Revue et Gazette Musicale de Paris*, XIV, #38, September 19, 1847, p. 308.
12. *Revue et Gazette Musicale de Paris*, XI, #51, December 22, 1844, p. 427.
13. *Revue et Gazette Musicale de Paris*, XI, #48, December 1, 1844, p. 401.
14. Lettres II, 1036, December 24, 1844, p. 13.
15. *La France Musicale*, VII, #51, December 22, 1844.
16. Lettres V, #2132, January 16, 1852, to Mr. Fontmichel in Grasse.
17. *Revue et Gazette Musicale de Paris*, X, #9, February 26, 1843, p. 73.
18. *Revue et Gazette Musicale de Paris*, X, #17, April 23, 1843, p. 143.
19. *Revue et Gazette Musicale de Paris*, X, #28, July 9, 1843, p. 243.
20. *Revue et Gazette Musicale de Paris*, X, #29, July 16, 1843, pp. 252-53.
21. *Revue et Gazette Musicale de Paris*, X, #46, November 12, 1843, p. 389.
22. *Revue et Gazette Musicale de Paris*, XIII, #4, January 25, 1846, p. 29.
23. Lettres II, #1121, July 22, 1845.
24. For complete text of this letter see Appendix A.
25. See J. Adrien de La Fage, *Orgue de Saint-Eustache: sa reconstruction, emploi des produits de la loterie tirée à cette occasion; lettre addressée à M. Eugene Suë*, Paris, May 1845, p. 15.
26. *Revue et Gazette Musicale de Paris*, XIX, #17, April 25, 1852, p. 135.

CHAPTER FIVE

1. "De la facture d'orgue au XIXe siècle.", II, October 1846, pp. 344-358; November 1846, pp. 377-91.
2. *Revue de la Musique*, 1847, pp. 35-40.
3. *Revue de la Musique*, 1-II-47, pp. 81-84.
4. See E. G. T. Gregoir, *Historique de la facture et des facteurs d'orgue avec la Bibliographie Musicale*, Anvers, 1865, reprinted Amsterdam, 1972, p. 55 and p. 164.

CHAPTER SIX

1. Rev. de la Mus. Rel., 1847, p. 385.
2. Abbé H. J. Ply, *La Facture Moderne*, 1878, p. 82, n. 1.
3. from *Rapport sur les Travaux du grand orgue de l'église de la Madeleine à Paris*, Paris, 1846, pp. 10-11.
4. This information is from *Etats des Orgues*, p. 74.
5. Lettres II, #1244, June 24, 1846.
6. Pierre-Marie Hamel (1786-1879), a judge at Beauvais and amateur organ builder, had

"restored" the ancient organ at the Cathedral of Beauvais in 1827. The fifth manual keyboard, with a 54-note compass, was given over to free reeds called *Conoclyte, Euphone,* and *Termopèle.* Another on the pedal was named *Dermogloste.* In 1849, Roret published Hamel's *Nouveau manuel complet du facteur d'orgues,* a book that reproduced, with additions, part of the work of Dom Bédos. Hamel served most of his life on the *Commission des Orgues* under the *Ministre de l'Instruction publique et des Cultes.*

7. Devis II, #22, June 8, 1842.

8. On free reeds, see also Lettres II, #1240 bis, June 19, 1846.

9. For Cavaillé-Coll's letter of application, see Lettres II, #1182, p. 97, January 16, 1846.

10. 1869, p. 442.

CHAPTER SEVEN

1. *Revue et Gazette musicale de Paris,* III, #15, April 10, 1836, p. 119.

2. See *Exposition de l'Industrie en 1839,* No. 1052, Cavaillé-Coll, Père et fils, Paris, 1839, p. 4, n. 1.

3. See *Lettres I,* #51, April 8, 1840, p. 25.

4. See *Revue et Gazette,* XI, July 7, 1844, pp. 230-32.

5. See *Revue et Gazette,* XI, #23, June 9, 1844, p. 231.

6. This work on the great Cliquot instrument had been done by Ducroquet, under the direction of Barker, after the bankruptcy of Daublaine-Callinet. The number of manuals was reduced from five to four, the old wind system replaced, the *Récit* redone as a Swell, and the old pedal was discarded in favor of a German-style keyboard with a compass of 29 notes, C to E. See p. 39 for the account of Callinet's role in this restoration.

7. *Revue et Gazette,* XIII, #4, January 25, 1846, p. 29.

8. *Lettres II,* 1488, September 9, 1848.

9. *Lettres III,* #1754, May 21, 1850.

10. *Lettres III,* #1785, June 25, 1850.

11. Henri Blanchard, "Auditions musicales", *Revue et Gazette,* XXXIII, August 18, 1850, pp. 273-74.

CHAPTER NINE

1. *Revue et gazette,* XIX, #5, February 1, 1852, pp. 37-8.

2. *Lettres IV,* #2172, March 12, 1852, for Cavaillé-Coll's effusive report to Fétis on that visit.

3. Devis IV, p. 54, 1846; Devis IV, p. 102, 1850.

4. see Manuels-Roret, *Nouveau manuel complet de l'organiste, première partie,* Paris, 1855, p. 103

5. Cavaillé-Coll proposed two pedal keyboards of identical compass. He had just returned from his first trip to Frankfurt, where he had seen the famous organ with double pedalboard built at St. Paul's Church, Frankfurt, by Eberhard-Friederich Walcker in 1833. Of 74 stops, 22 were controlled by the two pedal divisions.

6. Concerning this compass of 30 notes, Cavaillé-Coll commented: "I followed your advice and gave the *Pèdale* two and one-half octaves of compass, although in my opinion this is unnecessary. In the largest organs we never have more than two, from C to C."

7. Note Cavaillè-Coll's comment: ". . . however, considering the size of the instrument, we have given (the *Pédale*) all the compass required for playing the great masters: 2 octaves plus 2 notes, from C to D, or 27 notes instead of 18."

8. *Revue et gazette musicale de Paris,* XXII, #22, May 28, 1854, pp. 174-75.

9. *Lettres IV,* #2771, June 3, 1854.

10. Cecile and Emmanuel Cavaillé-Coll, *Aristide Cavaillé-Coll*, Paris, 1929, p. 76.
11. *Revue et gazette musicale de Paris*, XXI, #31, July 30, 1854, p. 249.
12. *Lettres IV*, #2933, February 14, 1855.
13. *Lettres IV*, #2977, April 27, 1855
14. *Lettres IV*, #2990, June 5, 1855.
15. *Lettres IV*, #2993, June 6, 1855.
16. *Lettres V*. #3155, March 6, 1856.
17. *Revue et gazette musicale de Paris*, XXIII, #14, April 7, 1856, p. 104.
18. *Revue et gazette musicale de Paris*, XXIII, #18, May 4, 1856, pp. 140-41.

CHAPTER TEN

1. *Revue et gazette musicale de Paris*, XXIII, #31, August 3, 1856, p. 247-48.
2. *Lettres V*, #3547, November 15, 1857.
3. Cecile and Emmanuel Cavaillé-Coll, *Aristide Cavaillé-Coll . . .*, pp. 124-45.
4. see *Discours de M. Théodore Dubois, souvenir de César Franck du 22 Octobre, 1904*, Paris, 1904, p. 20: "Lorsque la place de professeur d'orgue fut vacante par la mort de Benoist, je vins de suite trouver mon maître Ambroise Thomas, alors directeur, et je lui dis: 'Il n'y a qu'un homme vraiment digne d'occuper aujourd'hui ce poste, c'est César Franck;' il me répondit ces seuls mots: 'c'est vrai,' et le fit nommer. Je tiens à dire cela, parce qu'on a attribué à Ambroise Thomas une certaine hostilité contre Franck. Cela n'etait pas; . . . il appréciait hautement l'exceptionelle valeur de César Franck." "When the organ professorship became vacant upon the death of Benoist, I went directly to my teacher Ambroise Thomas, then Director (of the *Conservatoire*), and said: 'There is only one person today truly worthy of occupying that post, and that is César Franck.' He replied with these words only: 'That is correct,' and had him named. I am anxious to record that because Ambroise Thomas is said to have been somewhat hostile to Franck. That was not true . . . he appreciated fully the exceptional worth of César Franck."
5. Léon Vallas, *César Franck* (trans. Foss), London, 1951, p. 112.
6. Place Louis XV was where the Guillotine was first set up — now Place de la Concorde.
7. *Lettres VI*, #4251, September 23, 1859.
8. *Le Menestrel*, 720-26e Année, October 2, 1859, p. 351.
9. *Revue et Gazette Musicals de Paris*, XXVII, January 1, 1860, pp. 4-5.

CHAPTER ELEVEN

1. *Lettres II*, #1490, September 15, 1848.
2. For the section on "Multi-pressure bellows," Cavaillé-Coll refers to Devis III, #306 (Agen Cathedral), from which the author has drawn.
3. Although the case was erected before the *Montre* pipes could be put in place, the sculpture was done separately and installed last by Pyanet and Lechesne.
4. See Appendix D, Devis V, April 26, 1856.
5. For the total number of pipes in the two 100-stop organs, see below page 160.
6. *Lettres II*, #1053.
7. *Lettres V*, #3273, see Appendix A.
8. Abbé Lamazou, *Etude sur l'orgue monumental de Saint-Sulpice*, 1863, p. 57.
9. *La France musicale*, XXIII, no. 52, December 25, 1859, p. 507.
10. See above, page 130.
11. This contrasts sharply with the record for St.-Vincent-de-Paul, an organ of the same size, for which there were four progress reports: November 10, 1849; April 6, 1850;

July 31, 1850; and November 15, 1851, the last having been submitted only two months before the inaugural concert.

11. See Devis V. #767.

12. *Lettres* V, #2194.

13. *Lettres* V, #3596.

14. See above, *Lettres* V, #4226.

15. *Lettres* VI, #3977.

16. See "Notice" in the program for the *Inaugeration du Grand Orgue de la Basalique Ste.-Clotilde de Paris,* June 13, 1933.

CHAPTER TWELVE

1. A. Peschard, *Notice biographique sur A. Cavaillé-Coll et les orgues électriques,* Paris, 1899.

2. J.W. Hinton, *Story of the electric organ,* London, 1909.

3. Marcel Dupré, *Recollections,* New York, 1972.

4. Cavaillé-Coll died on October 13, 1899. Peschard's *Notice biographique* appeared the next month.

5. Hinton, *op.cit.,* p. 75.

6. Could Hinton have forgotten that only a few years earlier his countryman William Gladstone was elected to his fourth term as prime minister of England at the age of eighty-three (1892)?

7. Dupré, *Recollections,* p. 18.

8. Quoted from a pamphlet: *Le grand orgue de la salle Pleyel,* 1930.

9. See Chapter 8.

10. Quoted from A. Dupré, *Étude sur Aristide Cavaillé-Coll,* Rouen, 1919, p. 32.

11. *Lettres* IV, #2998.

12. Georges Schmitt, *Nouveau manuel complet de l'organiste,* Manuels Roret, Paris, 1855. Georges Schmitt was organist at the church of St.-Sulpice, Paris.

13. *Lettres* IV, #3012.

14. *Lettres* IV, #3012.

15. Peschard, *Notice Biographique (op.cit.),* p. 9.

16. We recall that after the Revolution of 1848, when he was in similarly desperate straits, Cavaillé-Coll's men had been out of work for more than six months.

17. A. Peschard, *Premières applications de l'élèctricité aux grandes orgues,* Paris, 1890, p. 27.

18. J.W. Hinton, *Organ construction,* London, 1900, p. 102.

19. *L'Orgue électrique de l'église Notre-Dame à Valenciennes,* 1891, p. 14.

20. J. Bonnel, "Rapport sur le concours pour le prix du Prince Lebrun", from *Memoires de l'Académie des Sciences, Belles-Lettres et Arts (classe des Sciences) de Lyon,* XXVIII, 1885-1886, p. 10-11.

21. *L'Orgue de choeur de l'église Sainte Clotilde à Paris,* Paris, 1888, p. 3.

22. The following quotations are drawn from Geudon, *Nouveau manuel complet de l'or-ganiste, Manuels Roret,* Paris, 1905, p. 166.

23. From Progrès du Nord, June 27, 1891, as quoted in L'Orgue... à Valenciennes (op.cit.), p. 30.

24. See A. Peschard, *L'Orgue électrique n'est pas d'origine américaine,* Paris, 1892.

25. See Peschard, *Notice biographique (op.cit.),* p. 13.

26. Hinton, *Story of the electric organ,* p. 81.

Index

The Index includes references to all names and significant subjects which appear in the text and Appendices A and B. Institutions and instruments are listed under their geographical locations. Bold face numerals indicate specifications, names from whose stop lists are excluded from the index.